The Discourse of Courtly Love
in Seventeenth-Century
Spanish Theater

The Discourse of Courtly Love in Seventeenth-Century Spanish Theater

Robert Bayliss

Lewisburg
Bucknell University Press

Associated University Presses
2010 Eastpark Boulevard
Cranbury, NJ 08512

Library of Congress Cataloging-in-Publication Data

Bayliss, Robert.
   The discourse of courtly love in seventeenth-century Spanish theater / Robert Bayliss.
       p. cm.
   Includes bibliographical references and index.
   ISBN 978-0-8387-5714-7 (alk. paper)
   1. Spanish drama—Classical period, 1500–1700——History and criticism. 2. Courtly love in literature. I. Title.
   PQ6105.B33   2008
   862′.3093543—dc22

                                                                    2008001173

Contents

Acknowledgments

THE PUBLICATION OF THIS BOOK WAS MADE POSSIBLE BY THE SUPPORT and guidance of far too many individuals to enumerate here, but there are several whose involvement and intervention in the project is too important to escape mention. As a longtime mentor and friend, James McGregor at the University of Georgia should be thanked for his encouragement and enthusiasm. As my graduate advisor and mentor, Catherine Larson is responsible for guiding this project from its earliest stages. Among her colleagues at Indiana University to whom I owe my sincere gratitude are Steven Wagschal, Giancarlo Maiorino, and Rosemarie McGerr. Juan Carlos Conde must also be thanked for his vision and encouragement, as well as Charles Ganelin at Miami University for his support and enthusiasm for my work. Finally, without the support of my colleagues at the Department of Spanish and Portuguese at the University of Kansas, and in particular of my faculty mentor Vicky Unruh, completing this project would simply not have been possible.

I owe thanks to the University of Kansas for their institutional support as I redacted and revised this book, both for the funding I received through the New Faculty General Research Fund and the Jessie Marie Senor Cramer & Ann Cramer Root Faculty Award, and for the technical support I received from the Hall Center for the Humanities.

The Discourse of Courtly Love in Seventeenth-Century Spanish Theater

Introduction: Courtly Love
and the *Comedia* as Discourse

cuando he de escribir una comedia,
encierro los preceptos con seis llaves;
saco a Terencio y Plauto de mi estudio,
para que no me den voces (que suele
dar gritos la verdad en libros mudos),
y escribo por el arte que inventaron
los que el vulgar aplauso pretendieron,
porque, como las paga el vulgo, es justo
hablarle en necio para darle gusto.
       —Lope de Vega, *Arte nuevo de
hacer comedias en este tiempo*

[when I want to write a comedy, I lock up the precepts with six keys; I take Terence and Plautus out of my study, so they won't speak to me (because the truth in silent books tends to shout), and I write according to the art invented by those who seek the applause of the crowd, because, since they pay for it, it is right to speak simply in order to please them.][1]

No MODE OF CULTURAL EXPRESSION BETTER REFLECTS THE COMPRE-hensive social and economic developments in Spanish society during the early modern period than the secular theater, where production reflected the demands of an emerging market of consumption rather than traditional modes of patronage. The crowds paying to attend performances at the newly constructed public theaters or *corrales* were socially and economically diverse, and as Donald Gilbert-Santamaría has shown, Lope de Vega pioneered a mode of dramatic representation indicative of "a new poetics commensurate with the demands of writing for an audience that pays."[2] According to the above citation from his *Arte nuevo,* the new "art" of the *Comedia,* defined by the tastes of its popular audience, must ignore the standards and precepts of the

11

established classics; in other words, Lope would have us believe that classical literary authority and the aesthetic pleasure of his contemporaries (at least of the temperamental *vulgo* attending performances of his plays and, in effect, paying his salary) are mutually exclusive.

Given the context in which Lope's statement appears, however—at the beginning of a treatise that anatomizes the mechanics of dramatic composition, replete with references to Aristotelian precepts and other authoritative classical and neoclassical sources—the statement is disingenuous and ironic. Lope's rhetorical posturing is given the lie by a longstanding tradition of critical investigation that has explored the myriad ways in which seventeenth-century Spanish drama calls upon its classical and medieval literary antecedents to meet the market-driven demands of its socially heterogeneous public. The literary appropriations of Lope's own *oeuvre* have been well documented and shown to be indiscriminate of generic, historical, or geopolitical boundaries.[3] In the popular comedies authored by Lope and his followers, theatrical praxis constituted a profitable filtering process through which a panorama of literary sources was successfully packaged for popular taste. This appropriation and reformulation of literary sources is most immediately apparent in the *Comedia*'s diverse representations of love and desire.

In *L'amour et l'Occident,* Denis de Rougemont effectively argues that no literary tradition has had a more profound impact on the expression and representation of desire in Western culture than courtly love. He argued at the beginning of the twentieth century that its influence could still be perceived in his day, and even a superficial glance at Western popular culture at the beginning of the twenty-first century suggests that his claim still holds true. Concepts such as "courtesy" and "chivalry" (in the nonacademic parlance of our contemporary culture) are in fact references to the medieval love ethic established in the poetry of the troubadours and further developed and disseminated through a variety of medieval lyric and narrative traditions. After Gaston Paris coined the term "courtly love" toward the end of the nineteenth century, de Rougemont and C. S. Lewis led several generations of scholars who attached to this label a set of ideas and a code of conduct in medieval Provençal poetry; this scholarship was quickly disseminated throughout Europe and across the Atlantic.[4] Despite the efforts of later generations of scholars to unseat this master narrative of idealized medieval love, the term has stuck.

While much of mid-twentieth century academic discussions on the topic would question, debunk, or reinstate "courtly love" as a valid critical construct, the proliferation of theoretical approaches and perspectives since the end of Structuralism's popularity has clearly revealed the issue to be far more complex than scholars of the early twentieth century could have imagined, and new insights are continually being offered today regarding what one may or may not choose to call courtly love. The historical circumstances of twelfth-century Provence certainly differ significantly from those of France, Germany, Italy, England, and Spain in the following three centuries, all of which are generally implicated in the courtly love tradition. The specific cultural context of troubadour performances is unique and far-removed from the situations of later court poets in neighboring countries; still more varied are the political and ideological concerns of writers who for centuries would find inspiration from the troubadours and their literary descendents for their own literary production. Indeed the variety of texts and contexts often subsumed by the label "courtly love" suggests that it is a procrustean term exercised by modern scholars to create a tradition out of disparate texts that have been taken out of their original contexts.

At the same time, to utterly debunk the concept of courtly love is to deny the existence of a major shift in the literary representation of desire that began abruptly with the troubadours and extended well beyond early modern Spain. Contemporary critics have certainly demonstrated problems in the traditional notion and academic construct of courtly love, but these problems make the change in amatory discourse brought on by the troubadours no less real. Moreover, understanding courtly love as a strictly medieval phenomenon, as both the medievalist and the scholar of early modern literature often do, is to assign an arbitrary limit to troubadour influence that has more to do with conventional literary historiography than with the literary traditions it describes. To ignore that the passionate reverence paid to Inés by Don Alonso in Lope de Vega's *El caballero de Olmedo* echoes the anguish and idealization of many troubadour lyric poems is, I would argue, to miss a major feature of the play's negotiation and reformulation of the literary discourses that inspired it. Courtly love is a mode of expression well worth reconsidering, and the *Comedia*'s representations of desire are among its lasting legacies. The various and often conflicting ways in which it appears, even within the limits of seventeenth-century theatrical practice, is suggestive of a discursive malleability that merits a closer look. Our understanding of this literary phenomenon needs to be updated in a way that focuses less on the rules and technicalities of a courtly code and more on how that code has managed to be so adaptable under so many differing circumstances. By revisiting courtly love in this way, we may be in a position to replace the proverbial "procrustean bed" alluded to above with a more nuanced understanding that accounts for its diverse manifestations.

It is ironic that to offer such a pluralistic reading of courtly love, we must first revisit what remains constant in the tradition, an essential base from which any text that refers to courtly love will invariably begin: its performative and self-referential nature, its implicit construction of ideologically determined gender roles, and its dynamic treatment of the relationship between the sexes. The troubadours forged a revolutionary discourse of love that ultimately assumed a role in western culture that Michel Foucault would describe as that of a "discourse of power."[5] In its most basic (and male-authored) formulation, courtly discourse implies a predetermined role and place for its subjects, especially in terms of gender: the male lover actively voices his emotions to or about a silent, objectified, and idealized lady. Engaging such a discursive mode in the representation of desire places its subjects in an implicit ideological system, although in this book I will argue furthermore that courtly love's discursive polyvalence fosters a kind of subjectivity that can be voiced or performed from the periphery of the medieval and early modern patriarchy, in particular by women writers, just as easily as it can reflect the male fantasies of the dominant elite. Spanish dramatists of the Golden Age regularly employed courtly discourse's centuries-old conventions as a mode of expression easily recognized by their audiences—in other words as an invocation of literary authority—that somehow proved widely popular for a largely illiterate paying public. Thus while the *Comedia* lies outside the common notion of the courtly love tradition, it does exploit its discursive features, even if it is often for different purposes and with substantially different results. The notion of courtly love as discourse therefore allows for a view of the *Comedia*'s place in literary history that will be argued in the pages that follow. It is a comparative view that would place it within a trans-generic tradition of performing desire that resists the fossilized boundaries of literary historiography while recognizing the changing material conditions of its cultural production.

Over the last three decades, *Comedia* scholarship has reinvented itself: the field once known as "Spanish Golden Age Drama" is now more frequently referred to as "Early Modern Spanish Theater," a change in nomenclature that reflects a shift of emphasis from the "literariness" or qualitative merit of selected and canonical great works (*Fuente Ovejuna, El Burlador de Sevilla, La vida es sueño,* etc.) to the theater's function as a popular tradition, cultural phenomenon, and material industry.[6] Conventional modes of comedy such as the *capa y espada* (cape-and-sword) plays and the *comedias de enredo* (comedies of intrigue) have been reexamined in light of the cultural context in which they thrived and the ideological tensions they reflect and negotiate, spurred on by current theoretical models such as the New Historicism and Cultural and Gender Studies. Specifically, these more conventional and formulaic plays produced by the hundreds during the so-called Golden Age, whose plots invariably are based upon a love story in which complications are, at least on the surface, neatly resolved in a final betrothal scene, explore the nature and dynamics of human conjugal love in a way that reflects a cultural polemic.

In his recent monograph, Thomas Austin O'Connor treats the social discourse surrounding the *Comedia* at length.[7] The way in which love is represented, he argues, was perceived by the more conservative voices of institutional authority as a threat to the established social order. The ongoing debate inspired by this presentation of "conjugal spirituality" pitted this conservative perspective against the champions of the *Comedia,* who would "celebrate theater as a manifestation of nature's variety and abundance."[8] Among other things, at issue was the presentation of love as the impetus behind the social institution of marriage, suggesting that the conjugal destiny of the individual may be determined autonomously rather than as the consequence of a contractual arrangement between families. "In this regard the *Comedia* constitutes a critical statement, as well as an artistic and social document, attesting to the desirability of making more of marriage than a societally approved mating contract for the passing on and acquisition of wealth and for the guarantee and enhancement of social status."[9] Lope's *El caballero de Olmedo* may serve as a prototype for this new dramatic formula: while the villain Rodrigo pursues Inés's hand through the traditional process of negotiating a merger of noble estates with her father, an approach that reflects residual courtship practices of Spain's longstanding caste system, the play's heroic protagonist Alonso wins Inés's heart through the demonstration of his merit, an emergent model of subjective agency that resonated with the new paying public of the *corrales.* The fact that Alonso's demonstration of merit is, until the play's final act, almost exclusively tied to his performance of desire through the discourse of courtly love suggests that *Comedia* love stories bear substantial social, religious, and ideological implications, as O'Connor explains:

> This portrayal of life incorporated an individualized and self-affirming consciousness of an immanent purpose to each and every person's existence. Men and women of various social classes came to experience in their own lives the resonances of the *Comedia*'s great theme of human and profane love. And marriage would, therefore, take on a new importance and urgency as those who fought to affirm their own identities and individual destinies confronted traditional structures of belief and attitudes of mind that opposed any change in actual social discourse and practice.[10]

The discourse of courtly love therefore functions in the *Comedia* as a linguistic medium for the affirmation of individual identity and autonomy—or more precisely, the performance of desire through this discourse constituted a dramatization of the struggle for such affirmation. It is a function clearly at odds with the general abhorrence in medieval courtly love to marriage, a point that suggests how radically different the *Comedia*'s use of courtly discourse can be from that of its founding fathers. Because the *state* of marriage is not represented onstage (the final curtain falls with its lovers on the threshold of this state), in other words because the fulfillment of desire brings closure, this incongruity is sustainable—just as it had been in earlier centuries for theologically orthodox Christian writers like Dante.

An issue not explored in any depth by O'Connor's study is the fact that this presentation of conjugal love, and furthermore the debate it inspired, reflects an exclusively male perspective on the matter. Although he pays substantial attention to the particular issue of women's participation in the public performance and reception of the *Comedia* as a major point of ideological contention, O'Connor's discussion only addresses the issue in terms of what men had to say about it. And while the social discourse about the legitimacy and licitness of the public theater (in the form of official edicts and treatises) may well have been devoid of female voices, as best we know, the same cannot be said of the *Comedia* itself, whose canon has broadened in recent years to incorporate a number of women dramatists. Given this development in *Comedia* studies, the fact that all of the specific plays analyzed in O'Connor's study are authored by men, in my view, limits his literary analysis to only one of two possible gendered perspectives.

The established canon of Spanish Golden Age drama is an undeniably male enclave, a fact that places the period's extant plays of female authorship in a distinct and marginal position. In the last decade of the twentieth century, scholars such as Theresa Scott Soufas have broadened our access to and understanding of several women dramatists of seventeenth-century Spain, and through their efforts it is now well established that secular plays written by these *dramaturgas* negotiate their marginal position from within the established theatrical codes and conventions of the male-dominated public theater.[11] One such code that merits further attention in female-authored *comedias* is the discourse of courtly love, through which desire is performed and questioned in ways that this book will analyze as indicative of the gendered authorial perspective from which their plays are written. The critique of male performances of courtly desire from within the same discursive framework used in male performances of courtly desire is realized through a number of creative strategies by such *dramaturgas* as Sor Juana Inés de la Cruz, María de Zayas, and Leonor de la Cueva y Silva. It is a discursive appropriation and manipulation that is made possible by courtly love's consummate adaptability to new cultural and ideological circumstances that would have been unforeseeable by the troubadours. The gendered difference in how courtly discourse is used to represent love and desire will point us toward a view of the *Comedia* that incorporates feminine and feminist perspectives.

In this sense the *Comedia* can be read as a *tenso* between the sexes, a term I borrow from the medieval Provençal debate poems, a popular genre among the troubadours. The analogy is especially compelling because quite often these structured exchanges involved the voices of the male poet and a female interlocutor, sometimes a fabrication by the poet (as with the enduring *pastorela* tradition), but other times a known and historically documented female poet. From its very inception in the lyric tradition of Provence, then, courtly love itself can be considered a *tenso* between the troubadours and their female counterparts, known as the *trobairitz*. The dynamics of this dialogue between the sexes have been explored by a number of critics; as we will see, the growing body of scholarship dedicated to the *trobairitz* reads their use of courtly discourse as an attempt to question and ultimately undermine the male model. As with the seventeenth-century *dramaturgas,* this discursive subversion is achieved from within the conventions of the male code, a fact that further demonstrates both the discursive malleability of courtly love and the fact that this dialogic feature is as old as courtly love itself.

Incorporating a feminine (and arguably feminist) perspective in my reading of the discourse of courtly love suggests issues and problems with which contemporaries of Denis de Rougemont and C. S. Lewis were not concerned. From medieval Provence to Counter-Reformation Spain, an evolving and diachronic patriarchal tradition of courtly discourse can be traced; meanwhile, from the critiques voiced from the margins of that tradition by women writers through the centuries, a pattern emerges that suggests inherent ethical and ideological conflicts in the authoritative discourse of the male tradition. These conflicts have generally fascinated and perplexed critics, and they often contributed to arguments made against the validity of the very term "courtly love." If, on the one hand, the sexual overtones of Jean de Meun's conclusion to the *Roman de la Rose* seem ideologically opposed to the roughly contemporaneous "cult of Mary" poetry that represents courtly desire on a wholly spiritual plane, this kind of contradiction is readily visible even within the work of individual lyric poets like Petrarch and Juan Ruiz, narrative writers like Chrètien de Troyes and Cervantes, and playwrights like Calderón and Lope de Vega. It is, again, the mutable ideological grounding of courtly discourse as a mode of performing desire that allows for such incongruity, and for the intervention of the tradition's female interlocutors. A central premise of this book is that female-authored representations of courtly love from the medieval and early modern periods can shed new light on the patriarchal traditions to which they respond. Feminist approaches to women writers will help broaden the critical perspective from which we may trace this diachronic evolution of the male-dominated discursive tradition.

The first chapter explores these issues by focusing on what I am calling the discursive paradigm established by the troubadour lyric, a performative framework and rhetorical scaffolding for amatory verse whose influence can be seen both in the Italian *Dolce stil nuovo* and Petrarchan models and in Spain's *Cancionero* and Petrarchist lyric traditions. All of these lyric traditions share a stylized posture of the subject (the male speaker) in relation to its object (the lady, a silent and passive object of male desire). The male-authored discourse of desire is essentially subject-centered or self-absorbed; regardless of the endpoint or goal of the desire expressed in a particular text, be it sexual conquest or spiritual union, the male subject invariably focuses on *his* desire for the feminine object and the effects of that desire on him. In fact, such a critique of courtly discourse is implicitly made by the *trobairitz*. In reference to the troubadours' metaphor in which the lady is treated as the "mirror" of male desire, we may consider the collective voice of women poets contemporary to them as the mirror's response: the male poet's desire for the mirror is ultimately narcissistic, and his propensity for discursively containing and objectifying the feminine is effectively "shattered" by the *trobairitz* response.

Such a reassessment of courtly love may be applied to the idealized dramatization of love that is privileged in the *Comedia,* which operates from within the same discursive parameters as those that were established five centuries earlier across the Pyrenees. These parameters were preserved and further developed in the lyric poetry of Petrarch and his followers during the fifteenth and sixteenth centuries; it is through Petrarchism that the discourse of courtly love was most readily accessible to Golden Age dramatists. Petrarch is generally accepted as a major influence on the poetry of Golden Age Spain, and Spanish Petrarchism in turn is an influential and inspirational source for the verses that constitute *Comedia* discourse.[12] Meanwhile scholars of Petrarch have long since established the debt his poetry owes to Dante, and through him to the troubadours. To my knowledge, however, connecting this chain of influence from medieval Provence to Golden Age Spanish drama has yet to be done, and it is my belief that a discursive analysis of courtly love is the method by which such a lacuna may be filled. The performative self-absorption of the troubadours (discussed in depth in the next chapter) provides a discursive framework through which Petrarch developed his own revolutionary representation of the self, which is often heralded as a decisive contribution to Renaissance and early modern thought.

The notion of the self and its lyric representation by both Petrarch and Petrarchism is a direct source for the representation of desire in the *Comedia,* especially in terms of the male protagonist's expression of desire for a feminine object. As scholars since the 1970s have noted, in the formulaic *comedias de enredo* and *capa y espada* plays such as Lope de Vega's *La dama boba,* the lady or *dama* acquires a more active role than in other subgenres. Feminine prominence in action and onstage presence brings with it an increased *linguistic* presence as well: action is both male- *and* female-driven, and dialogue privileges the voices of both sexes. Accordingly, the representation of feminine voices in these plays is of particular interest to this study's reading of courtly discourse. If the *galán* inherits from the medieval tradition a self-absorbed rhetorical model in which the feminine object of desire is relegated to a passive and unvoiced role, how are the dynamics of courtly love affected when they operate within the *capa y espada* plays and *comedias de enredo,* in which female characters enjoy an equal if not greater share of amatory expression? This question will orient my reading of Lope de Vega's *La dama boba* as a dynamic negotiation of desire through courtly discourse between the sexes, and as such exemplary of the broader popular male convention to which it belongs. The same question orients my reading of *La traición en la amistad,* by María de Zayas y Sotomayor. By comparing the male and female dramatists' portrayal of how courtly discourse is manipulated in the theatrical representation of desire and courtship, I argue that the discourse of courtly love is in fact the locus of mistrust (between the sexes) and contest (between suitors) whose tensions must be resolved to achieve the standard "all's well that ends well" sense of closure expected of this form of comedy by the paying public. A comparison of male-authored and female-authored manipulations of this discourse suggests that while *La dama boba* ultimately affirms the ideological implications of the patriarchal conventions of courtly love, *La traición en la amistad* renegotiates these conventions and exposes their implicit misogynist ideology.

The second chapter examines the conflicts that arise from taking courtly discourse out of its original lyric context and placing it within the active and dynamic context of narrative. As the troubadour lyric focuses upon the plight of the male subject and thus renders the female object a marginal and passive figure, much of medieval romance approaches human love by focusing on the conflicts it creates for the male hero, with a similarly passive and marginal role assigned to the lady. The discourse of courtly love becomes especially problematic and creates conflict in the social worlds represented in romance. My reading of *Erec* by Chrétien de Troyes, the most canonical of medieval *roman* authors, focuses on how the personal desire for the feminine object that is expressed through courtly discourse is placed in direct conflict with public (chivalric) duty. Meanwhile Marie de France offers a feminine countervoice to male romance, one that (like the *trobairitz*) involves a response to the exclusive focus that the patriarchal tradition places on the male subject or hero. In her *Lais,* represented here by "Eliduc," both heroes and heroines work to overcome such conflicts, demonstrating a willingness to transgress the strict and gender-specific parameters for action imposed upon male romance by the discourse of courtly love. This reading of medieval romance, in which courtly discourse's incorporation into an active and dynamic narrative space is inextricably linked to gender, paves the way for a similar reading of the *praxis* of courtly discourse in the dramatic action of the *Comedia.*

The direct implications of this conflict in medieval romance between personal desire and public duty for the *Comedia* may be understood in terms of Golden Age explorations of honor. The institutionalized social convention of honor is not unlike the chivalric duty of the medieval knight in that both present personal and individual desire at odds with what society expects and demands of the individual. Again, the parameters of courtly love set in place by the troubadour lyric must confront social realities in drama from which the enclosed space of the lyric poem is isolated. The conflict may be most apparent in the so-called honor plays such as Calderón's *El médico de su honra,* as well as Lope's tragic *El castigo sin venganza* and tragicomic *Fuente Ovejuna:* in all of these plays, desire is subordinated to honor and social obligation. However, the presence of this tension in the *capa y espada* plays and the *comedia de enredo,* in which the individual subject's attainment of desire is the most salient generic feature, is no less vital.

My reading of *La dama duende* takes the play as exemplary of how early modern Spanish popular comedy foregrounds individual desire and its attainment. Calderón's plot complication or *enredo,* as in much of popular Spanish comedy, stems from the circumnavigation of social conventions and obligations in the pursuit of desire, achieved through Angela's deceit, trickery, and ingenuity. Such obstacles pertain directly to the system or code of honor in early modern Spain as they are represented in the *Comedia.* The above reading of medieval romance will therefore suggest how courtly discourse in the *capa y espada* plays is used to express desire in the face of social conventions that would repress it, and the inevitable denouement can be read as a triumph of said discourse in *La dama duende.* And yet again, as with the *trobairitz* and Marie de France, we may see in Leonor de la Cueva's *La firmeza en la ausencia* a gendered response to the patriarchal representation of women. In her play, the discourse of courtly love, employed for different purposes by the *dama* and the *galán,* renegotiates the conflicts between individual desire and honor in a new way that resists the patriarchal tradition's objectifying and essentialist reduction of all women to the fixed category of Woman.

Cueva's resistance to the role and conduct prescribed for her gender by the patriarchal ideology of Golden Age Spain is reflective of a deeper ideological tension in the *Comedia* that is examined in the final chapter in terms of the early modern concept of decorum. Ideological guidelines for feminine behavior are an important element in the sixteenth- and seventeenth-century debate over the licitness and morality of the professional theater, in which the representation of desire through the discourse of courtly love is directly implicated. The interpretation of such discursive representation, especially in terms of its conformity to orthodox Christian doctrine and the ideology of the absolutist Spanish state, is an issue that is as old as courtly love itself: the troubadours privileged rhetorical dexterity in their performances of desire, including the occlusion of an exact referent and the playful resistance to fixed signification, thereby creating room for ethical ambivalence, ambiguity, and pluralism in what Laura Kendrick calls "the game of love."[13] It is therefore more accurate to treat courtly love as a linguistic vehicle or mode of performance that the individual author may engage as s/he chooses. Thus *Le Roman de la Rose,* whose complex manipulation of medieval allegory ultimately celebrates sexual conquest, and Dante's *Vita Nuova* and *Divina Commedia,* which celebrate a disembodied lady for directing the poet toward divine love, represent opposite extremes of the moral and ideological spectrum from which one may choose to perform in or play the "game of love." This paradoxical continuum of possible referents for desire's object is ingeniously exploited in Juan Ruiz's *Libro de buen amor,* Fernando de Rojas's *Celestina,* and ultimately in such *comedias* as Lope's *El caballero de Olmedo.*

Courtly discourse's openness to varied interpretations is later exploited in the developing forms of novelistic discourse of the late medieval and early modern periods, represented in the final chapter by Boccaccio's *Decameron* and Cervantes's *Don Quijote.* Chivalric romance and its immediate successors like the Iberian *novela sentimental* may treat the ethical problems intrinsic to courtly love in relation to society, but Boccaccio begins a *novella* tradition that places romance's courtly discourse in contact with the amatory discourse of other source traditions (*exempla,* folktales or *fabliaux,* Apulean novel, and so on). What Boccaccio and eventually Cervantes contribute to this evolving literary representation of love is to problematize courtly discourse through its integration into or fusion with the discourses of other source models (be they Boccaccio's medieval or Cervantes's picaresque and Byzantine sources). If genre is in part a function of ideology, then the Boccaccian *novella* and Cervantine *novela* call into question both traditional modes of literary interpretation and the implicit ideological stance of prose fiction by fusing disparate discourses. Such manipulation privileges interpretation, especially as a function of entertainment and aesthetic pleasure, over authorial and ideological prescription.

This development foreshadows a similar discursive manipulation in the *Comedia,* which may be read in terms of contemporary interpretations of the classical precept of decorum. Such a mandate, which demanded that diction match character, implies an ideological categorization of subjects along social class and gender lines that is made explicit on the level of discourse. In *Love in the "Corral"* O'Connor emphasizes the representation of desire and of the feminine as key issues in the debate surrounding the legitimacy and social function of the *Comedia;* such a concern serves as the point of departure for this chapter's reading of Lope de Vega's *El caballero de Olmedo.* The ideological pressure brought to bear by social and religious institutional authority on Golden Age dramatists may ultimately be seen in terms of the moral exemplarity presented by a particular dramatic representation of love and desire. Like the *Decameron* and *Don Quijote,* Lope's comic tragedy destabilizes the ethical and ideological message of his representation of desire by placing the discourses of courtly love (as enunciated by the *galán* and *dama*) and "low" farce (the discourse of the fool or *gracioso* and other servants) in direct and dialogic contact with one another. Sor Juana Inés de la Cruz's *Los empeños de una casa* employs a similar discursive hybridity from within the generic conventions of the *capa y espada* comedies, but with a greater emphasis on the difference between gendered discourses that allows her to question the patriarchal *Comedia*'s representation of women.

The mixture of discourses in order to destabilize the notion of a text's fixed meaning or official interpretation goes right to the heart of what has made the *Comedia* the subject of such varying interpretations by modern critics. For José Antonio Maravall, the *Comedia* is an ideologically conservative means of propagating an institutionally sanctioned prescription for the spectator's behavior, while for Bruce Wardropper it is an essentially subversive and transgressive tradition that challenges such institutional control over the individual.[14] My approach to treating courtly discourse suggests why both interpretations are possible, and why no single ethical or ideological stance can be ascribed to the entire *Comedia* tradition. In terms of human sexuality and the prescribed role of women in society, courtly discourse should not be seen as offering "the last word" (i.e., it is not ideologically conclusive) but instead as the locus of contest and disagreement, or a model for performing desire that each character, text, and indeed each reader or spectator may engage in a unique way. By incorporating the particularly distinctive voices of the *dramaturgas* or female playwrights, I will argue that the *Comedia* is but another install-ment in a long and cacophonic line of texts and traditions, whose var-ied and often conflicting treatments of human sexuality and roman-tic love may be described as the discursive tradition of courtly love.

1
The Legacy of Troubadour Self-Absorption

DUARDO. La calidad elementar resiste
mi amor, que a la virtud celeste aspira,
y en las mentes angélicas se mira,
donde la idea del calor consiste.
No ya como elemento el fuego viste
el alma, cuyo vuelo al sol admira;
que de inferiores mundos se retira,
adonde el serafín ardiendo asiste.
No puede elementar fuego abrasarme.
La virtud celestial que vivifica,
envidia el verme a la suprema alzarme;
que donde el fuego angélico me aplica,
¿cómo podrá mortal poder tocarme,
que eterno y fin contradición implica?

NISE. Ni una palabra entendí.

DUARDO. My love resists the elemental heat
and aspires to celestial virtue,
its image seen in angelic minds,
where the very concept of heat exists.
Fire, no longer an element,
garbs the soul whose flight the sun admires;
the soul in flight retreats from lesser worlds
to where the seraphim ardently assist.
Elemental flame no longer burns me!
Life-giving and celestial, virtue
envies seeing me reach the heights supreme!
For there, enveloped in angelic flame,
how can mortal power touch me,
who, eternal and incontrovertible, resist?

NISE. I didn't understand a word.][1]

(Lope de Vega, *La dama boba*, lines 525–39)

THE ABOVE EXCHANGE IN LOPE DE VEGA'S *LA DAMA BOBA* DRAWS ITS humor from the play's presentation of sexual difference as discursive alienation. Duardo and his fellow would-be courtiers proudly present a Petrarchan sonnet to Nise, fully expecting to be praised for its "profundos conceptos" (profound conceits). The sonnet itself is ostensibly a love poem, but its focus on Neoplatonic spiritual cosmography and Petrarchan psychological self-portraiture excludes any explicit mention of the (presumably female) object of desire. A series of attempts by the frustrated poets to explicate the poem meet with responses by Nise that echo her above statement, until their persistence forces her to exclaim: "Yo no escucho más, / de no entenderte corrida. / ¡Escribe fácil!" [I'll listen no more, / for I don't understand your harangue. / Write simply!] (576–78); Nise later further privileges unadorned language in the oft-cited statement "Yo quiero hablar claro" [I want to speak clearly] (line 2738).[2] Her unexpected criticism of the sonnet's obscure language is rationalized by Duardo and company as symptomatic of her gender: while Plato wrote of divine things through "matemáticas figuras y enigmas" (mathematical figures and enigmas), women are afraid of such "cosas oscuras" (obscure things).

This chapter will trace such a gap or disjuncture between male and female discourse back to the provençal origins of courtly love. Duardo's performance is in fact a seventeenth-century manifestation of a discourse of medieval origin, in which one finds the same obscurity and self-reflexivity that Lope deemed worthy of parody centuries later.[3] While Petrarch and his Spanish Renaissance imitators may be the immediate inspiration behind Lope's parody, the discursive paradigm dictating their performance of desire (that of a male subject only peripherally concerned with the feminine object of desire) is ultimately an inheritance of troubadour poetry. Such a connection between twelfth-century Provence and Golden Age Spain is supported by the recent critical focus, despite traditional associations of courtly love with an elevation of the lady's status (C. S. Lewis's "feudalization of love"), on how language and the first-person male subject position of the courtly lyric are the true foci of troubadour attention.

The consequence of troubadour self-absorption is a marginalization of the feminine from the parameters of courtly discourse. If the (male) self is the true epicenter of troubadour discourse, the *domna*'s role is determined by it and is at its service. For the troubadours, this role frequently was to remain outside the margins of the enclosed lyric space. This "poetics of exclusion" (as Simon Gaunt has called it) exercised a decisive influence on future traditions of love poetry in Western Europe, from the Italian *dolce stil nuovo* through the Spanish Renaissance's Petrarchan school, established in the sixteenth century by Boscán and Garcilaso de la Vega. As the notion of the self (in lyric discourse performed by the speaking male subject) develops from the Middle Ages through the Renaissance and into the seventeenth century, so too develops a representation of the feminine object of desire that renders her increasingly spiritualized and disembodied. The lady's passivity and the exclusion of her voice remain constants throughout the male-dominant lyric tradition, but as the late medieval and early modern notion of the self emerges through Dante and especially Petrarch, her function within the discursive parameters of courtly love develops and evolves to accommodate the increasingly introspective male subject. In light of this legacy left by the troubadours, the aforementioned resistance of Lope's Nise to Duardo's amatory discourse is indeed symptomatic of her gender, in that it reflects the centuries-old alienation of women from a patriarchal courtly love tradition.[4]

Furthermore, Nise's expression of her disdain—her vocalization of and response to that alienation—reflects the equally old (although only recently recovered and critically examined) counter-discourse of the *trobairitz* or women troubadours. Their response to male troubadour performances of desire, like Nise's complaints to Duardo, involves a shift in the subject position of the courtly lyric from masculine to feminine—a shift with radical discursive implications. Lope scripts the performance of desire onstage through both the voiced feminine subject and the more traditional male subject of courtly discourse in a way that makes light of medieval and Petrarchan courtly love. However, Lope's own Neoplatonic vision of love, which he would put in place of the dated and fossilized system of the medieval and Renaissance lyric, retains the same patriarchal parameters of performance that were originally established by that system.[5] His treatment of love is still a masculine construct, operating from within a phallogocentric discursive framework—a point that is not lost on several early modern women dramatists who wrote plays according to Lope's institutionalized formula.

The aim of this chapter is to establish a broad and diachronic context from within which the exchange of gendered approaches to courtly discourse in the *Comedia* may be considered. Looking beyond the narrow parameters of the patriarchal tradition to treat the resistance to it offered by female voices will suggest a connection between the medieval Provençal lyric and early modern Spanish popular comedy that has been long overlooked. While the above-cited exchange between Nise and Duardo is indicative of how Lope's play parodies troubadour and Petrarchan self-absorption, the discursive and ideological parameters of courtly discourse are ultimately affirmed by him—a point that is substantiated by his reliance on the Petrarchan model in his own lyric poetry, especially that of his *Rimas*. With the aim of comparing the dramatic representations of courtly discourse by male and female dramatists of the *Comedia* in light of the troubadour legacy of male narcissism and female alienation, a rereading of *La dama boba* will be offered in light of the alternate gendered perspective from which María de Zayas wrote her only extant play, *La traición en la amistad*.

Troubadour Self-absorption

> Per re non es om tan prenzans
> com per amor e per domnei,
> que d'aquí mou deportz e chans
> e tot can a proez' abau.
> Nuls om ses amor re no vau
> per qu'eu no volh, sia mia
> del mon tota.lh senhoria,
> si ja joi no.n sabi' aver.
>
>   (Bernart de Ventadorn, "Ges de chantar
>   no.m pren talans," lines 25–32)

[Nothing renders man so praiseworthy as love and the service of ladies, for from these one finds sport and song, and all that which has to do with his accomplishments. Without love, a person is worthless, and I would refuse to rule all the universe if it were necessary to not know the joy of love.][6]

The traditional critical approach to the troubadours and their poetry over the last eight centuries has taken the above lines as an accurate descriptor of how the troubadours conceived the enterprise of writing songs. Even well into the twentieth century such claims of female inspiration were generally accepted, and critics focused on the terms in which the troubadours expressed such profound love. Because it became academically codified in the critical climate of the late nineteenth and early twentieth centuries, and especially because of its conception of *poesis* as a sincere and authentic "spontaneous overflow of powerful emotions," this perspective may appropriately be called "romantic." C. S. Lewis's *The Allegory of Love* is perhaps the most famous example of the "romantic" interpretation of troubadour poetry, in which concepts such as "love feudalized" and "Ovid misunderstood" are discussed at length in an attempt to explain the "allegory" of courtly love.[7]

But the basic premise behind the modern concept of courtly love as it was codified by the likes of Lewis, Gaston Paris, and Denis de Rougemont—that love for the lady or *domna* is the inspiration behind troubadour poetry—is problematic in light of how little lyric attention is actually paid to her. More recent scholarship has thus shifted its focus to the troubadours' foregrounding of language and to the rhetorical strategy and posture implicit in their poetry. These features are now understood as a function not of poetic inspiration or emotion but of the ludic pageantry of courtly life in Occitania. This shift in critical focus from an ahistorical construction of meaning to the recovery of the cultural context and the social conditions of troubadour performance involved putting aside the question of sincerity, which Sarah Kay persuasively argues is a critical strategy that is more problematic than productive.[8] Along similar lines, Matilda Bruckner considers the sincerity issue to be the "red herring" of troubadour criticism.[9] We may say for certain that, regardless of the sincerity issue, troubadour discourse is far more complicated than its original critics would have us believe, and far more tied to its original conditions of performance than such a romantic reading would admit. Laura Kendrick's *The Game of Love* marks a pivotal turning point in troubadour scholarship: her "thick description" of the cultural context of troubadour performance allows for a reading of the tradition's oblique and elusive language as part of the courtly competition between poets.[10] In other words, the difficulty of assigning fixed meaning and intentionality to the troubadors' often contradictory performances of desire is not a "problem" as critics had seen it for decades; indeed it is an aesthetic value that was celebrated as a reflection of poetic ingenuity. Audience reception was an essential part of the courtly game, and Kendrick's book effectively invites us to reconsider the original context of courtly discourse in all its complexity.

A preoccupation with the first-person male subject and his own use of language is a distinctive feature that offers a point of departure for treating this complexity. Since the mid-twentieth century, critics have also focused on the implications regarding gender in this discourse's representation of the feminine, which has also been called the troubadours' "portrait of the lady."[11] Extant lyric texts embracing the stylized code of *fin' amors* authored by male writers have been read with special attention paid to the objectification of the *domna* as a literary construct, which is seen as a projection of male desire manipulated by the poet. The goal of this manipulation has been called into question and has even been described as self-serving. In other words, it is considered doubtful that the objectified literary lady of the troubadours is constructed for the purposes of advancing the social position of women, or even that (as more cynical critics would have it) her elevation to the position of *midons* is merely a rhetorical flourish for the purposes of sexual conquest; in fact it is now generally considered doubtful that it is done "for her sake" at all.[12]

Kendrick's treatment of the social and cultural context from within which the troubadours originally composed their lyric poetry supports the notion that the simplistic or "romantic" approach of earlier troubadour critics needs substantial revision. The ludic and competitive atmosphere of troubadour performance, as her title emphasizes, certainly undermines the treatment of troubadour discourse as a "spontaneous overflow" of idealized love—that is, as a direct communication and expression of desire between speaking male subject and feminine object. Rather than take the ostensible lyric paradigm of speaker-to-addressee correspondence at face value, Kendrick establishes that in public performance, Provençal poets employed this paradigm as a rhetorical posture, as a trope taken as the point of departure for demonstrating one's wit and skill, and indeed as a highly stylized literary convention that established the rules governing "the game of love": "The object of the twelfth-century game of love was to win with words, just as the object of medieval war games was to win with weapons. The player's goal was not to win the lady, but to win the game, to conquer the masculine opponent(s)."

Furthermore, she explains, both written and oral reproduction of earlier troubadour songs would in turn serve as the basis for revisions, re-readings, and parodies by other (often competing) troubadours and jongleurs: "The real object of the troubadours' game of love was to assert personal prowess by wielding words to attack and destroy opponents' words, reversing or modifying their meaning by dismembering or 'cutting them up' or by reframing and reinterpreting them in one's own new context . . . Once a written text had traveled beyond its original performance situation, there was no controlling its interpretation. Almost any counterkey—even if it did not match the composer's—would work to unlock the treasure of textual meaning."[13] From its original conception, then, the discourse of courtly love was intricately linked with public performance and with the persuasion of an audience. It is therefore not surprising that centuries later the dramatists of Golden Age Spain would find in this discursive tradition material rich with dramatic possibilities.

Kendrick persuasively argues for the need to update troubadour scholarship in light of what we now know of the performance culture of twelfth-century Provence; we will see in this chapter how well this argument resonates with the performance of courtly desire in the public theaters of seventeenth-century Spain. We should first recognize, however, that neither Lope de Vega nor Calderón de la Barca, nor for that matter Dante or Petrarch, would likely have been aware of the details of the troubadours' cultural milieu such as Kendrick's exhaustive research has uncovered, nor would they share the theoretically informed perspective of twenty-first-century scholarship on such data. The survival of courtly love over the centuries did not depend on a persistent awareness of its jocular and performance-based origins; indeed one might argue that ignorance of such contextual details facilitated its more enduring manifestations, such as the Italian poetry of the *dolce stil nuovo* or Spanish *petrarquismo*. The spiritual and ethereal treatment of the lady in such cases is indeed a poetics of exclusion of a different kind than that of the troubadour game. What survives the transformation, beyond a persistent emphasis on the subjective experience of the male lyric subject, is the marginal role of the female object of desire.

Nor should we assume, however, that the literary elites of early modern Spain were unaware of the practice of *fin amors* in the context of courtly competitions: such a performance tradition survived in Spain at least well into the fifteenth century, as a number of compiled songbooks or *Cancioneros* attest.[14] We might then posit that Lope associated courtly love with the notion of a competitive performance of desire, as Duardo's sonnet performance in the first act of *La dama boba* would seem to suggest. It may well vary from one playwright to the next (and indeed from one play to the next, if not from one speech-act to the next within an individual play) the extent to which the *Comedia*'s invocation of courtly discourse involves the element of play intrinsic to its original performance context or, conversely, the extent to which it assumes a more "naïve" (from the theoretically informed perspective of twenty-first century scholarship) understanding of courtly love akin to the "romantic" interpretation outlined above. Between the two dominant lyric traditions in Spain during the fifteenth and sixteenth century informed by medieval courtly love—Petrarchism and the so-called *cancionero* tradition—there is considerable difference in how easily one can recognize such play. Lest we revisit the proverbial red herring of the sincerity issue, we should recognize that this plurality of performances exists, and that it is accommodated by the underlying discursive dynamics of the troubadour code.

Bernart de Ventadorn and Jaufre Rudel illustrate how, despite the implicit assumptions of the "romantic" interpretation of troubadour verse, this original instance of courtly discourse tends to focus on the poetic self and his craft. Like their contemporaries, Bernart and Jaufre foreground language, in that great concern is shown for the manipulation and interpretation of words, for the rhetorical positioning that the speaking subject assumes vis-à-vis the desire he feels for his *domna*. Apart from the attention paid to language, the troubadour poem tends to describe the effects of love on the poet, whether joy or suffering. This concern for the self and self-expression results in the female object's assumption of a role that is at best peripheral.

Jaufre Rudel's significance in the troubadour legacy, as Rosenstein and Wolf argue, is intimately tied to his legendary long-distance love affair with the Countess of Tripoli.[15] The circumstances of this amorous relationship (as legend has it) are conducive to his most frequent theme: the suffering of the male lover separated from his lady. The tropes of "distant love" or "love from afar" give way to the speaking subject's isolation, and the tendency in Jaufre's poetry is to focus on what is close at hand (the effects of that isolation and the nature of love in the abstract) rather than what is distant (the *domna* herself). Wolf and Rosenstein explain that "it is still the idea of love and its ethic, rather than the lady, which is the focus of attention."[16]

Love and its ethic are therefore the objects of direct address in Jaufre's "Qan lo rius de la fontana," while the lady is discussed in the third person.

> Amors de terra loindana,
> per vos toz lo cors mi dol;
> e non puosc trobar meizina
> si non vau al sieu reclam,
> ab atraich d'amor doussana,
> dinz vergier o sotz cortina
> ab desirada compaigna.

(lines 8–14)

[Love from a distant land, for you my whole self aches; and I can find no remedy unless I go at her call, with the lure of sweet love, in a garden or beneath a curtain with a desired companion.][17]

There is a subtle but significant difference between this discourse and the conventional belief that the lady is at the center of the troubadour cosmos. Love is not treated here as the effect caused by the lady; instead the lady is considered the remedy *(meizina)* for the suffering caused by Love—a remedy that the speaker finds *(trobar)* through his song *(trobar)*. Love and the speaker are engaged in speaker-interlocutor discourse (a discourse which often, as in the above citation, consists mainly of the poet's complaints about how love torments him), while the *domna* is a third party merely referred to, objectified as the *desiderada compaigna* but certainly not directly addressed.

Again, this discourse promotes a consideration of the abstract concept of love. Such abstraction explains the tendency to interpret Jaufre's poetry as an expression of "Platonic" or nonphysical love. Courtly love is often considered idealistic and chaste, and the lady's absence from Jaufre's poetry—the absence of the body—creates space for such notions. This is by no means to suggest that sensuality and physical desire are not present in troubadour poetry; it is apparent, however, that at least for Jaufre, physical distance from the object of desire creates a space to consider love in abstract terms. But rather than fill this space with an idealized and nonphysical expression of love for the *domna,* Jaufre focuses his attention squarely on himself, as for example in "No sap chantar qui so non di":

> Colps de joi me fer que m'ausi,
> e ponha d'amor que.m sostra
> la carn, don lo cors magrira;
> et anc mais tan greu no.m feri,
> ni per nuill colp tan no langui,
> quar no cove ni no s'esca.

(lines 13–18)

[A stroke of joy strikes and kills me, as does a prick of love which ravages my flesh, and makes me grow thin; and never have I been so stricken or weakened by any blow, for it is not right, and does not happen.]

It should be noted that along with the focus on the male subject noted above, Jaufre's poetry is consistent with the troubadour tradition in demonstrating a concern for his craft within each song, as in the first stanza of the poem cited above:

> No sap chantar qui so non di,
> ni vers trobar qui motz no fa,
> ni conois de rima co•s va
> si razo non enten en si;
> mas lo mieus chans comens' aisi:
> con plus l'auziretz, mais valra.
>
> (lines 13–18)

[He cannot sing who makes no tune, and he cannot write songs who makes no words, and does not know how a rhyme works if he does not understand the matter; but my own song begins like this: the more you hear it, the better it becomes.]

Through such metalanguage the speaking subject discusses the quality of his verse and his reasons for composing it. Because of this rhetorical posturing and the focus on the plight of the poet, the attention paid to Jaufre's lady is miniscule.

The lady is marginalized in a similar manner by Bernart de Ventadorn, as for example in his "Amors, e que.us es vejaire?" As seen in Jaufre, Love is addressed in the second person, leaving the *domna* on the periphery of the poet's concerns.

> Amors, e que.us es vejaire?
> Trobatz mais fol mas can me?
> Cuidatz vos qu'eu si' amaire
> e que ja no trop merce?
> Que que.m comandetz a faire,
> farai o c'assi.s cove,
> mas vos non estai ges be
> que.m fassatz tostems mal traire.
>
> (lines 1–8)

[Love, what does it seem like to you? Have you ever found one more foolish than I? Do you think I should love without ever finding grace? All you order me to do, I do, since one must do so. But it is not fitting that you mistreat me every day.]

Over the course of his extant songs, Bernart explores his relationship with Amors. The most frequent analogy chosen is that of slave to master, as images of binding and lost control are present throughout his songs. "En cossirer et en esmai / sui d'un amor que.m lass'e.m te, / que tan no vau ni sai ni lai/qu'ilh ades no.m tenh' en so fre . . ." [In anguish and torment am I because of a love that grips and holds me so that I can go neither here nor there without her holding me in her harness . . .] ("En cossirer e en esmai," 1–4). The lady is treated directly in this case, but as is true of most of Bernart's poetry, discussion of the lady generally consists of lamenting her failure to reward the speaker and scolding her for her cruelty—it is a means of explaining his plight, which is the real subject of discussion.

Self-absorption in Bernart's poetry is perhaps the most apparent in "Can vei la lauzeta mover." The third stanza leaves little room to doubt that Bernart recognizes love's greatest effect on the lover as a cause for him to consider himself; in other words, what love inspires above all else is self-reflection.

> Anc non agui de me poder
> ni no fui meus de l'or' en sai
> que.m laisset en sos olhs vezer
> en un miralh que mout me plai.
> Miralhs, pus me mirei en te,
> m'an mort li sospir de preon
> c'aissi.m perdei com perdet se
> lo bels Narcisus en la fon.

(lines 17–24)

[Never have I had power over myself, nor have I to this day been mine, since the hour when she let me look into her eyes, into a mirror which pleases me greatly. Mirror, since I gazed at myself in you, sighs from deep down have killed me; and so I lost myself, just as the beautiful Narcissus lost himself in the fountain.][18]

This striking passage also speaks of the poet's loss of control (reminiscent of the Ovidian tale of Narcissus), a motif to which Bernart continually returns. Desire for the lady is explained here as closely involved with self-love—which in turn results in the same loss of control that is implicit in the love-as-slavery *topos*. In other words, desire does exactly what its greatest opponents in the institution of classical rhetoric claim: Cicero, for example, begins his *De inventione* by narrating rhetoric's original conception for the purpose of controlling desire, to extinguish the fires of desire which governed uncivilized man. These same fires are the cause of Bernart's destruction. But absent from the elaborate mirror image is any substantial treatment of the lady as an independent construct in her own right. Her eyes captivate the poet because they reflect his true concern—namely, himself. The lady (through her eyes) is a self-referent to the poet rather than a separate, autonomous, or other self that draws his attention.

We may actually consider "Lo rossinhols s'esbaudeya," the poem by Bernart in which the *domna* is paid the most lyric attention, as further evidence of the tendency toward self-reflection. The lady is again discussed in the third person; but more important is what is revealed in the opening lines of the song:

> Lo rossinhols s'esbaudeya
> josta la flor el verjan,
> e pren m'en tan grans enveya
> qu'eu no posc mudar no chan
> Mas no sai de que ni de cui
>   Car eu non am me ni autrui
> e fatz esfortz car sai faire
> bo vers, pois no sui amaire.

(lines 1–8)

[The nightingale rejoices among the flowers in the garden, and such great trouble comes to me thereby that I cannot help singing; and I know not of what or of whom, for I do not love myself or anyone else, and I make an effort because I know how to make a good song when I am not a lover.]

Paradoxically but not coincidentally, Bernart's speaking subject discusses an *ilh* (a "she") at the greatest length in a song begun with the admission that no such *ilh* actually exists. If Bernart is indeed not in love at this moment, he is likewise not affected by love or "enslaved" by it. There is no self-referential plight to express, and such an absence leaves open the space normally reserved for complaints about his situation. In other words without such a situation to lament (or without any *joi* to praise), the lover is able to direct his attention outward to the lady (even though she does not exist). This suggests that when he is in love, when there is in fact an actual pair of eyes that provide the function of narcissistic mirror, the lady serves as a mere pretext for the song. In a sense she does inspire the song because she causes the poet to experience the emotions on which his verse normally focuses. But her importance to the troubadour does not extend beyond that of a means to a self-referential end.

Over the course of this textual analysis of troubadour verse, it has been noted that focus on the subjective experience of the male subject is often realized through the recurring conventional images of slavery, isolation, and loss of control. Such a concurrence is especially true in the poetry of Bernart, whose verses tend to end in frustration rather than triumph. The troubadours' consciousness of their language, audience, and rhetorical strategies is at the heart of their isolation from the lady, from the exclusion of her body and voice from the lyric space. The tradition pays an unprecedented amount of attention to such linguistic and rhetorical issues, whether in discussing which style of *trobar* the poet has chosen or in commenting on his skill within a given style.[19] Language therefore becomes more than a medium for desire; it becomes a self-reflexive medium (and, as Kendrick emphasizes, a ludic and competitive one). One might say it is a linguistic and rhetorical game played by the troubadours, and the objectives of this game exclude any serious treatment of the *domna* or her (nonreflecting) qualities.

This is apparent in Raimbaut de Vaqueiras's *tenso* "Domna, tant vos ai preiada." According to Simon Gaunt's commentary on the bilingual *tenso* or dialogic exchange between two voices, Raimbaut speaks in courtly Provençal but the unidentified lady replies in a Genoese dialect of Italian. Gaunt argues that Raimbaut's stanzas disregard the comments of his interlocutor—in other words, if one were to extract her lines, his stanzas could still stand alone as a conventional troubadour *canso*. "Raimbaut continues to ignore his interlocutor; the accumulation of *topoi* could thus be addressed to any *domna* and consequently increasingly depersonalize the woman who is trying so hard to communicate her disdain to him."[20] Gaunt is primarily concerned with the linguistic differences between masculine and feminine (grammatical gender) as a marker of sexual difference (biological gender), a concern echoed by Kay's *Subjectivity in Troubadour Poetry,* but the discursive and rhetorical disjuncture between male and female speakers alone is striking and not unlike the lines from *La dama boba* cited at the beginning of this chapter.

Bogin explains that the troubadours expressed the exclusionary ideology of male linguistic community that they represented by means of "a language that voiced beneath its surface the deepest longings of their audience."[21] In other words, the male linguistic community of the troubadours does more than rhetorically mark its sexual difference from the *domna:* it establishes an ideology implicit behind the language (an "ideolect," Bakhtin would say) that excludes the feminine and ignores the existence of her voice. Raimbaut, as was the case with Bernart and Jaufre, is so utterly caught up in playing his linguistic game that the lady's presence is ignored, her voice unrecognized. Implicit in Bernart and Jaufre but explicit in Raimbaut's *tenso* is the fact that the *domna* does not play the same rhetorical Occitan lyric game—she literally does not speak his language. In these poems, the Provençal lyric appears to be something akin to an artistic and linguistic club whose membership is exclusively male. We will see, however, that one need not look outside the geographical and linguistic borders of Provençe to find a dissenting voice (one that asserts itself in spite of troubadour male linguistic hegemony) when we consider the response of the *trobairitz* to the troubadour tradition. These women poets demonstrate the paradox of speaking the same dialect while not operating from within the same implicit ideolect.

Sarah Spence suggests that the troubadours are responsible for a refiguring of rhetoric that incorporates desire, including the desire for the body so disdained by Augustine. The influence of Augustine on early medieval rhetoric would therefore be challenged by the new poetics introduced in the troubadour "game of love" in a way that reincorporates desire into the rhetorical art of poetry. The point here is that this desire is in fact born of self-love, and in rhetorically creating space for it, the lady is a casualty: the concern for desire, and especially for its effect on the self, overrides any concern for treating woman as a subject of textual space. Courtly love in its "original" male-authored Provençal manifestations, then, is a self-reflexive and linguistically self-aware discourse. The ideology implicit in the convention, we have seen, does more than idealize and praise the lady: it objectifies her and excludes her voice. When she is described, moreover, the function of narcissistic mirror reflects any attention paid to her back upon the poet: "What we see in the Lady of troubadour lyric is thus not a woman at all. She is a projection of the poet/lover's desire and a reflection of his fears; and the lyric itself displays the workings of an erotic fantasy based on male attraction to and repulsion from the female."[22]

It is important to note that, while Burns's analysis is compelling, it antedates Kendrick's *The Game of Love* and thus stops short of considering the cultural context in which such an "erotic fantasy" was originally performed. Before such considerations of cultural production were on the critical radar, Roger Boase had already argued in *The Troubadour Revival* that Spain witnessed a continuation of the courtly love lyric well into the fifteenth century, given the formal and thematic common ground between troubadour poetry and the Galician-Portuguese, Catalán, and Castillian love lyric traditions of the waning Middle Ages.[23] More recently, critical attention toward the *cancionero* (songbook) tradition of Trastamaran Spain has shed new light on what is, especially in terms of its social and performance context, the most direct descendent of troubadour discourse.[24]

SPEAKING FROM THE MARGINS: THE *TROBAIRITZ*

The renewed vigor with which critics have explored the Provençal lyric of female authorship has resulted in the discovery of a distinct feminine voice, which offers a different and refreshing perspective on the discourse of courtly love. The *trobairitz* offer songs presenting the lady's subjective point of view to voice a response to male troubadour poetry, an act that is in direct opposition to the troubadour construction of a silent, passive, and dehumanized object (or even "mirror," as the *domna* is often described). They reject the male construct of the courtly lady and engage their discourse in a renegotiation of the lady's role in relationships governed by the rules of courtly love. As a result, the very goals of courtly discourse are redefined.

For the *trobairitz* to attempt to work from within the discursive conventions established by the troubadours is problematic. Indeed, for the female poet to assume the same ideology discussed above (based on feminine exclusion and objectification through self-reflection and linguistic self-awareness), she would be forced to objectify and exclude her own feminine identity, thereby assuming a "male" poetic voice. Really, the very idea of a self-expressive or in any other way "voiced" lady is abhorrent to the troubadour system. The *trobairitz* are marginalized by the patriarchal tradition, left to compose their verses from the periphery of this male-constructed lyric world. A closer look at their extant works (and the critical assessments made of them by modern scholars) demonstrates that the response of the *trobairitz* to the male construct of courtly love lays bare the self-absorption that has been discussed, and it also seeks to set itself apart as an autonomous mode of discourse, not submissive to the aims and conventions of the male tradition and in fact antagonistic toward it. The *trobairitz* represent the gender objectified by the troubadours, and they reject the passive role of mirror that Bernart's male subject would have them assume. As such their very existence as a literary phenomenon is a rupture in the troubadour tradition; *sui generis* they fall outside of the scope of the male institution.

For this reason, critical attention has been largely concerned with the differences that set the women troubadours apart from the male tradition. This focus has led to a thorough treatment of their sense of identity, self-awareness, and autonomy.[25] Bogin offers the following reading of the texts in her anthology: "the women seek two things in their relationships: to be acknowledged for who they are, as women and as individuals, and a determining voice in how the relationship is conducted; the women argue for a *real,* as opposed to a *symbolic* acknowledgement of their importance."[26] The real social and political position of the twelfth-century woman in Provençe, although notably higher at this particular moment in history than the predominant position of women during most of the Middle Ages, has very little to do with her symbolic position as *midons.* Rosenn interprets this exchange—the real position of social inferiority for the idealized status of the male fiction of the *domna*—as central to the process of self-definition in *trobairitz* poetry: "There is, moreover, a contradiction of foundations in the contrast between the representation of women as powerful in the literary discourse of the male troubadours and the representation of women as powerless in the literary discourse of the female trobairitz, a discourse that in its very existence constitutes an act of empowerment."[27] The act of empowerment, then, paradoxically involves assuming the role of victim, through which the *trobairitz* create space for their own voices and forge a sense of autonomous artistic identity.

Because such a space is used to express an explicit rejection of the troubadour love ethic, there are of course substantial discursive ramifications to this responsive or countertraditional posture. In exposing the troubadour representation of *midons* as disingenuous and exclusionary, or as a patriarchal master narrative imposed upon a silent feminine object with which she does not identify, the female poetic voice identifies male courtly discourse as a closed system from which she feels alienated, thus making necessary a counterdiscourse that places itself in dialogue with that system. Bakhtin's terminology, although originally conceived in the context of prose narrative, seems both fitting and pertinent here: the troubadours forge a *monologic* tradition that serves as an "authoritative discourse," while the *trobairitz* engage in a mode of "internally persuasive" discourse more appropriately considered *dialogic,* since it exists as a response and corrective.[28] Bruckner specifically points to the "multivoicedness" of the woman poet's discourse, which constitutes the "kaleidoscope of her song."[29] This difference between male and female courtly discourse appears most evident in the latter's refusal to play the verbal and rhetorical game prescribed by the former.

In another subversion of the male construct, the *trobairitz* contrast troubadour rhetorical strategy and the intentional obscurity of *trobar clus* (closed style of composition) with what Bogin refers to as "plain speaking" or a "conversational style" and Bruckner calls a "lack of ceremony." Artistry through ornate language with ambiguous meaning is replaced by an attempt at communication of the *domna*'s position: "Their verse is rhymed, but there is less word play and less interest in the exercise of craft than in the men's poems; the women prefer the more straight-forward speech of conversation. Perhaps this is because the women, unlike the men, do not idealize the relationships they write about, nor do they use the lover and the lady as allegorical figures."[30] The parallels are clear between such a rejection of *trobar clus* and, as I will discuss later in this chapter, the *hablar claro* of *La dama boba*'s Nise. The *Comedia*'s portrayal of female subjects confronting the role of passive object assigned to them by the men who court them is therefore another installment of the longstanding discursive dynamics of the discourse of courtly love.

In place of such an allegorical treatment, the *trobairitz* express different concerns and different agendas. Nappholz identifies trust and betrayal as key issues for the anonymous lady of Bertran del Pojet's *tenso* and then expands the scope of the observation: "evidence exists to show that a similar concern with trust and betrayal is shared by most of the historical trobairitz."[31] In more general terms, the subject matter of many songs involves specific complaints regarding what is expected of them by men, how they are treated by men, and how they are sung about by men. Traditional images of courtly love give way to complaints against the injustice done to them, whether in a specific example involving a specific lover or in the more general sense regarding troubadour masculine discourse (and, again, its implicit ideology). As Bogin states, "the women do not want to be transcended."[32] Indeed Bruckner perceives their agenda to be a subversion of the hierarchical structures implicit in the male troubadour ideolect, which is replaced by a "balance of difference and sameness."[33] But whatever a given critical opinion may isolate as the major themes of this feminine discourse, there is a clear shift from the themes and arguments of the troubadours' game of love, and from the (male) gender-inflected discourse from which they are enunciated, to a more critical examination of the inherent problems and contradictions of the game itself.

Such a discursive rupture is particularly evident in Lombarda's *tenso* with Bernart Arnaut, one of the more celebrated examples of the *trobairitz* response.[34] In her response to Bernart's opening verses, Lombarda makes explicit reference to the role of "mirror" that the troubadours would have her assume: the presence of such an image signifies for her a denial of her voice that, in order to assume the voiced first-person subject position of lyric verse, she must overcome. The *tenso* is indeed quite indicative of the discursive difference between the male and female traditions that we have observed. Bernart's standard stanzas follow the obscure style of *trobar clus,* making meaning ambiguous and word play the central exercise; Lombarda's response begins with a subversive manipulation of the same *clus* style that mirrors the lines of her co-conversant. More importantly, she then breaks from the strategy of imitation to speak in direct and unambiguous terms about her resentment of how he has represented her: "Voil qe'm digaz / cals mais vos plaz / ses cuberta selada / e.l mirail on miratz" (I want to know / your true opinion: / which one you prefer, and what's / the mirror where you stare). Lombarda sees the troubadour convention of lady as "mirror" in the same narcissistic terms that we have used to describe it, and she makes it clear that this very image, if she were to conform to it, would render her both voiceless and nameless. If she were to accept the troubadour model, she would relinquish both her art and her identity. "Car lo mirailz e no veser descorda / tan mon acord c'ab pauc no.l desacorda, / mas can record so qu'l meus noms recorda, / en bon acord totz mons pensars s'acorda" (For the mirror with no image so disrupts / that it almost interrupts it; / but then when I remember what my name records, / all my thoughts unite in one accord).[35] And in a parting subversive gesture, Lombarda omits the final stanza that would have been necessary to make complete and perfect her mirroring of Bernart's stanzas. Her ultimate rejection of the phallocentric discursive practice (the *tenso* convention dictating that she mirror the male poet's verses), after having established her own voice within her own countertraditional lyric space, asserts the authority of her silence and her autonomous choice to not play the game, at least to its conventional conclusion. The gesture confirms her rejection of male discourse and, *in absentia,* it effectively establishes the autonomy and authority of the female poetic voice.

If the troubadours lay the foundations of a patriarchal literary institution (courtly love), and if their poetry constitutes a literary tradition, Lombarda and her fellow *trobairitz* make clear the conflation of gender roles and discursive roles implicit in that tradition. Writing from the margins implies a necessary reversal of such roles for the female subject to emerge as an alternative mode of performance, and the *trobairitz* make explicit reference to male-defined courtly love in the process of expressing a dissenting perspective. In effect, the *trobairitz* refuse to play the "game of love" that constitutes the foundation of the courtly love tradition. Yet they ostensibly compose from within the same cultural circumstances and base their amatory discourse on the same conventions of the male construct, in effect manipulating troubadour discourse so as to engender an alternate mode of subjectivity that contradicts its original gendered power dynamics. Perhaps it is more accurate to say that they find themselves placed there by the male tradition: they express their voice and subvert their objectification from the margins of the troubadour system, just as the *domna* finds herself objectified and relegated to the margins of the troubadour poem. Eva Rosenn expresses a similar opinion as she discusses the *trobairitz*'s "adopting the discourse of the troubadours but ultimately [being] confined by the paradigm of that discourse."[36]

To the feminist critic interested in arguing for an autonomous *trobairitz* discourse as a medieval manifestation of *écriture féminine*, such an assessment may be objectionable, but it should be emphasized that this contrastive analysis is a means of understanding the broader context in which both male and female voices were originally sounded. Ultimately we must ask: *can* a woman write from within the confines of the courtly lyric tradition, marked as it is by female objectification and exclusion, if by writing (voicing) she changes her role from object to subject? If the tradition of courtly discourse, which exercised a decisive influence over imaginative literature for centuries, is defined by a male canon (one that objectifies the feminine and uses this object for questionable ends), can the poetry of the *trobairitz* (which replaces the objectification with a distinctly subjective representation, in its turn manipulated for a divergent purpose) really be placed within the same tradition?

Certainly the *fin' amors* represented by women writers is of a different sort from that of the troubadours. It is a common argument that what we call "courtly love" is merely a modern construct, projected onto a wide range of amatory medieval literature that did not necessarily identify itself as part of a common "courtly love" tradition in its own day. Indeed, the argument that women writers employ courtly rhetoric and conventions for distinct purposes would lend support to such a contention, especially if "courtly love" is understood in the romantic sense of de Rougemont and Lewis. But if we instead treat courtly love as a discursive mode not necessarily delimited to a patriarchal master narrative, then the *trobairitz* may be seen as a tradition employing this discourse toward ends that diverge from those of their male contemporaries. By forging their own gendered forms of discourse in response to male courtly discourse, they offer us a perspective from which to reexamine the male-authored canon of courtly literature. For if the troubadours establish this mode of discourse with a set of misogynist patriarchal parameters, the *trobairitz* liberate it from those parameters by objecting to (and thus exposing) their implicit ideology. Simply put, the discourse of courtly love is invariably gender-inflected. Establishing the feminine as "other" implies the self as masculine and thus identifies one by gender, just as does the assumption by the women troubadours of the position of first-person female subject. What the *trobairitz* offer, apart from the alternative voice of the female subject, is a perspective from which to reexamine the male troubadour lyric, and indeed the troubadour legacy of courtly love, as equally inflected by gender.

The Troubadour Legacy: Dante, Petrarch, and Lyric Poetry in the Spanish Renaissance

The engagement of male courtly discourse in dialogue by the *trobairitz* has only recently been studied by literary scholars; it is the monologic male troubadour tradition that exercised influence on future generations and schools of lyric poets through the early modern period. Unlike the troubadours, whose mythic status as pioneers in the love poetry of the western world would endure for centuries, widespread dissemination of *trobairitz* poetry (with the exception of the occasional entry in medieval and Renaissance anthologies of lyric poetry) would not occur for seven hundred years. Implicit in the supposition that early modern Spanish comedy's representation of desire ultimately owes its paradigm to the troubadours is the notion that such a paradigm, earlier referred to as the legacy of the troubadours, persisted through the Middle Ages and into early modernity via the texts and traditions that exercised a more direct influence on the *Comedia*. Because the manifestation of this discursive paradigm in the Dantean *stilnovisti* and Petrarchan schools of lyric poetry informs the *Comedia's* representation of desire, both directly (in the case of Spanish Petrarchism) and through intermediary Spanish *romancero* and *cancionero* sources, a brief consideration of these Italian influences will illustrate the connection between medieval Provence and early modern Spain.

Dante was the first major literary figure after the decline of medieval Occitan culture to privilege the troubadours. His own importance in the history of vernacular literature is incontrovertible, but his *De Vulgari Eloquentia* and *Divina Commedia* demonstrate an awareness that his elevation of the vernacular to the status of a literary language on par with Latin was in fact a continuation of the pioneering troubadour lyric. It is worth noting that despite earning his place in literary history as the author of the *Divina Commedia* and the *Vita Nuova*—both narratives—Dante's earliest contemporary fame was earned for his lyric poetry. The debt owed by the poets of the *dolce stil nuovo* (sweet new style) to the troubadours is suggested when in the *Purgatorio* Dante names Arnaut Daniel as the "miglior fabbro del parlar materno" (best craftsman of the mother tongue)[37]—that is, the best wordsmith in the vernacular. Such deference makes sense in light of the troubadour influence on the poetic school within which his literary career began.

Dante's poetic mentor and role model, Guido Guinizelli, pioneered the sweet new style in response to an established Italian lyric tradition (first made famous by the Sicilian School of poets) in which he himself had earlier participated. The Sicilians, according to Douglas Radcliff-Umstead, "slavishly adapted the language and ideas of the Provençal tradition for their own needs," and Guittone D'Arezzo led a group of northern Italian poets who (in the view of the *stilnovisti* poets) "servilely copied the work of the Sicilian school."[38] Rather than exercise a repetitive mastery over the preestablished forms of the troubadours, Guinizelli and his followers pursued the "pure" expression of love as their new aesthetic. In other words, the goal became not form but content. This position is in fact an appeal to return to the essence of courtly love as they conceived it (and not unlike how Lewis would later conceive it): a sincere and devotional desire for the lady. "Slavish" or "servile" imitation, Dante would later explain in the *Purgatorio,* became for his predecessors an impediment (a *nodo* [knot]) to expression: among the gluttons in the twenty-fourth canto is one such pre-*stilnovisti* poet, Bonagiunta Orbicciani, who admits "Io veggio ben come le vostre penne / di retro al dittator sen vanno strette, / che delle nostre certo non avvenne" (I see well how your pens follow close behind the dictator, which assuredly did not happen with ours).[39] Dante has the poet literally repent posthumously of this mechanical practice, and in the process name his more famous contemporary Guittone d'Arezzo, calling him a "notario" (notary)[40] or transparent medium through which the subjective experience of desire was recorded, in order to underscore the mechanical nature of prominent pre-*stilnovisti* Italian lyric poetry. The consequences of this shift toward the more "inspired" *dolce stil nuovo* for literary history were to be substantial, for out of the sweet new style would emerge an idealization of love and of the feminine object of desire that would eventually influence Petrarch and his followers.

When compared to the self-reflexive language of the Provençal lyric, it would appear at first glance that the more "genuine" poetry of the *stilnovisti* would imply a move away from troubadour self-absorption, but in fact the lyric paradigm centered on a male subject experiencing love—the discursive legacy of the troubadours—is in fact taken more seriously and therefore legitimized. There is in this literary context no ludic competition played out between poet-performers, and Dante's idealized vision of love can hardly be considered a game. The *Vita Nuova* narrates the composition process of his more famous *stilnovisti* lyrics with a focus on the moments in which Beatrice inspired them. Again in the twenty-fourth canto of the *Purgatorio* he explains his notion of *poesis* in simple terms: "I' mi son un che, quando / Amor mi spira, noto, e a quell modo / ch'e' ditta dentro vo significando" (I am one who, / when Love inspires me, takes note, / and as he dictates within, I write).[41] As with Bernart de Ventadorn and Jaufre, Dante's paradigm directly implicates himself in the first person, along with the abstract personification of Love, leaving the lady who inspires his desire on the periphery. A Dantean scholar may take issue with the notion that Beatrice is ultimately peripheral, but in Dante's lyric poetry she does serve the function of the courtly discourse *domna:* to reflect back upon the male subject, indeed often as the pretext for the poet's experience of desire, and at best "a projection of the poet/lover's desire and a reflection of his fears."[42]

Guinizelli's famous "Al cor gentil rempaira sempre amore" asserts an important departure from the troubadour notion of love as an ennobling force that further privileges the male subject: the lover's intrinsic nobility is what makes love possible in the first place. "Al cor gentil rempaira sempre amore / come l'ausello in selva a la verdura; / nè fe' amore anti che gentil core, nè gentil core anti ch'amor, natura: / ch'adesso con' fu 'l sole" (To the gentle heart Love betakes itself / As to the wood the bird amidst the foliage: / Before the gentle heart, in Nature's scheme, / Love was not, nor the gentle heart before Love).[43] It should be pointed out that *gentil* connotes nobility for Guinizelli, not unlike the traditional English connotation of *gentility*. Rather than lift up a humble lover to an elevated status, this reconfiguration of love is the exclusive domain of a noble elite. In the fourth stanza of the *canzone* Guinizelli specifies that the nobility of which he speaks is a "nobility of the soul" as opposed to social rank, but the implication is that the male subject possesses an inherent quality that renders him worthy of love. Discussion of intrinsic masculine worth is but one more topic through which the discourse of courtly love treats the masculine exclusively at the expense of the feminine: once again there is minimal reference to an actual lady in this poem, as the lyric focuses on the qualities of the male subject and his relation to Love. When in the fifth stanza a *donna* is finally discussed, it is to compare her effect on him with that of God's divine radiance.

Guinizelli initiates a divinization of the lady, and a spiritualization of the male subject's love for her, that would be developed and amplified by Dante, whose treatment of Beatrice would later be adapted by Petrarch. The elevation of the lady to mythic and religious stature is an augmentation of the troubadour rhetorical posture whereby the lady is put on a pedestal, and its discursive implications include a similar objectification and essentialization of Woman. If, as in the view of Bogin, the *trobairitz* objected to "being transcended" by the troubadours, if they sought from them "a real, as opposed to a symbolic acknowledgement of their importance," one can assume that their reception of Dante's divinization and allegorization of Beatrice would involve a similar reaction. Hence while Dante would only apply the rhetoric of praise to Beatrice (she is quite literally blameless, as the *Paradiso* would ultimately affirm), his representation of her is ultimately self-reflexive and self-serving: it is again a projection and allegorization of his ideals and desires, and it serves to perpetuate the discursive paradigm set in motion by the troubadours. Ultimately, and well after the death of the flesh-and-blood woman to whom she originally corresponded, the angelic Beatrice would assume a major role in Dante's *Vita Nuova* and in his drama of self-discovery and epic journey through the divine cosmos led by her and her intermediary Virgil—in his *Divina Commedia*. The figure of Beatrice and the self-absorbed discourse through which she is realized are co-substantial, as for Guinizelli are *amore* and *il cor gentil*, the noble heart of the male subject.

Petrarch may be seen as the dominant voice through whom the two disparate traditions of the medieval love lyric and early modern Spanish drama are connected. His lyric poetry both formally and thematically serves as a source for Spain's Renaissance lyric poets, such as Garcilaso and Boscán, and (even if as a paradigmatic model against which to rebel) the poets contemporary to the *Comedia*—including Quevedo, Góngora, and even Lope de Vega himself. It is important to note that the Petrarch of *petrarquismo*—the portion of his overall *corpus* that began a western European lyric school bearing his name—represents only a portion of his work, only that portion of the *Canzoniere* that most closely draws upon the troubadour postures of love from afar and love-as-suffering. In these skillfully crafted sonnets, *canzones,* ballads, madrigals, and *sestinas,* the conventions of troubadour poetry are revised in a manner that reflects a Dantean influence. Much of the later portions of the *Canzoniere,* the *Trionfi,* and some of his Latin works (notably the *Secretum*) treat Laura and his experience of love for her in a manner that is less indebted to the discourse of courtly love, indeed in some instances in a manner that refutes the nearly exclusive lyric focus on the self being traced in this chapter. But what Lope and his followers in Spanish drama associated with Petrarch—the vernacular lyric that influenced their own representation of desire—does serve to perpetuate the discursive legacy of troubadour poetry.

The model of Beatrice was certainly an early influence on Petrarch and subsequently on Petrarchism, as was the self-absorbed discourse through which she was realized. In a manner similar to Dante's treatment of Beatrice, Laura is spiritualized and elevated to the status of a messianic figure. While her physicality is paradoxically incorporated into the divinization process—her hair, her eyes, and so on—to the extent that Petrarch would later repent of having so privileged the body in the poetry of his youth, it is still fair to say that the Laura of the *Canzoniere* comes to represent for the poet far more than the flesh-and-blood woman who died almost thirty years before Petrarch's own death (he continued to revise the collection of poems during his entire lifetime). Along similar lines, Mark Musa argues that the *Canzoniere* is less a study of Petrarch's relationship with Laura than a study of Petrarch in love: "who Laura was, married or unmarried, is not important, since such information does not provide us with a better understanding of the *Canzoniere.*"[44] "Di pensier in pensier / di monte i monte" (From thought to thought, mountain top to mountain top), *canzon* #129, exemplifies how Laura is a projection of the poet's desire and a function of his own psychological state.

> E quanto in più selvaggio
> Loco mi trovo e'n più deserto lido,
> Tanto più bella il mio pensier l'adombra.
> Poi quando il vero sgombra
> Quel dolce error, pur lì medesmo assido
> Me freddo, pietra morta in pietra viva,
> In guisa d'uom che pensi e pianga e scriva.[45]

[The wilder the place is, the more barren the shore where I may be, the more lovely do my thoughts depict her image; but when the truth dispels that sweet mistake, right then and there I sit down cold as dead stone set on living rock, a statue that can think and weep and write.] (trans. Musa 48)

It is the psychological landscape of the poet that gives way to her representation. Musa adds that "Laura is not the main subject of the work. Petrarch himself is its subject and centre, and the work itself is his own psychoanalytical notebook, an ever-changing portrait of the self."[46] Thus while Petrarch's innovations to the vernacular love lyric cannot be overstated, the self-reflexive discourse of courtly love provides the framework for this portrait of the self.

To be sure, lyric poetry in Spain during the fifteenth and sixteenth centuries bears the stamp of Petrarchan influence—a legacy that for Ignacio Navarrete reflects underlying cultural anxieties in the Spanish empire.[47] The intensified psychological self-examination and the mystification/divinization of the *dama,* seen above as part and parcel of the same self-absorbed discourse, are perpetuated by the Spanish Petrarchan tradition. Iris M. Zavala characterizes the poets of this school as "noble warriors who play music and seek poetry to sing about a lady that is always the superlative of beauty"; Garcilaso in particular is the "crier of the poet-warrior's glory, and his hyperboles have that bliss of a poetry that is born from a vast tradition." Such self-glorification, again, is achieved through an objectified portrait of the female object of male desire as "a surface very much infused with metaphors, images, and myths."[48] Zavala's identification of the poet-warrior's glory as the ultimate aim of *poesis* in the Spanish Petrarchan mode suggests that the discursive analysis of courtly love that has been traced thus far in this chapter, especially in terms of its focus on the self-absorbed male subject, is equally applicable to these Spanish "orphans" that would prove so influential for Lope de Vega and the *Comedia.*

The opening stanza of Garcilaso's thirty-second sonnet exemplifies the persistence of the egoistic Petrarchan posture of the lover/poet: "Estoy continuo en lágrimas bañando, / rompiendo el aire siempre con sospiros"[49] (I am continually bathed in tears, always rending the air with sighs). Petrarchan influence may lead Garcilaso and his contemporaries to a more psychologically intense version of troubadour self-absorption than was the case in the medieval Spanish lyric of the *cancionero* tradition, but the discursive framework seen above in Bernart and Jaufre remains nonetheless intact. The discourse of courtly love continues to be grounded in the male subject's experience of desire, in his "dulce lamentar" (sweet lament). We may certainly read the famous refrain of Garcilaso's first eclogue in these terms: "Salid sin duelo, lágrimas, corriendo" (Flow forth, tears, painlessly).[50] The tears that flow from love-as-suffering are the physical substance most closely connected to *poesis.*

Such a reading of Garciliaso's work puts aside questions of correspondence between the poet's lyric production and his biography, a longstanding preoccupation for Garcilaso scholars that has only recently been questioned.[51] In keeping with a "romantic" reading of courtly love as the sincere expression of the poet's personal experience of desire, scholars mined the scarce biographical information uncovered over the centuries in order to attribute Garcilaso's amorous relationships, especially one involving Isabel Freire, a lady of the Portuguese court, as the direct inspiration of his lyric poetry. What the present study suggests is that the discursive dynamics of the troubadour paradigm, especially in terms of the introspective and self-absorbed male poetic subject position from which he performs desire, are more important for this founding father of Spanish Petrarchism than is any particular woman with whom he may or may not have been romantically involved.

COURTLY DISCOURSE IN THE *COMEDIA:*
THE CASE OF *LA DAMA BOBA*

The persistence of the discursive paradigm forged by the troubadours that this chapter has traced thus far, in part with the help of a perspective of gendered alterity supplied by the *trobairitz,* has prepared the way for a reconsideration of the relationship between medieval courtly love and seventeenth-century Spanish theatrical performances of desire. In the realm of lyric poetry, Zavala argues that the Petrarchan strain of courtly love persisted as a dominant literary discourse until the Counter-Reformation. Thus Góngora, Quevedo, and Lope de Vega are the first major Spanish poets to move away from faithfully following the thematics of Dante, Petrarch, and the troubadours, insofar as they parody and even deconstruct courtly conventions in their own lyric poetry. While Zavala's emphasis on the self-awareness of Spanish Baroque poets as "post-Petrarchan" is well taken, however, we would do well to not overstate the distance between these early modern poets and Petrarch: their experimentation takes Petrarchan discourse as its base and point of departure, and often as an object of imitation as in Góngora's *arte mayor* poems. More importantly, the resilience of the courtly model as a discursive paradigm is such that, regardless of how "post-Petrarchan" the critical and objective engagement of the tradition may be, male-authored lyric and dramatic poetry retain such features as the self-absorbed, desiring male subject, as the case of *La dama boba* will illustrate. Such discursive resilience explains how, as Zavala puts it, "courtly love and its variants tend to become undone, to be burned and then reconstructed" as the Church reacts to the threat of Protestantism at the end of the sixteenth century.[52] One such reconstruction is the religious and mystical poetry of Fray Luis de León and San Juan de la Cruz, a conservative approach to love poetry that reconciles it to Christian ideology by replacing the divinized lady with God Himself. Another approach to literary love widely popular in the wake of Petrarchism upon which Zavala does not focus is Neoplatonism. León Hebreo's *Dialoghi de Amore* is philosophically and conceptually influential, notably so for Lope de Vega, but the ideas of Neoplatonism never fueled an alternate lyric tradition or distinctive poetic language to rival those of Petrarchism. It would be more accurate to consider Neoplatonic concepts as a later addition to the poetic repertoire of Spanish Petrarchism.

From another perspective, one could argue that Petrarchism became a victim of its own success: so widespread and popular was the Petrarchan lyric (especially the sonnet) that its language and conventions came to constitute what A. A. Parker has called "a rhetoric of orthodoxy."[53] In a *Comedia* tradition well known for its tendency toward the self-reflexive and metatheatrical, it is not surprising that the rhetoric of orthodoxy that courtly discourse had come to represent would be scrutinized, parodied, and reconfigured. Such treatment of courtly love makes sense in light of the change in audi-

ence from Renaissance courtly lyric to the early modern public theater; having fun with the cultured language of an aristocratic elite
(the literally "courtly" or socially elite readership of Petrarchan poetry)
was by all accounts well received by the popular audience (what Lope
calls the *vulgo*) at the *corrales*. The rise of the professional theater in
Spain that allows the *Comedia* to thrive and proliferate occurs at a time
when Spanish Petrarchism has long stood for the literary establishment, making the latter an easy target for the former to subvert in its
own representations and performances of desire.

It is especially the more formulaic and conventional comedies
derived from classical Roman and Renaissance Italian comedy, the
popular and stylized *capa y espada* plays and the *comedias de enredo*, for
example, that most directly confront and undermine the conventions and rhetorical postures of courtly love. The following pages will
demonstrate the ways in which *La dama boba* participates in this subversion. Of interest, however, is not merely whether or not the *Comedia* offers a vision of love that departs from the courtly and Petrarchan model, but also whether or not this departure extends to the
level of discourse. In other words, our concern is not limited to
Lope's undermining of the "ethic" of courtly love and its Petrarchan
conceits and motifs; of greater importance to our concerns is what
becomes of the discursive self-absorption and subsequent objectifi-
cation/exclusion of the feminine that have been traced thus far.[54]
The language and rhetorical postures of courtly love (as practiced by
several male characters in the play) are subject to critique and parody in this play, but in defining his own concept of idealized love
through the transformation of Finea (and, notably, through Finea's
verbal performance of desire), the courtly model's patriarchal discursive parameters are ultimately reaffirmed. Moreover, the play's
conclusion demonstrates the persuasive power of courtly discourse, as
both male protagonists do ultimately attain the women they desire.[55]

The plot of *La dama boba* hinges on the effects of love on its female
protagonist. The resolution to the conflict that Lope weaves is dependent on Finea's transformation at the hands of love, or her education
by love, which has generally been accepted as most directly indebted
to the Neoplatonism widely popular in the Spanish Golden Age.[56]
But what merits further attention are the terms through which this
transformative, transcendental, and idealized love is defined in the
work. *La dama boba* defines love to a great extent by the negotiation,
through female voices, of what it is *not*—namely the discourse of courtly

love and all of its rhetorical trappings. Consider Nise's early description of poetic discourse:

> NISE. Hay dos prosas diferentes:
> poética y historial.
> La historial, lisa y leal,
> cuenta verdades patentes,
>   con frase y terminos claros;
> la poética es hermosa,
> varia, culta, licenciosa,
> y escura aun a ingenios raros.
> Tiene mil exornaciones
> y retóricas figuras [. . .]
> así corre el engaño del mundo.

(lines 293–302)

[There are two kinds of prose: poetic and historical. The historical, plain and truthful, reveals patent truths with clear phrases and terms. The poetical is beautiful, varied, cultured, licentious, and obscure even to rare geniuses. It has a thousand embellishments and rhetorical figures [. . .] such is how the world is deceived.]

Nise appears to be making the distinction between poetic and historical truth that had been drawn at least as far back as Plato and Aristotle; over the course of the play it becomes clear that her use of language aspires to historical truth, while her distrust of male discourse has much to do with its resemblance to the poetic courtly love tradition, both for its inaccessibility ("escura aun a ingenios raros" [obscure even to rare geniuses]) and for its deception ("el engaño del mundo" [the ruse of the world]). Accordingly, the sisters (each in her own way) disparage the rhetoric of courtly love, but at the same time their own expression of desire is forged out of a dialogue with that discourse.

Nise rejects the obscure courtly lyric offered by Duardo; her criticism of that discourse for its inaccessibility (despite her own education and erudition, she claims to understand "ni una palabra" [not a single word]) is as applicable to the intentionally opaque *trobar clus* of Provence as it is to Petrarchan poetry. Duardo's self-focused verses, rhetorically ornamented and obscure by design, stand in striking contrast to Nise's declaration: "Yo quiero hablar claro." Her anti-rhetorical stance is a direct response to the courtly rhetoric of Duardo, Laurencio, and Liseo, and her plain-speaking makes clear that the "hablar oscuro" (*trobar clus*) of courtly rhetoric serves no purpose for her. Her cautious acceptance of Laurencio's gesticulations and advances is sharply halted when she learns that, behind her back, he has chosen to court Finea for her larger dowry. Nise's worst suspicions are confirmed: the courtly rhetoric of male courtship is devoid of the commitment (couched in terms of servile devotion) it claims to express. First frustration with Nise's resistance (her failure to be persuaded by courtly rhetoric) and then economic concerns are the motives behind Laurencio's change of heart, which in essence is an exchange of one feminine object for another, more profitable one—as Friedman puts it, "a shift from pure love to cash nexus."[57] The play's male performances of desire, then, dramatize Lope's critique of Petrarchism by exposing its potential for abuse. The language of courtship—the discourse of courtly love—maintains its original linguistic properties, but the motives behind its employment are fickle and potentially corrupt.[58]

Liseo, with whom Nise ultimately finds herself matched, proves to be equally self-absorbed in his courtship of Finea. He approaches Octavio to arrange the marriage for financial reasons: the fame of her dowry led him to seek her out. When overwhelmed by Finea's dim-wittedness, however, he considers other alternatives. His conception of the proposed marriage is clearly as a financial and legal arrangement, and her stupidity renders the contract null and void: "Aunque estuviera casado / por poder, en causa propia / me pudiera descasar. / La ley es llana y notoria" [Even if I were married by force, in self defense I could annul it. The law is clear and explicit] (lines 1001–4). In a discussion of his problem with his lackey Turín, he expresses the concern that his offspring may prove as idiotic as their mother. He then considers the possibility of instead courting Nise, and Turín's reaction is telling.

> ¡Oh, qué bien te reportas!
> Dicen que si a un hombre airado,
> que colérico se arroja,
> le pusiesen un espejo,
> en mirando en él la sombra
> que representa su cara,
> se tiempla y desapasiona;
> así tú, como tu gusto
> miraste en su hermana hermosa
> —que el gusto es cara del alma,
> pues su libertad se nombra—,
> luego templaste la tuya.

(lines 1034–45)

[Oh, how clearly you reveal yourself! An angry man, when he sees his image in a mirror, regains control of himself and his passion subsides. So you, as you saw your pleasure reflected in her beautiful sister's face—for pleasure is the face of the soul—you calmed your anger.]

The reference to Nise as a mirror may not be as explicit as was the case in Bernart de Ventadorn, but clearly Liseo's attraction is not to Nise but to the objectified qualities that she represents. She is, in other words, a projection of his desire for an estate and progeny, in effect relegating the *dama* to the passive role of mirror that the troubadours had assigned to the *domna*.[59]

In broad terms, the plot of *La dama boba* itself reflects this process of subverting courtly discourse through a dialogue with it: the male construct of love that functions within the play, of which Duardo's verses cited above are emblematic, leads Liseo and Laurencio to a series of decisions that generate the *enredo* and conflict. Female negotiation of that conflict, largely through language that takes great pains to mock and belittle male courtly discourse, leads to its resolution. Nise, we have seen, challenges the sincerity of the courtly rhetoric used to woo her, employed first by Laurencio and later by Liseo.

Finea's own reaction to courtly language at the beginning of the play serves two purposes: first, to demonstrate her idiocy, and second, to expose the ridiculous ornamentation of courtly discourse by interpreting it literally. As Emilie Bergmann explains, Finea "refuses to participate in the interpretation and use of an arbitrary system of symbols."[60] In other words, her dimwittedness renders her capable only of a literal interpretation of language—a limitation comically juxtaposed against the very figurative language of courtly discourse. The result is a communicative failure that echoes the *tenso* between Raimbaut de Vaqueiras and the anonymous Genoese woman discussed above, in which the *domna* literally does not speak the troubadour language. In Finea's case, the discursive incompatibility or language barrier between male and female is based on the latter's incompatibility with the metaphors and obscure references of courtly love:

LAURENCIO.   Agora
conozco, hermosa señora,
que no solamente viene
el sol de las orientales
partes, pues de vuestros ojos
sale con rayos más rojos
y luces piramidales;

pero si, cuando salís
tan grande fuerza traéis,
al medio día, ¿qué haréis?

FINEA.   Comer, como vos decís,
No pirámides ni peros,
Sino cosas provechosas.

(lines 746–758)

[LAURENCIO. Now, beautiful lady, I know that the sun does not only rise from the East, since it comes from your eyes in rosier rays and pyramidal lights. But if you rise with such intensity, what will you do at midday? FINEA. Eat lunch, but not, as you say, pyramids or such things, but good, healthy food.]

Eventually, however, Laurencio's persuasive courtly rhetoric does awaken a corresponding desire in Finea. Her soliloquy at the beginning of the final act, in which she confirms both her transformation from *boba* to *discreta* and that desire for Laurencio is its cause, is delivered as a direct address to Love—a familiar rhetorical posture of male courtly discourse. From this point forward, her speech acquires an increasing resemblance to the male rhetoric that she had previously been unable to interpret properly.[61] Once love, the "catedrático divino" (divine professor), has granted Finea the intellectual tools with which to interpret the discourse of courtly love, she embraces that system as the means of expressing her own desire. And with the disappearance of that which had previously led Finea to disregard courtly language (her inability to interpret figurative language), the play's subversion of male discourse is halted in a series of exchanges and events that serve to reaffirm it. Finea agrees to marry Laurencio. At the same time Nise, who earlier rejected Liseo's attempts to persuade her to love him, *is* persuaded and falls in love with him. With these betrothals, the standard and expected denouement of Lope's popular comedies, the subversive posture taken against male courtly discourse in the first two acts is undermined.

For Finea it may be "true love" that she feels for Laurencio, but for the reader/spectator it is only through the words with which she defines love's effect on her that we can understand that love. The literary construct of courtly love that was earlier rejected as a mere "rhetoric of orthodoxy" (in other words it is not what it appears to be; it is illusory), is replaced by an expression of desire that is equally grounded in discursive performance in a way that maintains the troubadour paradigm. When close attention is paid to the verbal performance of the transformed Finea in the play's final two acts, one could argue that she assumes the same rhetorically ornamented discourse as her lover. She explains to Laurencio that

> el alma, que te ve
>   por mil vidrios y cristales,
> por donde quiera que vas,
> porque en mis ojos estás
> con memorias inmortales.
>   Todo este grande lugar
> tiene colgado de espejos
> mi amor, juntos y parejos,
> para poderte mirar.
>   Si vuelvo el rostro allí, veo
> tu imagen; si a estotra parte,
> también; y ansí viene a darte
> nombre de sol mi deseo;
> que en cuantos espejos mira
> y fuentes de pura plata,
> su bello rostro retrata
> y su luz divina espira.

(lines 2410–26)

[My soul beholds your image in a thousand crystals and looking glasses, and follows you wherever you go, for you are in my eyes with immortal memories. This whole place is lined with mirrors of my love so I may gaze upon you. When I turn my face in this direction, I see your image; in that direction, also; and so my desire names you the sun, for however many mirrors and fountains of pure silver capture your image, they all glow from your light.]

In a clear echo of courtly discourse, Finea refers to Laurencio as the sun (just as he had earlier referred to her). What these lines express, again, is the subjective experience of desire and the effects of love upon the speaker: Finea's male object of desire is described as a static image that causes such effects. Whereas her earlier misunderstanding of courtly language established a distance between herself and male discourse (while she was *boba*), her own performance of desire (now that she is *discreta*) echoes the self-reflexivity of male lyric performances of desire in the courtly mode. Her choice of the mirror *topos* is a telling symptom of her discursive reliance on the male paradigm.

There is, of course, an important difference in Finea's use of the metaphor: the mirror in this case is not narcissistic. It reflects the image of the beloved (Laurencio) rather than being the beloved himself reflecting for Finea her own likeness. Indeed one could even read Finea's lines as an acceptance of the passive (reflecting) role that Bernart had assigned to his unnamed *domna*. Her eyes carry with her the image of her lover—not her own image—which would allow Laurencio (like Bernart) to enjoy his own image through her eyes. In a similar manner, Nise eventually allows Liseo's courtly language to succeed in persuading her to love him, thereby validating the position that the troubadour lyric offers its *domna*.

Finea's departure from the male narcissistic model can also be understood as the result of her more "pure" motives for employing the metaphor in the first place: Finea is inspired by love to adopt the lofty discourse, while Laurencio has made a conscious decision to employ it for the sake of financial gain. Finea's words make it apparent that Lope's Neoplatonic, idealized, and educative love owes a great deal to the discourse of courtly love. At the same time, though, Laurencio's use of such language is deliberate artifice. Finea employs courtly discourse for the same reasons that the troubadours would have us believe inspire them; Laurencio employs the same discourse as many argue the troubadours did in reality employ it, as a rhetorical strategy for social and financial gain.

We must therefore ask: is it courtly love itself that Lope criticizes, or merely its employment for dubious ends? Given his literary context, in the wake of a fossilized Petrarchism with which he often plays, it would make sense that the mechanization and endless repetition of Petrarchan forms would be the object of his critique. Despite its terminology of devotion and spiritual love, it is used (or abused) for highly questionable ends by Liseo, Laurencio, and Duardo to persuade the play's women. And yet when Nise and Finea verbally perform desire more "sincerely," the parameters established in the discourse of the troubadours still remain in effect. Returning to the notion that courtly love is an "ideolect," a discourse that bears an implicit ideology, we may say that the objectification and exclusion of women implicit in male courtly discourse are at first threatened by a subversive feminine counterdiscourse, but that ultimately this subversion is coopted by the male paradigm.[62] The patriarchal and literary authority of courtly love is reaffirmed by Lope, whose own attempts to offer a corrective vision of ideal love cannot escape being discursively grounded in the paradigm established by the troubadours.

Lope de Vega's representation of desire is therefore simultaneously within and without the courtly love tradition. This chapter's diachronic examination of courtly discourse further supports the notion that Lope's Neoplatonic conception of love, although set against Petrarchan love in an effort to supplant it, is no less dependent on the courtly model. Dante and his fellow *stilnovisti* poets had taken issue with the mechanical repetition of troubadour conventions by the Sicilian School. When the tired rhetoric of an outdated mode of expression was employed purely for the sake of demonstrating one's ability to imitate its verbal ornamentation, they saw fit to depart from the tradition and seek a new means of expressing the spirit of desire that had (as they saw it) originally inspired troubadour poetry. Lope finds himself in a similar situation in relation to Spanish Petrarchism: while quick to lay bare its inherent rhetoricity, his effort at representing desire in a more pure and sincere manner is ultimately unable to escape the same discursive parameters. Whether willingly or not, and whether consciously or not, Lope confirms the legacy of the troubadours in his new dramatic invocation of courtly discourse.

THE *DRAMATURGA'S* RESPONSE: *LA TRAICIÓN EN LA AMISTAD*

Lope's critique in *La dama boba* is of a particular manifestation of courtly discourse (mechanical Petrarchism), while his own representation of love proved equally grounded in the self-focused subjectivity and objectification of the beloved intrinsic to courtly discourse from the troubadours through Petrarchism. The perspective of a woman dramatist contemporary to Lope substantiates such a reading: in *La traición en la amistad*, María de Zayas points to the same issue of the rhetorical manipulation of courtly love. Her confrontation with its patriarchal and authoritative discourse, however, takes a different approach and yields very different results. Zayas's play dramatizes a subversion of male discourse through female characters whose performance of heterosexual desire (dramatized as *traición* [treason]) is ultimately subordinated to the homosocial bonds of *amistad* [friendship]. In this way, Zayas manipulates the discourse of courtly love so as to respond to it, a strategy that suggests clear parallels with the *trobairitz*.[63] What both plays share in common is a view of courtly discourse as a negative force, in both cases by portraying the insincere employment of courtly language for less than idealistic purposes.[64]

Like Lope de Vega, Zayas establishes through her male protagonists that courtly love is a linguistic register whose message should be received with skepticism. Liseo, the object of desire for Fenisa, Marcia, and Laura, openly admits to his servant that his use of courtly discourse is disingenuous: "León, si yo a Fenisa galanteo, / es con engaños, burlas, y mentiras, / no más de cumplir con mi deseo" [León, if I am courting Fenisa, it is with deception, tricks and lies, and only to satisfy my desire] (1298–1300).[65] He, Gerardo, and Don Juan have all inherited the legacy of troubadour self-absorption in their own expression of desire, although the degree to which each man abuses courtly discourse varies. When they are confronted by the various women in the play to whom their rhetoric is addressed, their efforts to seduce and persuade are overtly identified as sophistic and deceitful. While Juan and Gerardo are ultimately rewarded for the sincerity and devotion that they consistently demonstrate to be the motive behind their use of this language, Liseo's deceitful manipulation of courtly discourse with multiple women is dealt with collectively by those women, who conspire to force him to honor his commitments. Ultimately, collective female agency subverts the male discourse of courtly love when the triple alliance of Marcia-Belisa-Laura succeeds in holding Liseo accountable for the consequences of his behavior.

In *La traición en la amistad,* courtly discourse is associated with desire for the feminine object, but what is especially foregrounded is the desire for conquest and possession—the cause more than the effect. And not unlike the appetite for conquest of the Spanish monarchy in the new world, there is a financial base to the drive behind male courtly discourse to conquer and possess the feminine. Fenisa's comment to Marcia in the opening scene reflects a shift in the object of male desire from the female body to the economic capital it represents: "¿Qué piensas sacar de amar / en tiempo que no se mira / ni belleza, ni virtudes? / Sólo la hacienda se estima" [what do you think you will gain from falling in love these days, when money is valued more than beauty and virtue?] (lines 55–58). To this extent, Zayas's social satire is not unlike that of *La dama boba.*

Where the two comedies diverge is the reaction by female characters to the suspicious performances of male desire. The relationship between Lope's two sisters is competitive and antagonistic, as they are literally divided and conquered by courtly discourse. In Zayas's play, however, we witness both positive or "sincere" and negative or deceitful male performances of desire, and the latter case is successfully countered by female homosocial bonds. If the general rule governing the movement of the play is that male conquest is resisted and subverted by female agency,[66] a further important exception is that a female protagonist also adopts the male appetite for conquest. Zayas builds her plot around the deceitful manipulation of courtly discourse by the equally abusive Liseo and Fenisa. The play's leading *galán* and *dama* both perform polygamous desire, each directing courtly discourse (with its rhetoric of exclusive devotion and submission) to multiple addressees. Indeed Fenisa, a female Don Juan whose manipulation of language is no less suspect than that of men, is a marked departure from the other leading women in the play (Marcia, Belisa, and Laura). These three friends more closely resemble the traditional *dama* of the *Comedia,* in that they walk the gender-inflected tightrope of resisting the passive role assigned to them by male courtly discourse while still conforming to appropriate feminine behavior as prescribed by the patriarchal norms of decorum.[67] Meanwhile Fenisa breaks from decorum by adopting the ethically tenuous and discursively manipulative posture of the traditional *galán.* Because Zayas represents women as equally capable of deceit and manipulation, egotism is foregrounded in her association of the discourse of courtly love with conquest. This association focuses less on the objectification of women per se and more on its socially destructive consequences.

Zayas's perspective further differs from that of Lope (in *La dama boba*) in two ways: first, in her focus on the personal and social implications for women when they allow themselves to be persuaded and seduced; and second, in her portrayal of women who are equally active in realizing their own desires. While the latter difference is especially noteworthy in Fenisa, the former is treated the most extensively in the case of Laura, whose persuasion by Liseo leads her to surrender her honor. She explains the circumstances of her plight, namely her deception by Liseo before the action of the play begins, to Marcia and Belisa as follows:

LAURA.   Puso los ojos en mí
un generoso mancebo,
tan galán como alevoso,
desleal y lisonjero;
como mi esposo alcanzó
los favores, con que pienso
que si tuve algún valor
sin honra y sin valor quedo.

(lines 957–64)

[A noble youth eyed me, as gallant as he was treacherous, faithless and flattering. He gained my favors as only a husband should, leaving me, a woman who used to be valiant, with neither honor nor valor.]

The rigid code of honor and the use of marriage as an economic exchange between father and son-in-law (often referred to by critics today as "men trafficking in women") under which seventeenth-century Spanish society operated dictated that an unmarried woman's honor and worth were dependent on her virginity (her purity). By manipulating courtly discourse, the "lisonjero" (flatterer) Liseo persuades Laura to exchange that honor for his pleasure, under the false pretense that he will then marry her. Courtly language here becomes the instrument of the conqueror, whose victory bears with it dire social consequences for the conquered.

La traición en la amistad is a satire that targets the social customs and conventions governing courtship and relations between the sexes in the upper echelons of society in seventeenth-century Madrid (although the verbal representation of this target is ultimately indebted to the discursive legacy of the troubadours). Fenisa's lines quoted above (that men seek in women above all else a dowry) suggest a cynical view of current social practice that is not unlike that presented in *La dama boba:* men employ the language of courtly love in order to procure the wealth that marriage to a well-off woman brings with it. Fenisa refers to a previous state of affairs in which women were objectified by men for their beauty and virtue rather than for their dowries, implicitly suggesting that the change in women's roles from physical and spiritual objects (as was the case with the troubadours, Dante, and Petrarch) to economic objects (as was the case with *La dama boba*'s Liseo and Laurencio) has not been a positive one. It should be noted that, although she presents these symbolic roles (the physical and the economic) in terms of one having been exchanged for the other (a "before" and an "after"), the actions of Liseo do not support such a claim: he seduces Laura for sexual gratification and then abandons her. Male conquest therefore has not shifted but only expanded its objectives to include, when appropriate, money. And while this manipulation of courtly discourse is a marked departure from Dante and Petrarch, the troubadours' pleas for mercy can similarly be read as the solicitation of physical and/or material reward.

In either case, only the ends for which the language is manipulated are subject to change—not the language itself, nor its self-centeredness, nor its objectification of women. The employment of courtly discourse for the egoistic end of conquest is treated here as a transgression, and its victims (its objects), usually female, suffer for it. The play is therefore a convergence of the social and the literary: Zayas's satire of a deplorable social practice depends upon the discourse of courtly love for its verbal representation. While the posture assumed by the *galán* courting the *dama* (or by Fenisa courting various men) is "literary," an appeal to the cultural authority of a centuries-old literary discourse, the consequences of allowing oneself to be persuaded by that posture are very much grounded in social reality. Because of courtly deception's dire social consequences for women (the loss of honor), the male drive for female conquest—the motive behind courtly discourse—is socially destructive, as Laura testifies.

If the discursive manipulation of courtly love for egoistic purposes of conquest is a male pattern of behavior, and if Zayas's satire gives the lie to that practice because of its negative impact on the lives of women, then what are we to make of Fenisa? Ironically, her adoption of the strategy of male conquest—she claims to have room in her heart for "un millón de amadores" [a million lovers] (line 192)—is treated as the worst transgression of all. It is in fact a double transgression, against both the men she supposedly "conquers" and the women who get in her way. She ironically advises Marcia that she should reciprocate Gerardo's love rather than court Liseo, under the pretense that "de aqueste puedes, / fingiendo amor, cortesía, / estimación, y finezas / burlarte [. . .]") [by feigning love, courtesy, esteem, and charm, you can play a trick on him and have a little fun] (lines 129–32). Fenisa's counsel is in fact a description of her own behavior toward men, and it is further hypocritical in that it is made to Marcia only in order to dissuade her from courting the man that Fenisa wants for herself. Her warning about male discursive deception is in itself a deceptive speech act, and it is indicative of how her participation in the male strategy of conquest isolates her from the other women in the play.

When the collective agency of Belisa, Marcia, and Laura ultimately subverts the male drive for conquest embedded in male courtly discourse, Fenisa is a casualty of their success. If there is an overt gesture of "poetic justice" in the play's denouement,[68] it would be that Fenisa is the only character—lackeys included—who remains single when the final curtain falls.[69] The *gracioso* concludes the play with an announcement to the audience that further punctuates her punishment at the hands of poetic justice: "Señores míos, Fenisa, / qual ven, sin amantes queda. / Si alguno la quiere, avise / para que su casa sepa" [My lords, as you can see, Fenisa is left alone without a single lover. If one of you is interested, let me know and I will pass on her address] (lines 2911–14). Hers is literally the sin after which the play is named, friendship betrayed, and her treatment in the final scene even resembles that of the comic buffoon of ancient Roman comedy (a kind of inverted tragic hero). It is indeed a fitting reward for a character whose adoption of male egotism at the expense of female friendship and solidarity is admitted in a monologue from the opening scene: "El amor y la amistad / furiosos golpes se tiran. / Cayó la amistad en tierra / y amor victoria apellida." [Love and friendship exchange furious blows; friendship is defeated and love emerges victorious] (lines 171–74).

The play presents three possible responses to male discursive aggression from which women may choose. The first is to take religious vows (as Liseo believes Laura has done after his conquest), which is tantamount to seeking refuge from one patriarchal institution (the literary institution of courtly love) by submission to another (the Counter-Reformation Church), although Zayas's prose fiction frequently refers to such a choice as a refuge from male abuse. Fenisa takes up the second response: to adopt the male practice of deception and use it against men. The third option, which ultimately proves successful in the play's denouement, is for women to form a united front against the threat of male courtly discourse. Marcia, Belisa, and Laura collectively act to identify and expose this threat, after a bond of solidarity develops between them in the second act.[70]

This relationship of allegiance and solidarity, in terms of the change it brings about in the women's words and actions, is presented as a move away from egoism. Prior to their alliance these women, as individual objects of male desire, were dependent on the discursive parameters of courtly love for their own expression of desire: the closing lines of the first act (a sonnet by Laura) and the opening lines of the second (a sonnet by Marcia) reflect the self-absorption of the male discursive model. Before forming their friendship, in other words, each woman was individually engaged by male amatory discourse; accordingly, each operated from within its narcissistic parameters and the objectification of the desired when speaking of her own desires. Laura expounds on her lover's eyes in her sonnet and relies upon the courtly rhetoric of love-as-suffering ("Que muera yo, Liseo, por tus ojos / y que gusten tus ojos de matarme!") [Liseo, let me die because of your eyes, and may your eyes take pleasure in killing me] (lines 849–50). The beloved of her sonnet has in fact treated Laura cruelly, which makes appropriate the application of the troubadours' rhetorical conventions. It therefore follows that Laura's monologue would focus exclusively on the subjective experience of love-as-suffering, referring to the beloved's eyes only to describe what they do to her.

Marcia assumes the same rhetorical posture at the very beginning of the second act ("Amar el día, aborrecer el día," 863–76), but her pre-alliance egoism is well demonstrated from the opening scene in her dialogue with Fenisa. She declares that her love for Liseo has forced her to join the "war of love": "en esta guerra de amor / he de emplearme atrevida" [I am going to leap bravely in this war of love] (37–38). His courtship with its flattering language has clearly succeeded as the play begins, and Marcia's response to it is equally self-centered: "a nadie estoy obligada, / sino a mi gusto" [I am not obligated to anyone or anything except my own pleasure] (lines 121–22). Marcia, Fenisa, and Laura all pine for the discursively manipulative Liseo in isolation through individual expressions of desire that mirror and validate the subject-centered discourse of courtly love. Each is a victim of Liseo's seductive discourse, and each seems for the first half of the play ideologically confined by it.

What breaks the cycle of narcissistic desire in isolation for the women is the homosocial bond between them, the solidarity they feel with one another. Recognizing that male conquest (via courtly discourse) is an enemy that they share in common, they work together to identify and expose its inherent self-service and deception. Marcia is the object of Liseo's latest project of female conquest in the play, and Laura's cautionary tale forewarns her of the dangers of trusting his discursive manipulation. She and Belisa subsequently agree to work for the restoration of Laura's honor, and in so doing they collectively counter the socially destructive discourse of courtly love with the socially constructive bonds of friendship and solidarity. Together they manipulate Liseo by tricking him into accepting responsibility for his seduction of Laura by way of a signed letter promising marriage. The individual feminine object in isolation may be powerless against the conquering force of courtly discourse, but the collective agency of women ultimately proves powerful enough to subvert it and to bring about a resolution of the conflict that restores Laura's honor.[71]

We may therefore say that with the exception of Fenisa, Zayas's female characters collectively resist the object position in which they find themselves placed by the discourse of courtly love. Their shift from egoistic isolation (as individuals responding to the male drive for conquest) to communal solidarity (as a collective force seeking a justice that transcends the individual) is a kind of (homo)social evolution that the more "primitive" Fenisa fails to experience. The closure and resolution to conflict are thus found by all of the play's characters except for Fenisa, who by contrast remains without a marriage partner, prompting Constance Wilkins to suggest that "León's joking invitation may imply a continuation of Fenisa's endless desire that will keep her in motion and continue to disturb society."[72] Fenisa's perpetual egoistic desire ultimately affirms her identity as a female Don Juan, and the play's critique of her more masculine social behavior, again in contrast to the homosocial bonds that unite Marcia, Laura, and Belisa, is in effect a critique of the customs of men in Zayas's society, not unlike the indictment of male comportment so frequently associated with her prose fiction. If the courtly love tradition is the propriety of an exclusively male perspective, as was suggested in the above analysis of the *trobairitz* (a club "for men only"), Zayas dramatizes a response by women to male discourse that rejects their objectification and exclusion. One may say that women gather together from the margins of courtly discourse and collectively refuse to be deceived by it, as the *trobairitz* had done centuries before.

Zayas's response, which implies a mistrust of men, is in effect a defensive posture. Beyond the social ramifications of male conquest, and beyond courtly love's rendering of women as spiritual, sexual, or economic objects, it is also a defense against the marginalization and exclusion of women's voices implicit in courtly discourse. Zayas is responding to a male tradition of exclusion in a way that mirrors the response of the *trobairitz* to the troubadours, although no evidence exists that she would have been familiar with their work. Even if the parallels between their poetry and Zayas's play are not a case of direct influence, they cannot be considered mere coincidence. That a female dramatist sees fit to reexamine and question the discourse of courtly love employed by the patriarchal establishment of Lope de Vega and his male followers is suggestive of how deeply embedded the legacy of the troubadours was in the amatory discourse of Spain's early modern cultural production. In other words, because the discourse of courtly love (and all its ideological implications) informs male-authored Spanish comedy's representation of love and desire, Zayas finds herself in the same position vis-à-vis the patriarchal canon that had previously been occupied by the *trobairitz*. The fact that this position had not substantially changed over the five hundred years between them (a notion that is supported by the few extant poems of Florencia Piñar, which were circulated in manuscript *cancionero* anthologies in the centuries leading up to the *Comedia*) suggests that the same ideological parameters of troubadour discourse were still very much in place.

2
Duty and Desire: The Discourses of Courtly Love, Chivalry, and Honor

THE PREVIOUS CHAPTER'S ANALYSIS OF *LA TRAICIÓN EN LA AMISTAD* focused on the play's depiction of a collective effort by women to resist or subvert the self-absorbed male discourse of courtly love. Zayas's conflict between male and female is also a conflict between the individual and a community; the collective voices of Belisa, Laura, and Marcia confront the narcissistic male subject (Liseo) in order to restore honor to one of its members. Female virtue (a social value prescribed by the code of honor) is represented in conflict with the personal desire of the male subject of courtly discourse, and the women's honor-centered goals exercise authority over Liseo's self-centered desires because they are more in harmony with Counter-Reformation ideology. The code of honor affirms this ideology and is regularly pitted against the transgressions of the individual throughout the *Comedia* tradition. The dominant storyline of the mass-produced cape-and-sword plays and *comedias de enredo,* the union of two young lovers despite the social obstacles (especially restrictions placed upon them for the sake of protecting honor) that must be overcome, certainly treats the demands of the community or social decorum as obstacles to the realization of individual desire.[1] Even the more canonical tragedies and tragicomedies like *El castigo sin venganza, El burlador de Sevilla,* and *El alcalde de Zalamea,* each in its own way, deal with the threat posed to social order by personal (and typically carnal) desire.[2] I will argue in the present chapter that this early modern Spanish theatrical convention is in large measure discursively grounded in the courtly love tradition. As with the implications for women of the courtly lyric's "poetics of exclusion," the conflict between public duty and personal desire is a consequence of the self-absorption inherent in the discourse of courtly love. It is in fact an extension of a larger literary problem since this discourse first influenced the representation of desire in medieval European verse and prose narrative.

Returning briefly to *La traición en la amistad,* it is worth noting that, when confronting Liseo in the dénouement, Marcia explicitly articulates a connection between the social and the divine: "Liseo, cosa imposible / es apartar lo que ordena / el cielo; pues Laura es tuya, / por mí tu mano merezca" [Liseo, it is impossible to undo what heaven orders; thus Laura is yours, for through me may she deserve your hand] (lines 2837–40). The implication is that honor is a divinely ordained social code. Once Liseo's seduction of Laura crosses the line from verbal courtship to physical consummation, he is responsible in the eyes of God and his earthly Christian community for preserving that honor by marriage. Marcia's appeal to divine and social authority, supported legally when Liseo is tricked into signing a written promise to marry Laura, meets with little resistance in the denouement. Liseo is indeed transformed from a philandering Don Juan to a committed (albeit unenthusiastic) husband: "Laura, mi ventura es esta [. . .] Esta es mi mano, y con ella / el alma, pues, será tuya" ["Laura, such is my fate . . . Here is my hand, and with it, my soul will be yours] (lines 2856–59).[3]

Throughout the *Comedia* tradition, the male subject, operating from within the parameters of courtly love's discourse of the self, is at odds with a community that privileges a notion of honor precluding the physical consummation of his desire. The chivalric hero of medieval romance faced a similar problem: the influence of troubadour poetry on the terms through which his desire is represented places him in direct conflict with the public demands of feudal chivalry.[4] The social forces of medieval chivalry and Counter-Reformation honor are naturally quite distinct, as is the cultural and political context to which each pertains, but both are manifestations of a dominant prescription for social order implicit in Christian patriarchal ideology. As such, and despite their obvious differences, both chivalry in medieval romance and honor in early modern Spanish drama favor the community over the individual.[5]

More to the point, both value systems are at odds with a mode of discourse that is inherently self-centered, that is to say individual-centered and dependent on the performance of a personal and subjective experience of desire. Transferring the view of love expressed by the troubadours (and later, by Petrarch and his followers) from the confines of the lyric poem into the dynamics of narrative (whether verse, prose, or dramatic) involves a shift in context, from the static isolation and enclosure of the lyric poem to the dynamic representation of a society whose demands do not necessarily privilege the individual's realization of his desire. Like the voice of the beloved, the demands of society may remain more or less outside the margins of the courtly lyric as the male subject discursively performs his desire. But when the subject experiences desire in the broader context of a fictional story (in which he is but one member of a larger cast of characters), and especially when the plot develops in such a way as to involve his acting on that desire, he is no longer hermetically sealed off from society—including the social forces from which the cocoonlike lyric space protects his subjectivity. Broadly speaking, the *dramatis personae* in narrative and drama consist of multiple subjects, each with his or her own personal agendas and desires. Collectively they represent society and demand of the male subject that he follow the same codes of conduct by which they are all expected to operate. Medieval chivalry and Counter-Reformation honor are two such codes. If the discursive legacy of the troubadours extended to Golden Age Spain and its secular theater, it should come as no surprise that the conflicts bred by courtly love within medieval romance[6] would share common ground with the conflicts at play in the *Comedia.*

Thomas A. O'Connor agrees that the *Comedia* is an early-modern manifestation of a longstanding literary conflict: "Love as a personal motivator of conduct, in conflict with an abstract and frequently impersonal force called honor, places the *Comedia* in the mainstream of Western literature stretching back to the romance of Tristan and Isolde and even to the plays of Menander and Terence."[7] The differences between desire's representation in the theatrical traditions of Rome and Greece in classical antiquity and early modern Spain are so substantial as to make an explicit connection with Terence and Menander on this issue problematic, but we can say with certainty that classical comedy and its Italian Renaissance descendants (such as Ariosto's *Lena* and Machiavelli's *Mandragula*) exercised a substantial influence on the plot structure of the cape-and-sword plays and *comedias de enredo* of early modern Spain. The terms and conventions through which amorous desire is represented in the *Comedia* differ significantly from the view of love expressed throughout most of the literature from classical antiquity, however, and this difference complicates such classical influence on the *Comedia.*[8]

Medieval romance faces a similar complication: the chivalric hero is in many ways a literary descendant of the classical epic hero (through such traditions as the Old French *chanson de geste,* including the *Chan-*

son de Roland). The most striking difference between Odysseus or Aeneas and Lancelot or Gawain, however, is the view of love that motivates his action. Virgil describes Aeneas's decision to leave Carthage and Dido in terms indicative of the negative view of erotic love that characterizes much of "high" classical literature: Mercury comes to deliver his divine message, and this "awakens" the hero from the "trance" that Dido had inspired. The message to Aeneas is one of correction, as his love affair has proven to be an obstacle to his mission. For Aeneas, desire is a digression from duty that must be corrected. Virgil's approach to desire is no doubt influenced by Homer, whose *Odyssey* includes a series of female obstacles that attempt to thwart the hero's return to Ithaca—from the supernatural Calypso and Circe to the seductive Sirens. Nor can we isolate this view of love as a destructive force to the epic tradition alone: Greek and Roman comedy reflects a similar view (although transgressive love in classical antiquity is often subversively successful), and it was noted in the previous chapter that Cicero considered the discipline of rhetoric to be another such "corrective" to the dangers of Eros.

This inherent distrust of desire had serious consequences in terms of female representation by male classical writers, who for the most part characterized women as either passively loyal, as in the case of Homer's Penelope, or as the source of desire's ill effects, as in the case of Virgil's Dido. The rejection of desire is of course a marked difference from the courtly love tradition, but both mainstream classical love and *fin' amours* conceive their feminine personages as objects (whether they are objects to be feared or desired). In the case of the classical tradition, the feminine represents an evil, or at least an obstacle to the quest of the male hero. This treatment of women resonates in chivalric romance, and treating women as destructive to the male heroic enterprise is reinforced in medieval culture by Augustine's perpetuation of Judeo-Christian misogyny, ultimately based on the portrayal of Eve in *Genesis*. Medieval chivalric romance, then, incorporates the marginalization and objectification of the feminine implicit in the discourse of courtly love into a heroic narrative framework inherited from the classical epic and in keeping with a misogynist ideological climate that explicitly excludes desire from the male heroic project. For male-authored romances such as those of Chrétien de Troyes, desire is far more than a distraction from a more appropriately masculine or virile quest; indeed romantic desire's privileged position in the medieval heroic enterprise is a clear departure from the classical epic, although such desire is articulated in terms that resemble the tendency of the troubadours to relegate the female object of desire to a silent and passive role. As this chapter's analysis of Chrétien will suggest, the narrative foregrounding of desire in the wake of the troubadour tradition does not signal a reversal of classical misogyny, but rather an intense conflict between the ideological legacy of the classical tradition and the interest of medieval romance authors in representing a desiring male hero.

The text of Marie de France's *Lais* therefore occupies a liminal space in the canon of chivalric romance: although it draws upon written Arthurian and oral Celtic source material that is very much in keeping with the misogyny discussed above, its authorship and the narrative voice through which the tales are told originate from the feminine margins of the male tradition. Specifically Marie problematizes the conflict between duty and desire with a nonconventional focus on the role of women characters in its resolution. *Lais* like *Guigemar* and *Laüstic* portray the convention of the *malmariée,* the female victim of an arranged marriage that places her under the restrictive control of an older and jealous husband, in order to portray her attempts to fulfill personal desire despite the demands of matrimonial duty imposed upon her. In this chapter I will pay special attention to *Eliduc* because of its focalization of the duty/desire polemic in a male subject more directly related to the canonical heroes of Chrétien's romances, while it depends upon a rupture from the male-authored mainstream, in the form of the agency of female personages, to resolve the male hero's dilemma.

This reading of Marie's *Lais* suggests that the *tenso* between the troubadours and the *trobairitz* examined in the previous chapter resonates in the intertextual dialogue between Marie and the male romance tradition in which she participates. In other words, while the *trobairitz* respond to the troubadours and in doing so challenge the passive and voiceless role that courtly discourse prescribes for their gender, Marie's rewriting of the duty/desire conflict to allow for a more active role by women is a similar response to the passive and generally unvoiced role that male-authored romance posits for its female personages. And in responding in this way, Marie offers us a perspective from which we may judge the male representation of the conflict as equally gender-inflected, or as only one approach (privileging the male hero) to the problems that arise when the subject of courtly discourse steps out of his lyric isolation and into the social worlds represented in romance narrative.

Connecting this duty/desire dialectic with the *Comedia* will in turn reveal a parallel *tenso* between male and female authors regarding the ways in which personal and individual desire must confront the public duty prescribed by the code of honor; this dialogue calls to our attention the gendered double standard at work in such conflicts. The honor plays of Calderón, based on the husband's enforcement of this code and thus often called the wife-murder plays, as well as other tragic or tragicomic works of the male-authored canon, localize honor's affirmation in the offended husband. For women, by contrast, honor is a thing to be protected and a thing to be lost. But the comic conventions of the cape-and-sword plays and the *comedias de enredo*, as exemplified in this chapter by Calderón's *La dama duende*, privilege action in which women and men both must confront social obstacles imposed by the system of honor as they attempt to unite with the object of their amorous desires. This dynamic setting, I would argue, is the reason why female dramatists in Golden Age Spain so frequently invoke such comic conventions in their plays, while there is no extant tragic "honor play" (in the Calderonian sense of the term) of female authorship; the extant secular dramas of female authorship from the *Comedia* tradition privilege the generic conventions of popular urban comedy. It is within this comic world that the *tenso* between male and female playwrights is based in large measure. Leonor de la Cueva's *La firmeza en la ausencia* demonstrates how from within *Comedia* conventions a woman dramatist may treat the impositions placed by patriarchal honor on feminine behavior.

DUTY AND DESIRE IN MEDIEVAL ROMANCE:
CHRÉTIEN'S *EREC ET ENIDE*

Love plays a role in the heroism of medieval chivalric romance that clearly differs from that of classical antiquity, despite the literary influence of the latter in medieval narrative. Any knight worthy of being the protagonist of a romance must of course be worthy in virtue and especially in skill. But this public excellence does not guarantee universally virtuous conduct in the private realm of (courtly) love, and the romance narrative's focus on love is substantially stronger than that of the classical epic. Ideally, the virtues of loyalty, honesty, and courage that help the knight win the approval of his professional peers would likewise prove him a loyal, honest, and constant lover; but this is quite often not the case. That chivalric virtues do not inform amorous conduct makes it clear that these two realms are considered distinct by the authors and often even incompatible. We will see that a good example of this incongruity is Marie's *Eliduc:* the protagonist can do no wrong in military situations but is able neither to remain faithful to his wife nor to inform his new lover of his marital status. For Marie de France and Chrétien de Troyes alike, chivalric duty and courtly love are isolated realms of existence. Indeed, when these two realms do become intertwined, the result is disastrous more often than not.

Such a conflict between duty and desire seems omnipresent in the Arthurian romance cycle. The most obvious example would be the case of Lancelot and Guinevere, in which the ethical conflict between duty to one's lord and king and the desire for his wife is the substance of the male hero's dilemma. Chrétien de Troyes's *Lancelot* presents the conflict in such a way as to problematize the protagonist's heroism: the text's portrayal of his successful defense of Guinevere from her abductors is the prelude to a more serious and internalized psychological conflict whose social consequences are left unresolved as the narrative concludes. Even romances like *Parcival, Yvain,* and *Erec et Enide* (henceforth *Erec*), in which Arthur and his famous "love triangle" are peripheral characters, demonstrate that the conflict between duty and desire is the inevitable result of a presentation of chivalric heroism that involves courtly love. Chrétien offers a *corpus* of texts written in the immediate aftermath of the flourishing of the troubadour lyric, which thus invokes the ethic of courtly love in its representation of desire within the male system of chivalric honor and duty. The discourse of courtly love, as with the troubadours, objectifies the desired woman and renders her for the most part passive and silent. Chrétien treats the ethical and psychological conflicts resulting from desire as an exclusively male concern, and his characterization of women excludes any autonomous action by them.

Erec certainly illustrates this problem. From the very first scene the hero prefers to pass his time in the queen's company as the other knights of Arthur's court sharpen their skills by hunting (Erec has forgotten his armor). The hero is portrayed from the beginning of the narrative as unengaged in the day-to-day knightly activity of his male peers. It is only a wandering knight's affront to Queen Guinevere, a transgression of courtly behavior too egregious to be ignored, that spurs him to action. His behavior, from when he wins Enide in chivalric contest to the end of the narrative, is even more clearly motivated by this conflict. Blissfully enjoying his new marriage, Erec neglects the kingdom for the bedroom. It is a decadent phase in the course of his chivalric career.

> Mais tant l'ama Erec d'amors
> Que d'armes mais ne li chaloit,
> N'a tornoiement mais n'aloit.
> N'avoit mais soing de tornoier:
> A sa fame aloit dosnoier,
> De li fist s'amie et sa drue;
> Tot met son cuer et s'entendue
> En li acoler et baisier,
> Ne se queroit d'el aaisier.
>   Si compaignon duel en menoient;
> Entr'ax sovent se dementoient
> De ce que trop l'amoit assez.
> Sovant estoit midi[s] passez
> Ainçois que de lez li levast;
> Lui estoit bel, cui qu'il pesast.[9]

(pp. 200–202)

[But Erec was so deeply in love with her that he no longer took any interest in arms or attended tournaments: he no longer cared to joust, but spent his time playing the lover to his wife. He treated her as his sweetheart and mistress. He set his heart and mind only on embracing and kissing her, seeking no other pastime. His companions were sorry about this and often complained among themselves that he showed her far too much love. It was often midday when he rose from her side; but he was contented, whoever else was unhappy.] (32–33)[10]

In fact the reader is led to believe that Erec would have continued indefinitely to slight chivalric duty, explicitly linked here to his community of male peers, were it not for Enide's admonition; he is ignorant of the discontent of his court until she reluctantly reports it to him.

Erec's response to the problem is to take action. His "awakening" to the problem is not unlike that of Aeneas: Erec immediately leaves the castle with Enide and searches for adventures to repair his reputation and correct his conduct (indeed the decorations painted onto the trappings of Enide's palfrey depict scenes from the *Aeneid*). This quest, a response to the conflict between duty and desire, shapes the rest of the narrative. Enide must ride a good distance ahead of her husband in order to serve as bait for would-be abductors, and she is explicitly and repeatedly ordered not to speak out to forewarn her husband of imminent danger. That Erec demands silence from his wife only heightens our awareness that we have moved from the castle (the realm of the verbal exchanges of courtly love), and more specifically from the conjugal bedroom (where desire is fulfilled) to the field of chivalric action. It also demonstrates that Enide's role in the narrative is to provide an obstacle to the hero's chivalric duty.

In fact the behavior of most of the knights that Erec encounters in the course of the narrative can also be understood in terms of the conflict between chivalric duty and personal desire. The ceremonial hunt for the white stag is the activity in which Arthur's knights are immersed when the narrative opens. Arthur himself wins the prize and must therefore follow the custom of kissing the fairest lady of his court. The question of which lady he will choose presents a crisis within the court: each knight has a lady to defend and represent, and Gawain expresses concern to Arthur that his choice will anger those knights whose ladies are slighted. When Erec returns with Enide (after winning her through a similar competition), so beautiful that none will challenge that she is the fairest, he has averted the social disaster with which Arthur was flirting. This sequence of events establishes the mood of antagonism between courtly love and chivalric honor that permeates the rest of the narrative, in terms of both Erec's chivalric negligence and the knightly antagonists that he faces in his adventures. It is an antagonism between male would-be heroes over the female object, between knights competing for the prize of Erec's lady (who was originally won by Erec as first prize of a contest with other knights).

These knights either are willing to kill Erec out of desire for his wife or, in the case of the knight imprisoned in the "Joie de la Cort" (Joy of the Court), must fight the hero out of obligation to his lady. When the first such enemy of Erec is killed, he urges his companions to leave the couple alone. His dying admission of guilt, along with the prominent position he holds in his court, teach the reader a lesson: even powerful and normally well-mannered knights (his virtue is both redeemed and demonstrated in his confession) can turn to foul practices when so moved by desire. *Erec* therefore demonstrates that desire for a woman can cause a knight to neglect chivalric duty and even to openly defy it. The climactic duel of the romance demonstrates the antagonism between love and chivalric duty more clearly: the knight of the "Joie de la Cort" adventure is imprisoned in the castle and must fight any knight who approaches him—all because he promised an unnamed favor to his lady, who demands that he perpetually demonstrate his worth to her in combat. Ferrante writes that "The lovers of the *Joie* are an example of courtly love working against social responsibility: the service the lady demands of her knight not only bars him from human society, but also makes his only contacts with it destructive."[11] Both his promise and his fear of the lady's disdain confine him and force him to fight any knight that approaches him. Chrétien has thus made the troubadour rhetorical convention of being captivated or enslaved by love a reality within his romance.

What Chrétien's work demonstrates is how the coexistence of classical and troubadour influences on romance combine to make problematic the coexistence of courtly love's discourse of the self with the demands of chivalry and the social order it prescribes. As a consequence of treating this conflict as an exclusively male problem, the action of *Erec* (and of the larger *corpus* of Chrétien's romances) tends to marginalize the role of the heroine. It is difficult to illustrate this marginalization explicitly because it is realized in what is *not* in the text. The roles that are explicitly played by female characters in the text tend to resemble that of Dido and Eve—that is to say, the role of obstacular temptress in the male quest for a heroic realization of chivalric duty. Guinevere's function in the tale is to give cause for Erec's initial action. Once Enide is discovered and won, the queen is no longer necessary and in fact is no longer involved in the narrative action, suggesting that Erec has simply exchanged one female object for another. The lady who commands Erec's final adversary to remain in the courtyard until defeated in combat is perhaps the most active female presence in the text, and her function in the story is merely a necessary step in establishing a final obstacle through which the male hero may prove himself. Enide herself is won in competition and then used by Erec to attract further competition, as if Erec's heroism depended on the female object's occasioning of a social threat for the affirmation of his prowess.

The absence of any nonobstacular, socially redeeming female agency (and female voice) is the result of Chrétien's exclusive focus on the conflictive duties and desires of the male knight. Attention paid to the male hero may therefore offer clearer results in terms of reading the motives or authorial agenda behind the romance's action, as Chrétien's tradition involves a heroine who acts neither decisively nor autonomously in the course of her story. Indeed in the larger tradition of male-authored chivalric romance, things tend to happen *to* women rather than be caused *by* them. They are won, lost, wooed, abducted, and invariably enclosed by male protagonists or antagonists. Thus while the lady is the ostensible center of the chivalric hero's cosmos, her appearance is generally dictated by male action (by male responses to the desire she engenders): placement, displacement, and replacement are the extent to which the female romance protagonist, a passive female object, is involved in her story's action.

The ideals of courtly love, it has already been suggested, present no difficulty to chivalric duty in the abstract: the lady ennobles and inspires the knight, who in turn performs chivalric deeds worthy of her. Dante would later draw his professional inspiration from Beatrice in analogous terms. How is it, then, that when placed in the social orders represented in chivalric romance, there is such incongruity? Ferrante links the problem to the legacy of classical antiquity: "In its final effects, then, there is little distinction between the ideal, inspiring lyric love and the immoral, destructive classical love."[12] This is no more apparent than in the case of the romance lady: set in a framework of courtly love (in which she is to ennoble and inspire the knight), her effect, especially in the romances of Chrétien, is socially suspect at best and often destructive. Is Enide any different from Dido? It is no coincidence that her palfrey's garment bears the scene of Aeneas and the Carthaginian queen consumed by destructive passion. It has already been mentioned that Erec awakens from a decadent period of sexual indulgence and violently turns to dutiful action in a manner strongly reminiscent of the Aeneas story. The notable difference between them is that Aeneas leaves Dido while Erec takes his wife with him, using her primarily as bait to elicit adventures by having her ride ahead of him. She is not allowed to speak and functions as little more than a lure riding ahead of Erec's lance. It is true that few significant actions in the narrative can be attributed to her, but her presence alone—because of its effect on Erec—is still a powerfully disruptive force. And yet Chrétien makes every effort to praise Enide, precisely because she serves the agenda of his male heroic world perfectly.

Ferrante observes a progressive shift in focus over the course of Chrétien's known romances that can be considered as his attempt to work out this very duty/desire problem. Her argument is that his earliest efforts such as *Erec* treat courtly love as central to the story, but that he gradually loses confidence in his ability to make such love "work" in his narratives. He eventually turns to the grail cycle, in which the grail replaces the lady as the central preoccupation, prize, and object of desire for the knight. Courtly love is therefore treated only with irony in his later romances. Ferrante also suggests that this shift in Chrétien's commitment to courtly love in the chivalric romance is discernible in chivalric romance as a whole.

One example in which this shift is clearly illustrated is the literary figure of Roland/Orlando. The *Chanson de Roland* predates the troubadours and thus offers no consideration of idealized love that would resemble courtly love, but Roland demonstrates the chivalric ideals that inform courtly romance. He is as successfully heroic as any literary knight, both in victory and in defeat. The character's literary future in Boiardo's *Orlando Inamorato* and Ariosto's *Orlando Furioso* is indicative of the problems that courtly love presents for the chivalric hero. From the idealized chivalry of the *chanson*, Roland/Orlando eventually falls victim to the force of courtly love to the point where it becomes his sole occupation. And while it would be inaccurate to treat Ariosto as simply another author of Chrétien's tradition—he offers a later, parodic reflection in light of Renaissance literary theory—Ariosto was well aware of this problem in the object of his parody. The *Orlando Furioso,* peripatetic and episodic to the point of narrative chaos, parodically demonstrates chivalry's dissolution by way of desire.

Thus when authors of medieval romance incorporate the Provençal "system" in their representations of chivalric adventure, duty and desire are pitted against one another—a conflict between the two distinct aesthetic concerns of narrative and lyric poetry. In this sense the joust replaces the troubadour lyric as the means to sing the praises of the lady. The problem that this presents is that the joust involves an opponent, so that two knights equally worthy of respect and friendship might be driven by the "rules" of courtly love to fight to the death. In this light Ferrante's assessment of courtly love as "socially destructive" seems justified. The fraternal spirit of chivalry must often butt heads with the individualistic agenda of the courtly lover, and the blame for this confrontation is squarely placed upon the lady. The misogynist message is reiterated by the lady's silence and lack of narrative attention.

Anita Benaim Lasry studies the romance heroine in terms of this denial of the feminine to act as a positive force in romance. Her project involves an analysis of those rare instances in romance (such as the *Roman de Silence*) in which women do play an active role in determining their own fate beyond being passively placed, displaced, and replaced objects. She describes what she considers to be the two types of ideal heroines: "The first type of heroine is the woman who, according to the moral standards of the romance, ought to have the ideal of being like a man . . . while the second type of heroine also exhibits an independent 'masculine' spirit and behavior."[13] Her assessment underscores that in the world of medieval chivalric romance, heroism and its subject position are indelibly gender-inflected.

Agency in romance is inherently male, and a woman's assumption of the heroic subject position must therefore involve a departure from her own gender or an adoption of male identity. The *Roman de Silence* fits the mold perfectly: Silence performs heroically, but only because she is raised and disguised as male. Her quest excludes love and even physical desire because of this androgyny; it centers instead on social and legal issues such as restoring the rights of women to the inheritance of a father's estate. But while assuming a male professional identity, allowing her to successfully meet the demands of chivalry, Silence cannot adopt the male sexual drive to conquer and possess a female object—a problem that ultimately causes her true identity to be revealed. She uncomfortably dodges the advances of women throughout the narrative, until her culminating refusal to sleep with the queen very nearly costs her her life. Silence is utterly devoid of courtly desire, and her marriage to the king in the romance's denouement is essentially a financial and social arrangement rather than a fulfillment of desire. We may take Silence's demonstration of Lasry's argument as indicative of the extent to which romance heroism is a function of masculinity.

DUTY AND DESIRE IN CHIVALRIC ROMANCE: *ELIDUC*

Such is the ideology implicit in the male romance tradition that Marie de France confronts. Rather than make her heroines aspire to a male ideal, which would in essence affirm the patriarchal marginalization of femininity, she avoids such a characterization of her female protagonists. Taking a more subtle approach, Marie works within the traditional confines of accepted gender roles in order to problematize and deconstruct them in response to the male tradition. Before we consider how this response is made explicit in *Eliduc,* some observations regarding Marie's body of *Lais* as a whole suggest an echo of the previous chapter's analysis of *trobairitz* poetry.

Of special interest to scholars has been Marie's choice of the *lai* over the traditional courtly *roman* narrative. Her citation of oral *Breton* sources immediately sets her narratives apart from the Latinate romances represented by Chrétien. In truth, the actual source material may not be so different as Marie would have us think: such is the position of Eva Rosenn, who offers a perceptive study of Marie's selection and manipulation of source material for the purposes of forging a distinct feminine discourse in the face of male hegemonic tradition.

"It is Marie's relation to (masculine) textual authority in the *Lais* that comprises a distinctly feminine discourse."[14] This is evident from the rhetorical posturing of the prologue, in which Marie discusses her project and her selection of the *lai*. Rosenn traces the convergence of literary Latin and folkloric Breton sources in Marie, noting that they often overlap—as in fact they do in Chrétien as well. Despite this qualification, Rosenn finds that privileging the *lai* as her primary source material offers for Marie an alternative to masculine discourse.

> In choosing the Breton *lais* as her source, Marie completely reverses the division and rejection that prescribes discourse. She privileges the *conte* over the *estoire*, the oral over the written, the *lai* over the *romaunz*, the Breton/Celtic over the *translatio imperii*, the vernacular over the Latin, the personal over the national, the feminine over the masculine. Marie includes rather than excludes (empowering the desires of the voiceless), defies rules (refusing to repeat the same hegemonic myths), and reappropriates literary discourse for herself.[15]

Marie privileges the oral Breton tradition, according to Rosenn's argument, as part of her strategy to separate herself from the male-authored chivalric romance. Such an argument implies that the ideology of gender implicit in the oral folkloric tradition offers a framework that allows room for Marie's voice in a manner denied to her by the patriarchal written romance. Chrétien himself associates the *lai* with female authorship and orality: in *Erec et Enide*, it is women who compose and sing the "Lai de Joie." In keeping with the male paradigm, however, Chrétien cannot dwell extensively on any expression of the female voice, as it would distract him from the self-absorbed chivalric hero around whom his male-centered *roman* is constructed. In contrast, Marie chooses to model her written narrative after the oral *lai*, thus subverting the male textual authority to which Chrétien clings. What is marginalized by the male author is privileged by the female, who according to Rosenn marginalizes in turn the Latin sources of her stories.

Within this newly forged discursive space, Marie addresses issues that reflect a different agenda from that of masculine exemplarity or propagandistic male hero-worship. The nature of love is explored not as an endorsement of the hero's virtue but as a means of representing her female personages' struggles to fulfill their amorous desires. For example, Marie focuses on the issue of communication between lovers in several *lais*, just as the *trobairitz* demonstrate a keen interest in effective and unambiguous communication. *Chevrefoil* narrates only a brief fragment of the Tristan legend, one that demonstrates the power of true and pure love to allow its practitioners to communicate on a level that approaches the preverbal. This "courtly" (and therefore extramarital) union stands in contrast to the utter lack of communication between husband and wife in the majority of the *lais*. Marie thus offers a counterview of love, whose function is in part to criticize the injustice of her culture's institution of marriage (this is clear when one considers the *malmarieé*, the unfortunate wives of *Yonec*, *Laüstic*, and *Guigemar*, who are locked up by possessive, jealous husbands). The function is also in part (as in *Eliduc*) to allow for the possibility of a woman's assumption of a heroic role. This distinct presentation of courtly love's integration into heroic narrative makes Marie de France's relationship with the established patriarchal courtly love tradition problematic.

At this point we should explore in more detail exactly how Marie's presentation of love differs. We have already seen that for male-authored romance, courtly love makes demands on its hero that often conflict with his professional obligations. *Eliduc* is the *lai* that best exemplifies the duty/desire problem of romance, but Marie manipulates the conflict in a way that subverts knightly heroism and, as a result, allows the two main female characters to assume more autonomous roles uncharacteristic of the ladies of Chrétien's romances. Marie's project involves, to borrow Rosenn's terminology, a sexual and textual politics that privileges the feminine and grants the heroine an importance in narrative plot and structure that is dramatically augmented from that of Chrétien's romance model. Here we see both the subversion of male authority and the ingenuity with which Marie achieves it: rather than reject outright the male model, she manipulates its inherent conflicts and tensions in order to achieve her end. In the process, moreover, she demonstrates a keen insight into the complexities of medieval chivalric romance that continue to occupy modern literary scholars. To begin our reading of *Eliduc* in terms of this subversion, we should turn our attention to exactly how the male heroic ideal is subverted by the female poet.

Faultless in military strategy and performance, Eliduc is unjustly dismissed from his Breton King's service and travels to England in search of an opportunity to restore his reputation. Once a new king is found to serve, the hero again proves his peerless skill in military matters, saving his new lord and his kingdom from his enemies. It is when he falls in love with the king's daughter that the true conflict of the story—a conflict between duty and desire—is introduced. By having this love affair (an affair justified by Eliduc on the grounds that he had not physically consummated it), the knight has violated his duty on two levels, that of remaining faithful to his wife (a social and religious obligation, not to mention a personal promise reflecting on his honor), and that of being honest and loyal to his new king.

> Une grant piece i demura;
> Puis prist cungé, si s'en ala;
> El li duna mut a enviz,
> Mes nepurquant s'en est partiz,
> A sun ostel s'en est alez.
> Tut est murnes e trespensez,
> Pur la belë est en esfrei,
> La fille sun seignur le rei,
> Que tant ducement l'apela,
> E de ceo ke ele suspira.
> Mut par se tient a entrepris
> Que tant ad esté al païs,
> Que ne l'ad veüe sovent.
> Quant ceo ot dit, si se repent:
> De sa femme li remembra
> E cum il li asseüra
> Que bone fei li portereit
> E lëaument se cuntendreit.[16]

(p. 135)

[He stayed there a long while, then took his leave and left. She granted him leave very unwillingly, but he nevertheless departed and returned to his lodging. He was very sad and pensive, and anxious because this little girl alarmed him, the daughter of his lord the King, had addressed him so gently and sighed. He considered himself most unfortunate to have been in the country for so long and to have seen so little. Having said this, he repented of it, for he remembered his wife, and how he had assured her that he would be faithful and behave loyally.] (115)[17]

Eliduc does hesitate to express his love to Guilliadun because of his wife, but this only emphasizes his awareness of right and wrong as he chooses the latter. The slighting of duty to his new patron is more puzzling: the king in fact encourages his daughter to meet and entertain the knight. There is no reason to suspect that the king would not be elated at their mutual love, as Eliduc has told no one that he is already married. Yet the lovers choose to keep their affair hidden from public view, and eventually Eliduc returns home and then back

to England to secretly carry the princess away. One must also wonder
what Eliduc plans to do with the princess once he has brought her
back to his homeland—and to his wife. At first faultless in his chivalric behavior, Eliduc has allowed his passion for Guilliadun to lead
him to violate his pledge of loyalty and service to his king. In the
process, Marie shows us a hero whose decisions and behavior call into
question his virtue and indeed his very heroism.

One can also discern a pattern in the narrative: when confronted
with a serious problem, Eliduc resorts to military action, to violence.
He is first faced with adversity in France when his name has been tar-
nished by the envy of other members of the court. The response is to
seek a chance to prove himself in battle elsewhere. His next crisis comes
upon realizing that he has fallen in love with the princess (the passage
cited above). Consider how the narrator describes his response to the
crisis.

> Tant s'est de la guere entremis
> Qu'il aveit retenu e pris
> Celiu ki le rei guerreia,
> E tute la tere aquita.
> Mut fu preisez par sa prüesce,
>
> Par sun sen e par sa largesce;
> Mut li esteit bien avenu.

(p. 141)

[His efforts in the war were so successful that he captured and retained
the King's adversary, and freed the whole land. He was greatly valued for
his prowess, his wisdom and his generosity. Good fortune had befallen
him.] (118)

That he may excel at war while tormented by personal crisis demonstrates the hero's understanding of the public and private as completely divorced from one another. One can excel in one realm regardless of his performance in the other, so polarized are the worlds of love
and military prowess. But the passage also demonstrates that Eliduc
can only respond to crisis in the private by further action in the public. When the distance between these sides of life collapses, the result
is disastrous. As Eliduc and the princess sail back to England, a storm
places their lives in jeopardy. When the boatman pronounces the
storm to be an act of divine justice in punishment of the knight's adul-
tery and suggests that they cast the princess overboard to calm the seas,

the crisis is further intensified: Guilliadun learns for the first time that Eliduc is married and faints from the shock of betrayal. Eliduc's response is true to form: he seizes the boatman and hurls him overboard. The physical strength of the knight is the professional attribute on which he continually falls back in any crisis, and with it he commits a violent murder when his private misconduct is exposed.

Eliduc's questionable male heroism has left him and his two female objects of desire in a seemingly irreconcilable dilemma. That there is no solution available by way of male heroic agency is of course by design, as it allows Marie's women characters to act autonomously and heroically, in effect subverting the male courtly and chivalric ideal. At the same time she rejects Lasry's definition of an "ideal heroine," based in the female character's approximation of masculine traits and behavior: rather than act as rivals in competition for Eliduc, Guildeluëc (Eliduc's first wife) and Guilliadun negotiate a resolution that ultimately leads all three characters to commit their lives not to personal desire, but rather to a religious vocation. At the women's first meeting, Guilliadun narrates her life in the terms of a cautionary tale, complete with an explicit moral to her story: "Mut est fole quë humme creit" (154) [She who trusts a man is extremely foolish (125)]. Guildeluëc responds by offering to remove herself from this triangle of earthly desire and enter a convent, a noble gesture of self-sacrifice that constitutes an alternative model of heroism outside the conventions of male agency in romance and, more to the point, antithetical to the egoistic male discourse of courtly love. Marie grants her heroine the narrative space traditionally denied her in male-authored romance, and in the process she reveals an approach to human love that is a marked departure from courtly love's discourse of the self:

> "Bele," la dame li respunt,
> "N'ad rien vivant en tut le munt
> Que joie li feïst aveir;
> Ceo vus peot hum dire pur veir.
> Il quide ke vus seez morte,
> A merveille se descunforte.
> Chescun jur vus ad regardee;
> Bien quid qu'il vus trova pasmee.
> Jo sui sa spuse vereiment,
> Mut ai pur lui mun quor dolent;
> Pur la dolur quë il menot
> Saveir voleie u il alot:

> Après lui vienc, si vus trovai.
> Que vive estes grant joie en ai;
> Ensemble od mei vus en merrai
> E a vostre ami vus rendrai.
> Del tut le voil quite clamer,
> E si ferai mun chef veler."
>
> (pp. 154–55)

["Fair one," the lady replied, "nothing on earth could make him joyful, you may be assured of that, for he thinks you are dead and is terribly distressed. He has come to look at you every day, but I assume he found you in a swoon. Truly, I am his wife and my heart grieves for him. Because of the grief he displayed, I wanted to know where he went, and came after him and found you. I am overjoyed that you are alive and shall take you with me and return you to your beloved. I shall set him free completely and take the veil."] (125)

Guildeluëc's behavior is a clear departure from the possessive and objectifying love of the troubadours and Chrétien. The *cupiditas* which has from the beginning made courtly love problematic for the Christian Church is replaced by a mode of discourse that reflects the Christian ideals of *agape* and especially *caritas*. There is no alternative possibility for Guildeluëc than to take a religious vow and "marry the church," given that the space of romance is one in which courtly love (courtly *cupiditas* borne of self-interest) is the generic convention. Marie tells the story of a heroine who not only rises above the traditionally silent role of her fictional predecessors but rises above the male discursive tradition of courtly love. It is no coincidence that once given a voice to speak, she operates with a discourse of love far removed from the possessive troubadour love ethic, as was the case with the *trobairitz*, choosing instead to demonstrate *caritas* through the foundation of a convent. The tale's narrator informs the reader at the conclusion that this heroic gesture eventually inspired Eliduc and Guilliadun to renounce their physical love and join her in taking religious vows.

This reading of *Eliduc* suggests a problematic relationship between Marie de France's representation of desire and the conventions and ideals of the patriarchal discourse of courtly love, just as was suggested of the *trobairitz* in the previous chapter. They, like Marie, subvert and manipulate a male discursive tradition in the process of defining a distinctive feminine voice. Also like Marie, the women troubadours assume a different rhetorical posture and use a different language to communicate their ends. These ends for Marie and the female lyric tradition may be subject to interpretation in terms of their particulars, but it is clear that in both cases the chief end is to respond to a male conception of love, in part to subvert this tradition's misogynist discourse and thus reject its objectification and marginalization of women, and in part to offer an alternative that does allow room for the representation of feminine voices and the subjective experiences they describe. Both the *trobairitz* and Marie de France offer an important perspective from which the discourse of courtly love may be reconsidered, precisely because of their refusal to conform to the same ideological parameters implicit in troubadour poetry and Chrétien's romances.

DUTY AND DESIRE IN THE *COMEDIA:* HONOR AND THE DISCOURSE OF COURTLY LOVE

While the influence of Chrétien's model for romance narrative on Spanish medieval literature is most explicit in the widely popular *libros de caballería* (books of chivalry), including the *Amadís* cycle, a parallel tradition in the late Middle Ages draws upon this paradigm with a more direct focus on the problems confronting the chivalric hero in his negotiation of duty and desire. The immensely popular *novela sentimental*[18] examines desire allegorically and constitutes important source material for Spanish dramatists through the early modern period. *Cárcel de amor* (Prison of Love) and *Siervo libre de amor* (Free Servant of Love) exemplify the genre's tendency to examine the potentially destructive social and moral implications of desire, further establishing the narrative context in which courtly discourse was first introduced to the Iberian peninsula.

As early as the *Celestina,* Spanish drama has reflected a tension between the public demands of honor[19] and the expression of the individual's desire discursively grounded in the courtly love tradition. Fernando de Rojas parodies the language and sentiment of courtly love-as-suffering, and Melibea's suicide in front of her father (after Calisto's "tragic fall") punctuates the conflict. Her choice to reciprocate Calisto's advances and to fulfill her own desire is an irreversible one, and the fact that it is her father to whom she confesses before committing suicide highlights that her decision is a transgression of familial honor (a transgression which, in keeping with the patriarchal ideology informing the code of honor, is only of concern when committed by a woman). While *Celestina* scholarship continues to offer new insights into Rojas's multilayered and highly nuanced treatment of courtly conventions,[20] the conclusion of the work is clearly presented in the terms of a cautionary tale: Calisto's comically presented tragic demise and Melibea's subsequent suicide bear the message that courtly love is all-consuming and socially destructive, a message that runs parallel to the socially problematic courtly love depicted by both Chrétien and Marie, not to mention the bulk of Spanish sentimental narratives of the fifteenth century. Cervantes's Don Quijote-Dulcinea parody of courtly love, published over a century after Rojas's tragicomedy, offers evidence that the discourse of courtly love retained this association with socially destructive behavior well into the early modern period: Don Quijote's interpretation of chivalric courtly love spurs him on to seek new challenges and adventures for the sake of his imaginary lady, to the consternation and often to the physical peril of innocent passersby. This tension continually reemerges throughout the seventeenth-century *Comedia*, although in a variety of generic manifestations that may resemble neither the *Celestina*'s nor the *Quijote*'s parodic treatment.

A major difference between Rojas's dramatization of courtly desire and that of the seventeenth-century *Comedia* is the influence of Renaissance Neoplatonism on the latter. The *Celestina* predates the sixteenth-century publication of Hebreo's translation of Ficino's *Dialoghi d'Amore* and is utterly devoid of its conception of human love as a stepping stone toward divine love. As the following chapter will discuss in greater depth, Renaissance Neoplatonism reconfigures desire in such a way as to reconcile human love with Counter-Reformation ideology. This does not mean, however, that early modern dramatists could simply adopt this "new" love ethic and therefore avoid the pitfalls of courtly love to which chivalric romance and the *Celestina* fall victim. Even courtly love itself as an abstract theory would have ennobled the medieval lover in a socially constructive way, inspiring feats of chivalry that would both fulfill his public duty and honor his lady. Like chivalric romance's engagement of courtly discourse, Neoplatonic love functions in harmony with the predominant cultural ideology of its day only as an abstract philosophical theory (such as Ficino's round-table discussion).[21] When put into narrative or dramatic practice, however, both courtly love in romance and Neoplatonic love in the *Comedia* prove socially problematic. The continuity of this tension results from what literary love in medieval romance and in early modern Spanish drama share in common: the representation of desire through the discourse of courtly love. Despite the philosophical and theoretical gaps between medieval courtly love and Renaissance Neoplatonism, the discursive self-centering originally established by the troubadours continues to operate in the *Comedia* as the means by which desire is performed as a function of personal and subjective experience.

Despite courtly love's early modern "evolution" by way of Neoplatonism, the dramatic staging of desire depends on the expression of subjective experience by individual characters. While prose or verse narrative may rely upon a third-person omniscient narrator to describe love from without, the theatrical *Comedia* is by nature the exchange of "first-person" speech acts; the substance of the *Comedia*'s love stories is grounded in subjectivity, in speaking subjects who are directly experiencing the emotional and psychological effects of love (including jealousy, lust, and bliss). Reconciling this subjectivity with Neoplatonism, which privileges union and ascent over courtly "love from afar" and self-absorption, is treated in multiple ways in the *Comedia*. My analysis of *La dama boba* in the previous chapter focused in part on Laurencio's disingenuous employment of courtly discourse to woo Finea, at least originally for the sole purpose of financial gain; what was not discussed was his ironic employment of Neoplatonic concepts in the process. His instruction of the still-*boba* Finea on the nature of love in the first act describes the union of two souls through the holy covenant of marriage—a lesson through which he hopes to seduce her and gain her dowry (as he eventually does). That Nise understands "ni una palabra" (not a single word) of Duardo's Neoplatonic sonnet underscores the extent to which the abstract concepts of Neoplatonism do not effectively or pragmatically communicate desire to the real women who ostensibly inspire it. We have also seen in the previous chapter how Finea's transformation from *boba* to *discreta,* a Neoplatonic ascent and ennoblement if ever there were one, by no means liberates her from the paradigmatic self-reflexivity of courtly discourse. Neoplatonism may therefore add to the complexity and tenor of love's representation in the *Comedia,* but the legacy of the troubadours maintains its decisive influence on the terms through which desire is performed. Although the philosophy of love (if one may be identified) of a given play might be deduced as Neoplatonic in orientation, the discourse of love still bears the stamp of the courtly model.

It is therefore no surprise that the tension and conflict between duty and desire that resulted from courtly love's integration into medieval chivalric romance would reemerge in the *Comedia*. Along the lines of the *Celestina* and Juan de la Cueva's *El infamador*, early modern Spanish tragedy (such as Lope's *El castigo sin venganza* and Calderón's honor plays) and many of its tragicomedies (including Lope's *Fuenteovejuna* and *Peribáñez*, Tirso de Molina's *El burlador de Sevilla*, and Calderón's *El alcalde de Zalamea*) deal with physical desire as a socially destructive *cupiditas*. Such a presentation of love clearly pits the individual male transgressor against the community of subjects, whose social order is circumscribed by the code of honor both onstage and in the audience. O'Connor reiterates that honor in the *Comedia* grounded the spectator's experience in the *corral* in his or her own social reality. "What is required so that successful communication take place between actors and spectators is agreement on the rules governing transmission of meaning, a set of previously established codes that mediate the gap between the real world of the audience and the fictional world represented on the stage."[22] The medieval duty/desire conflict outlined thus far reemerges in the early modern Spanish honor play as a threat to this shared cultural value.

Public duty and individual desire operate in conflict in the seventeenth-century Spanish theater even in popular comedy, where the ultimate end of love is most often marriage, presented as the socially constructive union of self-actualizing subjects based on *conformidad*, which O'Connor translates as "mutual reciprocity."[23] Female resistance to the male advance, such as Angela's opening-scene flight from Luis in Calderón's *La dama duende*, and even female acceptance of the male advance, as is the case with Inés's initially cautious response to Alonso in *El caballero de Olmedo*, are expressed invariably with reference made to the woman's honor. Especially for female characters, the desires of the individual must always be weighed against the social consequences of succumbing to them. And while the most generically comic cape-and-sword and *enredo* comedies resolve this tension harmoniously through promises to wed (usually made between multiple couples), the plots of these plays consist of the process by which the *galán* or *dama* wins the favor of his or her desire's object and the approval of the community through the social institution of marriage. It is only in the final scene, after three acts of tension and discord, that such closure is achieved. Put another way, seventeenth-century Spanish comedy achieves its harmonious and festive resolution primarily through the successful negotiation of an ongoing conflict between social duty, represented in terms of honor, and desire, represented through the discourse of courtly love.

La dama duende is representative of how the male authors of cape-and-sword plays construct the *enredo* (plot complication or "knot"), first engaged and then dissolved over the course of the play's action, around the confrontation of love and honor.[24] It also reflects the sub-genre's major departure from Golden Age tragedy and tragicomedy in its representation of gender roles: women play a more active role in bringing their amorous intentions to fruition.[25] As the social code of honor in Counter-Reformation society dictates, and as is reflected in other early modern dramatic genres, women are the depository of familial honor, an essentially passive and defensive role. Men may reaffirm and validate their social standing by acting honorably; women may do so by not acting dishonorably.[26] The challenge for the more active *dama* of Spanish comedy is to maintain the appearance of passivity (guarding her honor) while surreptitiously acting to make possible the union with her *galán* (pursuing her desire). Angela's active pursuit of Don Manuel must take into account both her personal need to make her intentions known to him and her public or social need to protect her anonymity for the sake of her family's honor. Discretion and invention are required to maintain this delicate balance—as they are required in order to offer the paying public an engaging *enredo*.

Angela's predicament stems from her brothers' containment of her, which denies her the freedom and autonomy to interact within her society. Other cape-and-sword plays, like Calderón's *Casa con dos puertas, mala es de guardar,* revolve around a concern by men to contain women and protect their honor, but in *La dama duende* the need for the containment and concealment of Angela is particularly urgent. She is widowed and has inherited considerable debt from her deceased spouse, so her enclosure is motivated by both the need to demonstrate a respectable period of mourning and the desire to hide her return to town from her husband's creditors. "Donde en efeto, encerrada / sin libertad he vivido, / porque enviudé de un marido, / con dos hermanos casada" [In effect I have lived locked in and without freedom, and because I became a widow, I am married to two brothers] (lines 389–92).[27] Angela's containment by the institution of marriage, dissolved with her husband's death, has been exchanged for containment by her brothers. Even the rare occasions in which a young woman would normally be permitted to appear in public are denied her, and she therefore must resort to slipping away from home, unbeknownst to her brothers and with her face hidden behind a veil, in order to have any contact with the world outside her immediate family. During the action of the play, yet another restriction is placed upon her that only further contains and conceals her: because her brother has invited his friend Manuel to stay with them, Angela's bedchamber is completely sealed off from the exterior guest room in which he stays, in the hopes that Manuel will come and go without ever having seen her. Angela is returning from one of her "illicit" ventures into town when she first meets Don Manuel in the play's opening scene, after having been spotted and pursued by her brother Luis, who wishes to know her identity. Her plea to Manuel focuses especially on her honor: "Honor y vida me importa / que aquel hidalgo no sepa / quién soy, y que no me siga" [My honor and life depend on that gentleman not knowing who I am, and on his not following me] (lines 105–7). From the very beginning, then, her need as an individual to interact with society and her familial obligation to remain hidden from public view are at odds.

Angela's existence as a social individual is repressed throughout the play and can only be realized surreptitiously. Her clandestine written correspondence with Manuel, delivered by her servant Isabel through a secret entrance to his room, successfully subverts the measures taken by her overzealous brothers to isolate her. They also dictate the action and ultimately the title of the play: her inexplicable entrance and departure from Manuel's locked bedroom is attributed, especially by the *gracioso* Cosme, to the supernatural powers of a *duende*. It is an appropriate term to describe a woman who must subvert male control for the sake of desire, and Angela herself adopts the name ("la dama duende") when signing her love letters. The humorous mock syllogism that Cosme offers at the close of the drama's second act further emphasizes the play's association of femininity with the demonic. After Angela's "apparition" and disappearance in the presence of Manuel, he confusedly asks his lackey for his opinion of what they have witnessed, to which Cosme replies:

> Que es mujer-diablo;
> pues que novedad no es,
> si la mujer es demonio
> todo el año, que una vez,
> por desquitarse de tantas,
> sea el demonio mujer.
>
> (lines 2236–41)

[It is a she-devil; it is nothing new, if woman is the devil all year long, that this time . . . the devil is a woman.]

The association of femininity with the demonic, especially when femininity subverts the attempts of the patriarchal power structure to contain and silence it, is by no means a parenthetical aside to this play's representation of gender offered by a *gracioso* for comic relief. Margaret Rich Greer observes that the association is made throughout the play by virtually all of its primary characters—including female characters. This "characteristic of patriarchal societies" leads Greer to the conclusion that "it would be a distortion to make of Calderón a defender of women's rights *avant la lettre*."[28] But while avoiding such a simplistic distortion of Calderón's complex representation of women, we must surely recognize that *La dama duende* makes light of the conservative and traditional association of women with the diabolical.[29]

A split identity emerges from Angela's character: Doña Angela (*angel*), the isolated and passive depository of male honor, and "la dama duende" (lady-phantom or *devil*), the subversively active female subject pursuing a male object. It is only in the denouement, when Manuel announces to her brothers his intention to marry her, that this dualism is erased. The anonymous "duende," in the presence of her brothers and the patriarchal authority they represent, may then finally recognize her desire at the same time as her identity. The honor/desire conflict she faces is externalized in her two identities, and her imminent reentry into the social and religious institution of marriage with the man she loves makes the subversive side of her split identity no longer necessary.

Angela's predilection for action and agency is especially important in a play in which the three male protagonists find the pursuit of their personal desire severely restricted by the rigors of male honor. One might even say that honor-driven male stasis causes female agency: Angela takes great care to hide her identity from Manuel, because his honor would prevent him from cultivating an amorous relationship with the sister of his host and friend. In fact his initial concern when reading her letters is that she is Don Luis's *dama*, in which case his loyalty would likewise keep him from pursuing her. Her next letter makes clear that Luis could not possibly court her, and only then does he begin to show anything approaching genuine interest in her. Knowing that his honor-code obligation to Juan and Luis would prevent him from courting her, she chooses to at least temporarily remove such an obstacle by hiding her identity from him. To maintain her anonymity, she must contrive and dictate the terms of their meeting. Manuel is compelled to comply with her demands by a curiosity that eventually develops into courtly desire.

Over the course of the play, the three male protagonists share the same basic conflict between honor and personal desire. Don Juan's approach to the conflict is duplicitous: as Angela's oldest brother and "padrino" (as he calls himself in the final scene), he is obsessed with protecting his sister from contact with the outside world for the sake of familial honor. At the same time, however, he pursues their cousin Beatriz with the wooing *finezas* of courtly love, unscrupulously betraying the trust that her father has placed in him by allowing her to come and go freely to Angela's house. This hypocrisy is augmented in the third act, when Beatriz is forced to seek refuge there after her irate father had discovered her at night outside her window with an unknown suitor (who is in fact Don Juan). Don Luis also shamelessly pursues Beatriz, although his advances are met with a level of disdain that borders on contempt. His love gives way to jealousy as he plots to impede his brother's amorous designs: "el fuego que me abrasa / ya no tiene otro remedio; / que el estorbar es el último remedio / de un celoso" [the fire that engulfs me has no other remedy; to prevent is the last remedy of a jealous man] (1821–24). Thus while desire drives Don Juan to hypocrisy, its destructive consumption of Don Luis pits him against his own brother's aspirations. Both subjective experiences of desire, though emotional polar opposites, are performed through the discourse of courtly love.

Don Manuel is the most successful negotiator of this conflict, in the sense that his choice to defend the honor of Angela, the object of his desire, leads to a fulfillment of that desire. It is apparent, however, that his desire for "la dama duende" would be more appropriately called a precocious curiosity than heartfelt passion. It is Angela who ardently yearns for their union: from her opening-scene appeal to him for protection to her closing-scene appearance, witnessed also by Don Luis, she continually places Manuel in a position where his sense of personal nobility and honor mandates that he protect her. In the latter case, just before offering his hand in marriage, he expresses his motive: "No receles, señora. / Noble soy, y estás conmigo ahora" [Never fear, lady. I am noble, and you are with me now] (lines 2993–94). Duty and desire appear to be reconciled in Manuel's character, but it is only because of the weakness of the latter.[30] When he is actually confronted with a situation in which public duty conflicts with his tepid desire, as when he is summoned away from the house to join the royal court at El Escorial, he refers to desire as mere "gusto" and chooses to subordinate it to his honor.

> Confuso me ausento
> por no llevar ya sabido
> esto, que ha de ser tan presto;
> pero uno importa al honor
> de mi casa y de mi aumento,
> y otro solamente a un gusto;
> y así, entre los dos extremos,
> donde el honor es lo más,
> todo lo demás es menos.
>
> (lines 1721–30)

[I take leave confused by not yet having come to know this (her identity), which is to be revealed so soon; but one thing pertains to the honor of my house and to my betterment, and the other merely to my pleasure; and so, between the two extremes, where honor is the concern, all else means less.]

Ultimately it is his chivalric sense of duty, not his rather dispassionate desire for Angela, that compels him to ask for her hand in marriage. In order to protect her from Luis's rage upon discovering them together (he has unsheathed a dagger, threatening to kill his sister for her impertinence), Manuel tells Luis (not Angela) of his intention to wed. After assuring Luis of his innocence (that it was Angela who had entered Manuel's room unbeknownst to him), he assures her brother that her honor remains intact: "Y para cumplir mejor / con la obligación jurada, / a tu hermana doy la mano" [And to better comply with my sworn obligation, I give to your sister my hand] (lines 3087–89).

If Manuel is simply complying with an obligation while Angela is responsible for making their union possible, is the play to be read as a triumph of female desire over the confinement imposed upon her by familial honor? Such a reading is attractive, but it must be kept in mind that Angela remains dependent on her *galán*'s sense of honor and duty for her liberation. This dependency is most apparent in the events that immediately lead up to the denouement. The strategies and plottings of the *duende,* made in secret with her friend Beatriz and her maid Isabel, are actually thwarted by the unexpected return of her brothers, just as she was to dine with Manuel. Angela's subversive agency therefore fails her, placing her honor and that of her would-be lover in peril. She has no choice but to reveal her identity to Manuel and warn him of this danger, so that he might defend her and himself. From this point forward her onstage presence recedes into the background; she assumes a role more like that of a traditional romance lady/object as Manuel and Luis begin their climactic duel. After Manuel disarms Luis and then allows him to leave in search of another sword (demonstrating first his physical skill and then his chivalric generosity), he manages to calm the brother's rage by making clear his innocence and the purity of his intentions. The male lover asserts to the lady's male guardian that, by marrying her, her honor will be preserved and transferred to his guardianship. Only then is Angela's desire for Manuel recognized as acceptable, legitimate, and ideologically orthodox. In short, Angela's attempt to subvert her brothers' containment of her has failed, and she is at the point of being violently punished by Luis for her transgression when the heroic Manuel comes to her rescue. The happy denouement is dependent on Manuel's honorable behavior to compensate for the potentially disastrous result of Angela's pursuit of him. After all of her machinations and strategies to subvert her brothers' authority over her, it is ironic that she is successful only upon assuming the role of soon-to-be victim (of Luis's vengeance), a literal damsel in distress. The standard neohistorical reading of early modern comedy seems well supported by *La dama duende:* an effort to subvert power is ultimately coopted by its dominant ideology, and the subversive individual is reintegrated into her proper function within this ideological system through the patriarchal institutions of honor and marriage.

La dama duende demonstrates the way in which the duty-desire conflict traced thus far has different implications for male and female subjects. Honor implies a distinct set of social obligations for each sex that in basic terms imply passive protection for women and active pursuit for men. This distinction leads to very different conflicts faced by Angela and Manuel, which explains why the former fails while the latter triumphs. The fact that Angela's failure gives occasion to Manuel's heroism suggests that Calderón affirms the established patriarchal and often misogynist worldview of the Counter-Reformation. How, then, is the representation of honor's conflict with individual desire changed when explored by a woman dramatist? Calderón's ideological affirmation does recognize in Angela's dual identity (angel/devil) that honor severely limits a woman's capacity to pursue her personal desire. He even recognizes that male guardianship of female honor may become overzealous and abusive, not to mention hypocritical, as Don Juan and Don Luis demonstrate. However, the fact that he represents the dilemma posed by this abuse (the dilemma that forces Angela to assume the subversive role of *duende*) as unresolvable without the intervention of a positive model of male honor ultimately subordinates subversive female action to heroic male action, in the end affirming male power. If such a conflict is written from the perspective of a woman, who according to Calderón's model is powerless and dependent on male intervention, may a similar ideological affirmation be expected?

DUTY AND DESIRE IN THE *COMEDIA*:
LA FIRMEZA EN LA AUSENCIA

Leonor de la Cueva y Silva's comedy *La firmeza en la ausencia*[31] portrays the conflict between love and honor in very different terms, making the play's ideological affirmation or subversion less immediately apparent.[32] The inherent differences in honor's implications for men and women are again the focus, but without the dependence of female honor on male heroism. Armesinda, the play's heroine, demonstrates a positive and heroic *firmeza* (resoluteness) that stands in stark contrast to the *flaqueza* (weakness) expected of her by the play's three male protagonists. Her insistence on maintaining autonomous control over her personal future pits her against the obligation demanded of her by the king whose sister she serves at court, and her *firmeza* even develops over the course of the play from an anxiously defensive posture to a confident and open defiance of the king's attempts to impose his will over hers. By the end of the play, Armesinda's *firmeza* has developed beyond its original impetus, fidelity to her lover, into a personal autonomy that she will defend even with her life. Thus while her *galán* Don Juan affirms honor as a function of male heroism in terms not unlike those of Calderón and even Chrétien, Armesinda's role is a departure from male-authored Spanish comedy in her successful resistance to male containment.

If *La dama duende* represents the negotiation of the duty/desire conflict by male characters with varying degrees of success (Manuel's heroic affirmation of honor contrasts with the failures of Juan and especially Luis), *La firmeza en la ausencia* does the same but through an even more extreme contrast offered by its male protagonists. The male characters appear to observe the Aristotelian notion of consistency or "unity" of character, unlike Chrétien's Erec or Marie de

France's Eliduc, who fluctuate between the weakness of personal indulgence and virtuous self-sacrifice for the sake of honor. From the opening scene Don Juan is a paragon of honor, both as the chaste and loyal suitor of Armesinda and especially as a military leader in the service of the king of Naples, Filiberto. In contrast, Filiberto is driven to deceit and manipulation by a jealous desire for Armesinda. Her disdain and *firmeza* only strengthen his obsession and the extent to which he will abuse his power to possess her. Don Juan's professional duty is fulfilled at the expense of his love for Armesinda, while Filiberto's desire breeds dishonorable and abusive behavior.[33]

The king's privileging of desire is especially unethical in that it spurs him to manipulate Don Juan's own sense of public duty and honor in order to remove his rival from court. Because Don Juan himself places duty above desire, Filiberto is able to send him away to fight on his behalf and thereby enjoy exclusive access to Armesinda. He confesses his passion in the first act to his sister Celidaura in language borrowed from courtly love-as-suffering: "No puede, hermana, ser más / lo que esta enemiga bella / me hace sufrir y penar" [The pain and suffering caused by this beautiful enemy could not be greater] (lines 495–97).[34] His further admission that jealousy has motivated his removal of Don Juan from the court is justified in terms that reveal a treacherous and tyrannical selfishness: love, he explains, holds sovereign power over him and is only subject to the law of *gusto* (pleasure). Filiberto is well aware of his transgression, but he is hopelessly controlled by desire.

> No estoy, Celidaura, en mí;
> quiero y amo con exceso
> aquesta ingrata hermosura,
> origen de mi locura,
> pues por ella pierdo el seso . . .
>
> (lines 516–20)

[Celidaura, I am not in control of myself; I love and desire in excess that ingrateful beauty, origin of my madness, since for her I am losing my sanity]

The employment of various *topoi* of courtly love (love causes misery, enslavement, and madness) is a telling choice for Leonor de la Cueva in her representation of Filiberto's desire. The courtly discourse of the self is represented as anything but an idealization of love. Instead it is the discourse of male deceit and manipulation, not unlike Liseo's *engaños* in *La traición en la amistad*.[35]

The king's destructive passion only increases in intensity as it feeds on the disdain it generates from her,[36] to the point where her *firmeza* is seen as a personal affront: "ya esa altivez me ofende" [now this haughtiness offends me] (line 1444). Armesinda's resistance constitutes a challenge to King Filiberto's authority and to the power he has over his subjects—authority and power that Don Juan never questions. A series of deceptive strategies employed by the king to conquer Armesinda's will all prove unsuccessful. After sending Don Juan away, the king first decides to intercept all of the letters he writes to her in expression of his continued fidelity; he then convinces her that Don Juan has betrayed her and married a princess; finally, he informs her (through Carlos) that her lover has been killed in battle. Filiberto's desperation reaches a climax in the play's final scene, when he threatens to force Armesinda into marriage: "Dame aquesa mano, acaba, / o tomaréla por fuerza" [Give me your hand, now, or I will take it by force] (lines 2129–30).

The imminent threat to Armesinda is averted by Don Juan's sudden return from battle, which exposes the king's deceptive maneuverings for what they are. His return also offers a solution for Filiberto's unhealthy desire, which up to this point has operated at the expense of his public duty as king: as part of the terms under which the king of France surrendered to Don Juan, Filiberto will marry his beautiful daughter Clara. The new arrangement would place Filiberto's personal desire for love and marriage at the service of his public duty as political and moral leader of his kingdom. Such a reversal of priorities better conforms to the model of male heroism exemplified in this play by Don Juan and in keeping with the longstanding heroic tradition, at least as old as that associated with Virgil's Aeneas, that places duty over desire for the male hero. A marriage to the socially inferior Armesinda, his sister's chamber maid, would have done little for the good of the kingdom; marriage to the daughter of a rival king, however, maintains the family's noble lineage and supports international peace. When Don Juan shows Filiberto a portrait of his new and more appropriately royal fiancée, the king is struck by her beauty and immediately accepts the proposed marriage, a response that underscores the superficially carnal and egoistic motives behind his pursuit of Armesinda.

Don Juan's heroic affirmation of duty and honor compensates for Filiberto's exploitation of these values in his loyal subject, an abuse of power driven by an obsessive desire for an unwilling female object. At the beginning of the play he has faithfully and honorably courted

Armesinda for six years. He is well aware of the king's motives for sending him away, but he is nonetheless duty-bound to obey at the expense of his desire. "Que obedezco; / y que tan sujeto estoy, / que mi vida y cuanto soy / a sus pies humilde ofrezco" [I shall obey; I am so subject to him that my life and all that I am are humbly offered at his feet] (lines 161–64). Don Juan lacks the power to ignore a royal command, and his desire to increase his fame and renown on the battlefield further weakens his ability to resist the order. His pre-departure soliloquy as the first act concludes expresses the nature of his conflict in terms borrowed from classical mythology, underscoring that he is not the first hero to face such a dilemma: "¡Ea, partid a la guerra, / cuidados y pensamientos, / seguid a Marte animoso, / dejad a Cupido tierno!" [Leave for war, cares and thoughts, and follow the powerful Mars, leaving behind tender Cupid!] (lines 809–12). The sentiment will no doubt remind the reader of Marie de France's similarly duty-bound hero Eliduc.

Because of his obedient departure, Don Juan's appearances until the closing scene are in absence from his lady and, aside from offering an account of his heroic military achievements, they consist of his lamenting this absence. Again, the self-focused discourse of courtly love-from-afar (a courtly motif first made famous by the troubadour Jaufre Rudel) serves to express his own constancy towards Armesinda. In a second-act soliloquy (a dramatic recourse that invites the lyric isolation and self-absorption of troubadour discourse), he addresses the absent object of his desire in the second person:

> Después que de tí partí,
> vivo con tantos enojos
> que no sé si estoy en mí,
> mas no es mucho si en tus ojos
> la primera vez me perdí.
>
> (lines 1265–69)

[Since I took leave of you, I am living with such exasperation that I no longer know if I am in my right mind; but this is nothing, since I lost myself the first time in your eyes.]

Like the troubadour lady, Armesinda exists for Don Juan as the pretext for his narcissistic experience of love. She also serves as his motivation for returning from military duty as soon as his duty allows him: "El ánimo es la esperanza / de gozar tu belleza" [My courage comes from the hope of enjoying your beauty] (lines 1285–86).

Don Juan is therefore a heroic figure whose professional and public achievements take precedence over his love for Armesinda, despite his fears (and Filiberto's hopes) that the natural *flaqueza* (weakness) of her sex will render her powerless to resist the king's advances. The standard misogynist generalization at play here is that over the course of time, a woman's loyalty will invariably falter—in other words, the quality privileged in fictional representations of women as early as Homer's Penelope, loyalty or fidelity to the male hero, is treated as suspect because of the inherent weakness of the female sex.[37] For Armesinda to remain loyal and withstand the king's advances, she must assume a measure of *firmeza* that she herself recognizes as uncharacteristic of her gender: "y he de amar hasta morir, / porque se pueda decir / que hay firme alguna mujer" [and I will love him until I die, so that it can be said that there exists at least one faithful woman] (lies 450–52). Don Juan's withdrawal from Naples places his heroism in the background of the final two acts (until his last-minute return for the denouement), while the play instead foregrounds the testing of Armesinda's fidelity and ultimately her independence from male control in the absence of Don Juan's protection. Don Juan privileges duty over desire, leaving Armesinda isolated and defenseless against her male aggressor; Filiberto sacrifices his public duty for the sake of desire and threatens to force her into marriage. The choices made by both men give rise to the play's *enredo* and to the challenge posed to the female protagonist.

That challenge is the basis for the bulk of the play's action, and the development of Armesinda's *firmeza* through the tests to which she is subjected assumes the primary dramatic focus that is traditionally reserved for male heroism, as is the case in *La dama duende* with Don Manuel's successful affirmation of male honor. Because she learns of Don Juan's imminent departure in her first appearance in the play, whereupon she makes her initial promise of *firmeza*, Armesinda's character is represented onstage exclusively in crisis, exclusively as offering resistance to the obsessive pursuit of Filiberto while maintaining fidelity to Don Juan. One can therefore consider *La firmeza en la ausencia* a heroic comedy, but of a different sort from that of the male-authored canon: the almost archetypal Armesinda is heroine, and her heroic resolution replaces the affirmation of male honor as the "exemplary" quality upon which the action is based.[38]

The development of Armesinda's character over the course of the play may be best described as a weaning, a process of transformation from male dependence to an autonomous self-awareness.[39] Her initial resistance from Filiberto's attempts to court her depends on her faith in Don Juan's quick return to her rescue, and the expression of her *firmeza* is accordingly made in reference to him. When Carlos is first sent to test her weakness by the king (he is to tell her that Don Juan has been married abroad), she greets him with the complaint that she has yet to hear from her lover. She asks her friend: is it right that she receive no word from him to repay her constancy, "no mujer, sino diamante, / firme roca, no veleta, / y siendo a tan grandes olas / inmóvil risco en firmeza" [being not a woman, but a diamond, hard as stone, not weak, and an unmovable pillar of fortitude against such strong waves] (lines 993–96)?

Her justifiable anger upon learning of Don Juan's supposed infidelity, however, does not yield the desired effect. Rather than soften her disdain for Filiberto, Carlos's lie only strengthens her resolve to resist the king. Her faith is lost not only in Don Juan but in all men: "Válgame Dios, lo que yerra / la que fía de quien tiene / tan varia naturaleza / como en el hombre se ve" [My God, how much in error is she who trusts one with such a fickle nature as is seen in men] (lines 1162–65).[40] Armesinda's *firmeza* is thus freed from its earlier dependence on male heroism, rendering her an autonomous subject who will resist her unwanted suitor for her own sake. It has in effect developed from a function of her desire for Don Juan to a function of her independent self-identity, suggesting that *firmeza* for Armesinda is in many ways similar to the *caritas* of Marie de France's Guildeluëc.

Because of her misinformation, then, Armesinda considers Don Juan, Filiberto, and all men to be her enemy. She accordingly dismisses the traditional association of her own gender with weakness: "Mal ha dicho quien ha dicho / que la mudanza se engendra / sólamente en las mujeres, / por su femenil flaqueza" [He spoke poorly who said that inconstancy is only engendered in women, because of their feminine weakness] (lines 1169–72). A final attempt to win her favor through deception is made by Filiberto when he tells her that Don Juan has been killed in battle. Armesinda's disassociation from love (from desire for a male object) defuses such an attempt, however, for she has chosen to take religious vows and live in complete isolation from men. In short, Armesinda's *firmeza* eventually constitutes a feminine resistance to male power.[41]

One could argue, however, that this act of subversion is eventually contained by Don Juan's triumphant return: Armesinda is informed of the king's deceptions and joyfully accepts her lover's proposal to marry. The true act of subversion, however, does stand: before being undeceived, she has thwarted the king's efforts to possess her. Don Juan appears as Armesinda has just offered the king the choice to either allow her to join a religious order or to kill her with his sword. Given the social reality of male power over and control of women, as well as the *Comedia*'s observance of verisimilitude, Armesinda's options for resistance are limited to either a heroic death or refuge in the Church (which constitutes another form of patriarchal containment). Don Juan's timely return only avoids what had appeared to be an imminent tragic conclusion; he is a *deus ex machina* (albeit a plausible one) by which the playwright may resolve her conflict according to the generic conventions within which she operates. Given that *La firmeza en la ausencia* is a comedy, which explains the presence of the *gracioso* Tristán and his female complement Leonor, multiple marriages in the play's denouement are the inevitable conclusion.

Leonor de la Cueva therefore works within the structural parameters of patriarchal Spanish comedy to offer an alternative representation of the conventional conflict between duty and desire. The same assessment has been made of Marie de France's *Eliduc,* which further suggests continuity in the response of women authors to medieval and early modern male representations of heroism grounded in the discourse of courtly love. In the patriarchal tradition of heroic narrative and drama, the influence of courtly love challenges the male hero to negotiate its exclusive demands on the male subject with his obligations to the established social order, whether manifested in terms of medieval chivalry or Counter-Reformation Spain's code of honor. It is again a struggle between a stylized discourse of subjectivity and a fictional representation of society informed by patriarchal ideology. A casualty in this struggle between the male individual and his community is the representation of women, who assume the same passive and objectified role as is assigned to them by the troubadour lyric, further burdened with the patriarchal assignment of women as depositories of honor.

The responses of Leonor and Marie are parallel in their shift of narrative or dramatic focus from the male hero to the women affected by his conflict. Both Calderón and Chrétien represent male heroism in a way that only superficially resolves the duty/desire conflict, for Don Manuel and Erec both succeed by controlling desire and subjugating it to their public obligations. Because such a resolution only further marginalizes women in this presentation of heroism, the female authors re-present the male hero in a more problematic light; their male heroes are instead dependent on the virtuous and distinctively heroic actions of women. In this way, the discourse of courtly love is manipulated toward a different ideological end from that for which it was originally conceived by its founding fathers: rather than direct its egocentric focus toward the affirmation of male power, the women writers discussed in this chapter expose the consequences of that power for the women subject to it, in the process creating a new discursive space for female representation.

3

Discursive Interplay: The Ethics of Courtly Love, Decorum, and Interpretation

THE CONFLICT TRACED IN THE PREVIOUS CHAPTER BETWEEN DESIRE and duty or honor implies a conflict of discourses. In *La dama duende,* for example, the discourse of honor is successfully invoked by Manuel in his final exchanges with Luis. Manuel's honorable actions, and the performative speech acts through which they are engendered, rescue Angela from the social peril in which she has placed herself after voicing her desire for him (through a series of speech acts that, as she is well aware, risk damaging familial honor).[1] This instance may serve as an example of how the function of courtly discourse in early modern Spanish drama can only be understood when one takes into consideration its interplay with the alternate and competing modes of discourse that George Mariscal has identified as characteristic of early modern Spanish literary expression.[2] We have seen that, unlike the enclosed space of the lyric poem, courtly love in the *Comedia* does not exist in a discursive vacuum. The pursuit of desire, whether by male or female subjects, is made dramatic through its representation in collision with other forces (in the case of honor, a social force) that threaten its success. In Aristotelian terms, speech *(lexis)* itself becomes the action being imitated *(praxis);*[3] rather than simply being the medium through which an action is represented, discursive exchanges constitute the action itself. The assertion of the anonymous *Memorial impreso dirigido al rey D. Felipe, para que levante la suspensión en las representaciones de comedias* (Published written request addressed to King Philip that the suspension in the representation of plays be lifted), that "de todo hay en la *Comedia*" (everything is in the *Comedia*),[4] can be read as more than a celebration of the tradition's great variety in subject matter; it can also be considered a discursive maxim that points to a major source of tension and *agon* in Golden Age drama.

104

For Michel Foucault, any discourse functions as an instrument of power insofar as it operates to create subject positions that classify and categorize individuals according to its implicit ideology.[5] Applying this perspective to the example of *La dama duende*, we can say that Manuel's discourse of honor assigns to Angela the role of wife, as opposed to the position of *domna* or *midons* prescribed by the discourse of courtly love. In dialogue with Luis, who invokes the same discourse of honor to challenge Manuel to a duel, Angela is effectively treated as a commodity exchanged between men. She is again a feminine object, the responsibility of whose honor is transferred from brother to husband. If to this point we have explored the implications of courtly discourse's representation of women as objects of desire, in light of how female writers like the *trobairitz*, Marie de France, and Spanish *dramaturgas* have responded to such treatment, it seems appropriate now to consider the ways in which that representation is refracted by the other discourses brought into contact with courtly love in the *Comedia*. With colliding discourses come colliding ideologies, and we must now consider the effects of such ideological cross-fertilization on the reader's or spectator's experience with a given text or spectacle. As we shall see, the ideological significance of the discourse of courtly love in a play, witnessed from within the context of the seventeenth-century Spanish *corral*, was subject to a wide range of interpretive possibilities.

A key concept for analyzing Golden Age drama in terms of its discursive hybridity and diversity is the Aristotelian precept of decorum. The citation from Lope de Vega's *Arte nuevo de hacer comedias en este tiempo* given at the very beginning of this study, in which Lope claims to lock up Terence and Plautus when writing for the *vulgo*, is difficult to take at face value when one considers his adherence to this classical precept. Even within the same treatise, he prescribes the style of speech appropriate for the social station of several stock *Comedia* characters.

> Si hablare el rey, imite cuando pueda
> la gravedad real; si el viejo hablare,
> procure una modestia sentenciosa;
>
> . . . .
>
> y si formare quejas, siempre guarde
> el debido decoro a las mujeres.
> Las damas no desdigan de su nombre . . .

(lines 269–80)

> [If the King speaks, imitate whenever possible
> royal solemnity; if the elderly speak,
> procure for them a modest sententiousness;
>
> .   .   .   .
>
> and if one offers a complaint, always respect
> the decorum owed to women.
> Ladies should not tarnish their good name . . .]

The first portion of the above citation offers two stock characters (the king and the old man, the latter usually a father) as examples to stand metonymically for the broad range of character types represented on the Golden Age stage, all of whom must be verbally represented in a way that is particular to their type; the last three lines are specific to the ways in which representing women runs the risk of impropriety. The two admonitions are reflective of two functions of the notion of decorum in the early modern period, one as a literary prescription that diction match character, disseminated through the millennia from Aristotle's *Poetics,* and the other as a notion of socially acceptable behavior.[6] Both senses of the term bear ideological implications: not only do norms and guidelines for socially acceptable behavior reflect ideology in their designation, but the literary representation of social difference can also be read as an ideological statement.

The *Comedia* offers a representation of seventeenth-century Spanish society that is explicit in plays of a contemporary and localized setting, such as the prevailing popular mode of urban comedy; society may also be represented implicitly in plays with a setting that is either historically or geographically distant (or both). In either case the ideological statement made by the society represented onstage is oriented from an authorial position that falls somewhere within its structure, and the statement itself will reflect that position vis-à-vis the social power structure's implicit ideology. Decorum as a literary precept therefore reflects ideology, and it would serve as a guide for dramatists throughout Western Europe during the early modern period. Lope's prescription that a character must act and speak in a decorous manner—that is, actions and language must appropriately reflect the "station" or position of the character—implicitly recognizes differences in social rank and gender, in turn discursively stratifying the social order and either affirming or critiquing the validity of its structure. The "message" of decorum for the dramatist is that the audience must be able to recognize the differences between a king and a peasant, a lady and a gentleman, or an aristocrat and a lackey. The audience must feel that each social position has been accurately and appropriately represented. By making the speech of each character reflect his or her social station, the precept of decorum assures that in early modern theater, and especially the forms of comedy and tragicomedy popular in Golden Age Spain (in which various social stations are brought into contact, from kings to peasant farmers), multiple styles of speech must be brought into dialogue.

Decorum's literary and social implications are of concern to Lope and indeed to all dramatists participating in the *Comedia*. As a literary precept, decorum was a rule handed down from the ultimate classical literary authority. It was essentially a call for "unity of character" that would contribute to the more general goal of plausibility and verisimilitude in early modern theater (i.e., "this is how people from such a social station *would* speak"). As a social precept, the observation of decorum also implied a didactic function in the *Comedia* (i.e., "this is how people of such a station *should* speak") that merits further explanation.

This didactic function—or more precisely the perception of such a function—needs to be contextualized in the cultural polemic surrounding the *Comedia* in Spain in the sixteenth and seventeenth centuries.[7] As representatives of both church and state argued passionately over the licitness and moral effect of the *Comedia*'s public performance on both audience and actor (on the spectators and those producing the spectacle), the presence or absence of moral exemplarity became a central issue in the debate. In addition to judging the *Comedia*'s representation of desire either as harmless entertainment or as lascivious and sinful carnality that could prey upon the public's inherent human weakness, those who weighed in on the debate would also argue for or against the presence of morally instructive content. Defenders of the theater, including Fray Manuel de Guerra y Rivera, argued for the "docent function of plays"[8] in an effort to avoid the kind of prohibition that was briefly placed on public performance at the end of the sixteenth century and twice during the seventeenth century. For the theater to survive the moral rigor of the Counter-Reformation, it became increasingly important to point to the moral edification that it could offer. The macrotext of the *Comedia*, in short, was the battlefield in a war of interpretation.

According to O'Connor, the conventional closure of early modern Spanish comedy with vows of matrimony became a central component in the arsenal of the theater's defenders. "Read in historical depth and with critical sensitivity to the underlying assumptions it questioned, marriage as a theatrical convention became the *Comedia*'s affirmation of a broader appreciation of humankind as well as a fundamental rejection of a dehumanizing tradition whose roots lay most immediately in Augustinian theology."[9] As the principal means of verbally representing the mutual desire between *galán* and *dama* that leads to this felicitous conclusion, the discourse of courtly love assumes an especially important role in the polemic. That decorum be observed while the Golden Age dramatist employs courtly discourse, in both the literary and the socially didactic senses of the term, is requisite for the *Comedia*'s interpretability as "docent."

Lope's admonition that "las damas no desdigan de su nombre," preceded by the directive that the dramatist practicing his new art of writing comedies "siempre guarde el debido decoro a las mujeres" (always observe due decorum with women), indicates the particular significance of decorum for women. As a professional author of comedies, he would no doubt have been well aware of the importance attached to the *Comedia*'s representation of women by those who found the tradition offensive and socially detrimental. O'Connor explains the implicit misogyny of the theater's critics as follows: "For many traditionalists good mores translated into either controlling women and their behavior or, when this failed, blaming them for the sorry state of humankind in general and of society in particular."[10] The ideological legacy of Augustine's condemnation of physical desire and his placement of blame for it on women served as a base for the arguments of those who called for the permanent closure of the *corrales*. This fact places the expression of desire through the discourse of courtly love in the *Comedia* squarely in the center of the battle. The representation of the feminine object of desire by a male subject through the language of courtly love, and the employment of this same amatory discourse by the female subject to express her own desire, are of special concern for those arguing both for and against the licitness of the public theater.

The diametrically opposed assessments made of the *Comedia* by the theater's proponents and opponents are contradictory acts of interpretation. Clergy and laymen alike participated in the debate on both sides of the divide, which suggests a more complicated set of circumstances was at play than if, for example, the theater's opponents were exclusively of religious vocations and its supporters were exclusively secular.[11] The religious vocations pursued by the most commonly acclaimed dramatists of the period—Lope de Vega, Tirso de Molina, and Calderón de la Barca—are in themselves indicative of the extent to which the professional world of the *Comedia* and the Church were mutually integrated. Clearly the amatory material contained especially in Golden Age comedy was subject to interpretation; for every ideologically driven construction of meaning that was made, another could be offered in direct contradiction to it. This chapter will posit that such ambiguity and open-endedness stem from the fact that the discourse of courtly love is refracted by the competing modes of discourse with which it would come into contact in any given play.

If the result of the *Comedia*'s polyglot nature is an undermining of its fixed meaning, the precept of decorum may serve as a useful tool for the analysis of such destabilization. The representation of both social position and gender is guided by decorum, which dictates that each category be represented verbally through its own distinctive discourse. Unlike classical drama, in which the generic divide between tragedy and comedy would isolate social classes (tragedy treats grave and serious matters involving the upper echelon of society, while comedy treats "low" matters involving the lower end of society),[12] the *Comedia* represents virtually all levels of the social spectrum, from servants to kings, in direct contact with one another. An example of this social diversity is the final scene of Lope de Vega's *El caballero de Olmedo,* in which Tello the lackey appears before the king of Spain to plead for justice. The *Comedia*'s more socially diverse cast of characters implies a similarly diverse array of linguistic registers—a plurality of discourses—by which they may be identified. The roots of such discursive variety lie in Renaissance Italy with the development of the hybrid tragicomedy genre, first exported to Spain by Fernando de Rojas's *Celestina* and further explored by sixteenth-century Spanish dramatists before the advent of Lope's *Comedia nueva.* The hybridization of "high" tragic and "low" comic discourses is therefore an innovation that predates the Golden Age *Comedia,* but this chapter will posit that *El caballero de Olmedo* manipulates multiple modes of discourse, each decorously gender and class-specific, in a way that departs from earlier models of tragicomedy. Alonso's expression of desire (and that of his beloved Inés) through the discourse of courtly love, a "high" register bearing the weight of literary authority accumulated over the centuries, is refracted in a new way when put into contact with alternate modes of discourse operating in the play.

Such a perspective suggests that the *Comedia* is, to borrow a term coined by Mikhail Bakhtin, polyphonic. Bakhtin's notions of polyphony and heteroglossia, central to his analysis of the dialogic principle of literary discourse, were made originally in reference to the modern novel rather than to drama; later critics who further explore dialogism have for the most part maintained this original context. Should we consider the "dialogic principle" in the context of the *Comedia,* however, we may go far in understanding the discursive *agon* upon which the tradition (at least in the early modern period) is based. Bakhtin's dialogic reading of the novel penetrates the surface of the multiple voices of its characters to reveal the fundamental discursive diversity upon which that surface is founded—that is to say, it is not simply a case of identifying the fact that different characters exchange utterances ("who says what"); it is indeed a question of establishing that these utterances reveal independent and diverse perspectives and identities ("who says what, and *how they say it*"). The *Comedia* may be analyzed in similar terms: by identifying the distinctive discourses at play in a given text, we may better grasp the nature of the conflicts realized through their collision and competition.

In "Discourse in the Novel," the essay in which his notions of dialogism and polyphony are most thoroughly treated, Bakhtin focuses on the development of the modern novel, a diachronic problem whose ultimate achievement he considers to be the work of Fyodor Dostoevsky. In his view, the earliest work to exhibit these qualities and thus constitute a modern novel by his criteria is *Don Quijote,* a text whose relationship with its contemporary theater is well known to scholars of both Cervantes and the *Comedia.*[13] Because the sources that informed and influenced Cervantes's prose fiction would constitute for Bakhtin a "prehistory" of novelistic discourse, he is generally more concerned with Cervantes's influence on future writers than with the texts and traditions that made *Don Quijote* possible. Taking his terminology from that context and applying it to the *Comedia* suggests a new way of treating the *Quijote/Comedia* relationship that privileges the resistance they both offer to being reduced to a fixed and ideologically predetermined interpretation. Cervantes's destabilization of the interpretive process, his surrender of authorial control over how his text is to be read and understood, comes in the midst of the debate over the propriety and licitness of the Spanish theater.

We shall see that the combination of the discourse of courtly love in the *Comedia* with alternate modes of discourse is mirrored in the *Quijote* and in the *Novelas ejemplares* (*Exemplary Novels*). To better understand this shared characteristic, we must also consider the common sources from which both Cervantes and Lope's *Comedia* draw. The polydiscursivity of Golden Age Spain's theater and its most important author of prose fiction did not appear from out of nowhere, but in fact represent a culmination of discursive interplay that can be traced at least as far back as Giovanni Boccaccio. The *Decameron* offers its own presentation of human love that is based upon the "contamination" of courtly love by other discursive modes. The connection between the Boccaccian, Cervantine, and *Comedia* presentations of love is most evident in their shared practice of destabilizing the ideological significance of desire's discursive representation—an achievement made possible through the recombination and fusion of disparate discursive systems into new organic unities. In other words, Boccaccio fosters a process of shifting the ideological function of literary discourse away from the monologic ethical purpose characteristic of medieval writers like Dante,[14] toward an ideologically open-ended mode of storytelling that privileges aesthetic pleasure over ideological utility.[15] The *Comedia* and Cervantes's prose fiction contribute to this process by amalgamating discourses (including that of courtly love) in such a way as to invite multiple interpretations, again privileging aesthetic pleasure. Lope's *Arte nuevo* claims that the primary goal of his professional theater is to satisfy the paying public; Cervantes urges his "idle reader" to interpret and judge his masterpiece *Don Quijote* as he or she sees fit. Both statements indicate how far removed Golden Age Spain is from the medieval culture in which the courtly love tradition originally flourished.

Cervantes's surrendering of authorial control over how his work is to be interpreted and received stands in stark contrast to Dante, whose *Divina Commedia* and *Vita Nuova* are anything but ideologically elusive. While twentieth-century literary theory, including hermeneutics, has stressed the open-endedness of any literary text or its dependence on the individual reader to construct meaning from it, the absolute confidence with which Dante's divine cosmography is presented in the great vernacular epic of the Middle Ages differs substantially from Boccaccio in the *Decameron*. Dante's treatment of the quasi-divine Beatrice, discussed in chapter 1 in the context of the *stilnovisti* lyric, is among other things an exercise of authority over how his reader should interpret his representation of desire. The desire for the feminine object implicit in courtly love is sublimated from a physical to a spiritual plane, the process of which is meticulously described in the *Vita Nuova*, a narrative gloss of his lyric poetry that points the reader to a fixed and ideologically orthodox interpretation. The allegorical treatment of Beatrice in the *Commedia* ascribes to the feminine object a Platonic function in the divine schema, as a conduit for divine love and providence in the tradition of Augustinian and Boethian Neoplatonic thought. Through both the sublimated desire for Beatrice and the divine punishment witnessed in the *Inferno* for the sin of unsublimated lust, the reader is left with little doubt as to the ideological stance the poet has taken; *caritas* has replaced troubadour *cupiditas,* and reading Dante is no ethically "idle" matter.

The destabilization of courtly discourse's interpretability by means of its collision with competing discourses is thus posterior to Dante, indeed first offered by Boccaccio in response to him. But Dante's firm stance as to how his use of courtly discourse is to be interpreted is itself a response to an ethical ambiguity intrinsic to the tradition of courtly discourse from its very origins. A common point of critical argument against the validity of the term "courtly love" has been the wide ethical disparity between its various medieval manifestations. The Neoplatonic philosophy and Christian ideology it serves in Dante contrasts sharply with the cupiditous and carnal desire that is generally accepted as the ends toward which Jean de Meun's narrator in his continuation of *Le Roman de la Rose,* and much of troubadour poetry, are directed. Such a problem underscores the utility of treating courtly love as a discourse, not as a monolithic phase in the "history of ideas." A discourse may embody an ideology, as Foucault would have it; but from one poet to the next, from one text to the next, the same discursive features may be employed to embody utterly antithetical ideologies, from the suggestive sexual imagery of Jean de Meun's narrator to the culmination of Dantean Platonism that appears in the poetry of the seventeenth-century Spanish mystic St. John of the Cross. Therefore, one can say that how to interpret the discourse of courtly love is a question that is as old as courtly love itself: the so-called "courts of love" in medieval Provence and France underscore that courtly discourse had functioned from the beginning as a language for the negotiation of its own interpretation. The tradition of the *tenso* itself reflects the instability of how courtly discourse can be interpreted and understood. Dante's attempts to solve the problem notwithstanding, courtly love's ethical ambiguity and ideological elusiveness persist from their medieval origins through the early modern period, first as an intertextual variance and later because of intratextual polydiscursivity. To fully understand the question of how its discourse functions in the *Comedia,* then, we must historically ground our analysis in courtly love's resistance to fixed signification—a resistance intensified after Dante by the hybridization of literary discourses to further destabilize the ideological parameters of interpretation for the reader or spectator.

CARITAS VS. CUPIDITAS: THE ETHICS OF MEDIEVAL COURTLY LOVE

> With respect to troubadour lyrics, our tendency was to idealize and reduce their meanings into a secular equivalent of *caritas;* we did this by focusing on the sameness of the lyrics, trying to read them all as if, albeit deviant in some ways that we tended to overlook as flaws, all troubadour lyrics were versions of an Ur-troubadour text that set the rules or conventions establishing the sublimation of erotic desire into verbal—poetic, artistic—aspiration for recognition by an unattainable lady. Behind the search for the "origin" of this refining, standardizing idea of "courtly love," which is largely the product of unifying interpretations of troubadour lyrics, lies a reductive, controlling intention.[16]

Laura Kendrick's assessment of traditional troubadour scholarship is made to contrast the thrust of her own argument, which instead privileges the Provençal school's resistance to fixed signification. "The troubadours realized what we scholars—preceded by contemporary artists—have been reemphasizing in the last few decades: that the meaning of a sign is determined by its use in a particular context, and that the most important context is the mind of the interpreter."[17] Her analysis suggests that the *discourse* of courtly love—not the "refining, standardizing idea of 'courtly love' "—thrived on double-entendre and sexual innuendo from its very inception. To be sure, the "standard" and idealistic meaning did have its place among the plurality of possible interpretations of courtly discourse, and some prominent troubadours like Marcabru argued for it exclusively, considering the more bawdy and sexually suggestive poetry of others contemporary to him to be an abuse of *fin amors*.[18]

The conservative and orthodox Christian reading of courtly love that Marcabru prescribes defines itself through the theological notion of *caritas,* love of God through love of another human being. It is this ennobling, Platonic conception of human love that guided much of twentieth-century critical interpretation of courtly love. An alternative interpretation of courtly language that has existed all along is that it is a rhetorical veil used to express sexual desire, *cupiditas,* in a refined and socially permissible manner. It is precisely this thin line between "good" and "bad" love, from the perspective of orthodox

Christian ideology, that Juan Ruiz exploits for comic effect in *El libro de buen amor*, a collection of lyric poems that celebrates sexual desire ostensibly to warn his reader to avoid it. Beyond the lyric tradition, this duality is well represented by Dante's *Divina Commedia* and Jean de Meun's continuation of *Le Roman de la Rose*.

Dante's representation of desire in his *stilnovisti* poetry, the *Vita Nuova*, and the *Divina Commedia* is firmly rooted in *caritas*. Love for Beatrice is a stepping-stone for love of God: she is an intermediary, a means to an end rather than an end unto herself. Desire is sublimated to a purely spiritual plane. If troubadour love sublimates physical desire through abstraction, it still represents a goal of physical and earthly union. Dante's Platonic courtly love, however, manipulates this sublimation in order to reconcile desire with medieval Christian morality. As the Augustinian framework offered in the *De doctrina Christiana* would suggest, it is a question of use versus abuse: is the lady an inspiration for a higher plane of divine love (proper use), or the endpoint of carnal desire (abuse)? In electing the latter alternative, Jean de Meun and many troubadours subvert Christian doctrine. In electing the former, Dante both "rescues" allegory from the profane conclusion and moral trajectory of *Le Roman de la Rose* and in the process establishes a narrative model for later vernacular treatments of courtly love and allegory, such as the late medieval Spanish *novela sentimental* tradition, which links the concrete specificity and subjectivity of personal experience to an allegorical mode of representation in keeping with Augustinian *caritas* (often through a "cautionary" representation and condemnation of *cupiditas*).

What these ethically antithetical narratives share is a discursive framework based upon what Gregory L. Lucente has called a "poetics of absence": "By tracing such fundamental themes as absence/desire and transgression/penitence . . . we can gauge the crucial shift that occurred in Italian Renaissance lyric in terms of the internal force of the poet's desire and will. This shift was accomplished even though many of the thematic concerns of the later lyrics appear to remain the same or to change only nominally. Despite the apparent similarities, their meanings and their effects are notably different."[19] In the case of Dante, then, the "internal force of the poet's will" is focused on describing through a mystical allegory his own personal experience of divine love through Beatrice. The corresponding "force" for Jean de Meun's narrator/protagonist is also driven by desire, but the conclusion to the narrative leaves little doubt that it is a physical desire whose object, the female (specifically virginal) body, is allegorically represented in the Rose.

Lucente explains that the absence of the beloved creates room for the manipulation of courtly discourse toward either end of the *caritas/cupiditas* polarity. The rhetorical posture assumed in the troubadour lyric depends on such absence, whereby the withdrawn lover may contemplate his desire's object from a distance—although above all else that distance allows for a self-absorbed expression of the suffering caused by absence. Jean de Meun allegorizes absence through the Tower of Shame, enclosed by a fortress and defended by allegorical personifications; it is a physical representation of the social barriers separating the speaker from his beloved. Absence for Dante appropriately assumes an earthly or literal level (Beatrice's death, the death of the body) and an allegorical level as well (the absence of God). This allegory of divine absence is first represented at the beginning of the *Inferno* in the pilgrim's having lost his way into the *selva oscura*. Absence of the beloved will later be represented through the allegorization of the courtly *topos* of imprisonment in Diego de San Pedro's *Cárcel de amor*. What Dante's *selva*, de Meun's tower, and San Pedro's prison share in common is their focus on the male subject's isolation and helplessness. The distance or absence and the self-absorption it invites render the identity and nature of the female object of desire ambiguous.

In turn, such ambiguity places a greater burden on the act of interpretation by the reader or listener. Of course, the nature of Western love poetry at least as far back as Ovid is to represent desire as potential, especially as absence: desire must necessarily be unfulfilled to be represented. The absence of desire's object, whether it is achieved through rhetorical or allegorical means, defers the object's identity to the act of interpretation. If we accept the authenticity and validity of the letter to Can Grande,[20] then Dante's intended interpretation corresponds with modern critical assessments—at least in terms of what Beatrice represents to the pilgrim in the *Paradiso*.

Le Roman de la Rose similarly defers the exact identity of the absent object of desire to the act of interpretation. We are told by Guilliame de Lorris's narrator in his portion of the romance that there is a "cele por qui je l'ai empris" (she for whom I write),[21] a literal muse whose literal name goes unmentioned. That absent object is projected allegorically onto the text as the rose. The rose itself is therefore the key to interpreting at which end of the *caritas/cupiditas* spectrum the text and the love it represents is to be located by the reader. When the reader interprets the description offered by Jean de Meun's narrator of the successful fulfillment of his desire in his continuation of de Lorris's text, the ostensible interpretive possibilities range from a union with God to an earthly, sexual union. The narrative depiction, however, treats the attainment of the allegorical rose with such blatant sexual innuendo as to make a Platonic, nonsexual interpretation implausible. The allegorical veil, so to speak, becomes transparent.

> Sovelement et sans moi poindre
> Le bouton pris a eslochier;
> Envis l'eüsse sans hochier.
> Toutes en fis par estevoir
> Les branches croler et movoir,
> Sans ja nul des rainz depecier,
> Car n'i voloie riens blecier;
> Et si m'en couvint il a force
> Entamer un poi de l'escorce;
> Autrement avoir ne savoie
> Ce dont si grant desir avoie.
>   En la parfin, tant vous en di,
> Un poi de grene y espandi,
> Quant j'oi le bouton eslochié.
> Ce fu quant dedens l'oi tochié [. . .]
> Si que tout le boutonnet tender
> En fis eslargir et estendre.[22]

> [Most gently, that I might avoid the thorns,
> I set myself to loosen that sweet bud
> That scarcely without shaking could be plucked.
> I did this all by sheer necessity.
> Trembling and soft vibration shook her limbs;
> But they were quite uninjured, for I strove
> To make no wound, although I could not avoid
> Breaking a trifling fissure in the skin,
> Since otherwise I could have found no way
> To gain the favor I so much desired.
>   This much more I'll tell you: at the end,
> When I dislodged the bud, a little seed
> I spilled just in the center, as I spread
> The petals to admire their loveliness (. . .)
> The consequence from all this play of mine
> Was that the bud expanded and enlarged.][23]

If we accept the climactic union described above as a sexual one, we may infer that the rose represents the female body, desired and possessed as an end unto itself (Augustine's "abuse") rather than as a Platonic mediator of love for God, or as an object through which *caritas* may be expressed. Jean de Meun's narrator establishes the cupiditous nature of his desire both in the citation above and in his extended dialogue with the female allegorical figure of Reason. Their dialogue,[24] dominated by Reason's speeches and illustrative stories, is perhaps the most intense and direct discussion of love in all its forms (both Platonic and carnal) of the entire narrative.

It should be noted that this extended dialogue with Reason[25] is in fact the second appearance of the allegorical figure, an expansion of the fifty-nine line dialogue composed by de Lorris. The shorter exchange focuses on Reason's promotion of a purely spiritual love, and this spirituality in reinforced by her own appearance: "El ne fu vielle ne chenue, / Ne fu trop haute ne trop basse, / Ne fu trop megre ne trop grasse. / Li oel qui en son chief estoient / A deus estoiles resembloient; / [. . .] Pert que fust faite en paradis" (She's not too young or too old, / Too fat or lean. Her eyes like two stars shone. / (. . .) An angel come, perhaps, from Paradise). For de Lorris, Reason visits the Lover on purely didactic terms, "De garder homme de folie, / Par quoi il soit tex qu'il la croie" (To rescue men from foolish acts, / Provided that her counsel they'll believe).[26]

In the more substantial encounter composed by Jean de Meun, which terminates with the Lover's rejection of her counsel, Reason's didactic posture is maintained but expanded. The extended discourse of the second encounter establishes two contrasting kinds of love, one borne of self-interest and the other, *amitié* (friendship), of mutual reciprocity. After a description of the spiritual union of hearts that is the latter, she pronounces an extensive condemnation of the former kind of love, which is carnal and self-centered. The contrast is directly implicated in the plight of the Lover/narrator when Reason offers her own love to him, to replace what was previously offered by the God of Love, Cupid: "Souffre que je sois ta serve, / Et tu li miens loiaus amis. / Le dieu lairas, qui ci t'a mis" (Let me serve you; but be my loyal friend. / Forsake the god who brought you to this pass).[27] Her spiritual alternative is expressed in terms that clearly link it to *caritas.*

> C'est bonne volenté commune
> De gens entr'eus sans demorance
> Selon la lor bon voillance.
> Et soit entr'eus communité
> De tous lor biens en charité,
> Si que par nulle excepcion . . .

> [Two hearts so close in mutual accord
> That no discord can interrupt their love,
> Which seems like the benevolence of God.
> 'Twixt such friends there should be community,
> In loving charity, of all their goods,
> That no exception they may think to make.][28]

But the Lover is so enslaved by *cupiditas* that he rejects Reason's offer. Early on in Jean de Meun's text, then, the Lover is driven by a desire for sexual pleasure to reject the possibility of sublimation to a spiritual plane. Indeed Reason is noted at the conclusion of the narrative as the figure to whom the narrator should *not* offer thanks for assisting him in his conquest. His later admission that the particular female body embodied in the rose is but one of the variety of buds that he has tasted drives the point home: love for Jean de Meun's narrator signifies the conquest of the female body. The most enjoyable aspect of this particular rose is its virginity: "Je le passai touz li premiers" (I was the first of men to tread that road).[29] The reader is left to conjecture that this will not be the last unpaved road upon which the Lover would tread. Through the narrator's self-congratulatory bravado, the allegorical function of the rose is rendered questionable: it represents a female body metaphorically, but not an abstraction of Woman or Virginity itself. In Platonic terms, the rose corresponds to the realm of appearances, a particular manifestation of the "essence" to which medieval allegory normally is pointed.

The final scene of sexual conquest punctuates a downward moral trajectory that was earlier noted in the Lover's rejection of Reason and her *caritas*. *Le Roman de la Rose* as a narrative therefore descends to an amoral (and, to orthodox Christian doctrine, immoral) plane that sharply contrasts the morally didactic function of the medieval allegorical tradition established by Augustine and fostered by the likes of Prudentius (*Psychomachia*), Boethius (*Consolatio*), and Alain de Lille (*Plaint of Nature*). In terms of the classical Horatian precept that assigns both aesthetic pleasure and moral instruction to literature, Jean de Meun appears to privilege pleasure at the expense of instruction (at least in the sense of propagating orthodox Christian ideology). The Lover's rejection of Reason and her *caritas* suggests that from his perspective, the two goals are mutually exclusive.

As the letter to Can Grande suggests, Dante's allegory attempts to balance the two demands of the Horatian precept, to champion a new allegorical mode of representation that combines a literal first person narrative of subjective experience with an allegorical representation of man's desire for the divine: "Nel mezzo del cammin di *nostra* vita / *mi ritrovai* per una selva oscura" (11)[30] [In the middle of the road of *our* life / *I found myself* in a dark forest] (*Inferno* I, 1–2, my emphasis). If the *selva oscura* is taken as an allegorical representation of a moral transgression (as the reading of the three beasts he encounters there as allegorical representations of vice would suggest), we might then say that the pilgrim's experience begins on morally questionable ground, in danger of losing his way to God, and with the poet in danger of representing and narrating his perdition. Such a moral descent would indeed mirror the downward moral trajectory of *Le Roman de la Rose.* Dante's poem begins, then, at a moral crossroads (the "mezzo"), and the pilgrim is without direction until Virgil presents himself. The path of moral ascent is made possible by the three feminine figures of Mary, Lucia, and finally Beatrice, who has sent Virgil as an intermediary.

Although a great deal has been said regarding the scope of Dante's project, we should focus especially on the fact that Beatrice is described from the outset as a representative of divine *caritas:* "amor mi mosse, che mi fa parlare" (love so moved me, it makes me speak).[31] Clearly Beatrice is celebrated as a locus of *caritas,* but just as important is the fact that divine love is identified from the outset as the "mover of all things," particularly of speech. *Caritas* literally makes him speak, which links the virtue with *poesis.* If carnal desire serves for Jean de Meun as the internal force behind his Lover's desire and will, as Lucente argues in a passage cited above, *caritas* descends from heaven to direct Dante's desire toward morally solid ground, in turn enabling him to refocus his allegory away from the cupiditous ends of the *Roman de la Rose.* In contrast to Jean de Meun's moral descent, the *Divina Commedia* follows a moral and ethical trajectory of ascent, literally from Hell to Paradise. Dante the pilgrim ascends from the cupiditous courtly love of chivalric romance represented in the fifth canto of the *Inferno* to Bernard's mystical love lyric in the thirty-third canto of the *Paradiso,* in effect witnessing the entire gamut of possible interpretations that can and have been applied to the discourse of courtly love. It is telling that Beatrice's appearance in the *Purgatorio* is itself only the *mezzo* of the pilgrim's journey: what for de Meun is the endpoint of desire is for Dante an intermediary step toward the ultimate goal of experiencing divine grace, which is to be visualized in part as a divine celestial rose in the *Paradiso.* The rose as divinely choreographed constellation is in effect a reversal of the rose's libidinous allegorical function for de Meun.

The love of God reaches Dante through a series of intermediaries, of which Beatrice is but one. The Virgin Mary is the first mediatrix, followed by St. Lucia, who in turn alerts Beatrice of her friend's moral plight. Because the journey for which Dante is destined must begin in Hell, a point to which the sanctified Beatrice may not descend, she employs the services of yet another mediator in Virgil, a pagan who guides Dante through the lowest regions of the divine cosmography until Beatrice can intervene. Virgil's tutelage and Dante's encounter in Limbo with the other great poets of antiquity (canto 4) are indicative of the importance Dante attributes to his project. It is to reconfigure allegory as an expression of *caritas* and therefore to unite the virtues of classical literature (Virgil and others) with those of vernacular literature (the medieval *roman* and the lyric tradition inspired by the troubadours) in a divine comedy. The *cupiditas* that moves Jean de Meun's narrator to celebrate sexual conquest, just as it motivates many troubadour lyric poems, is to be sublimated through the sweet new style.

The condemnation of medieval romances in the vein of *Le Roman de la Rose* is made explicit in the *Inferno:* Tristan's presence calls attention to chivalric romance, and he is placed alongside the characters from classical antiquity who were also driven by carnal desire. Dido, Paris, and Helen of the pagan epic tradition, condemned by Augustine as morally destructive in his *Confessions,* are joined by the cupidity-driven heroes of post-Augustine medieval romance. Dante may be suggesting how Augustine would have judged the romances, but the reaction of the pilgrim himself does not suggest such categorical disdain: "Poscia ch'io ebbi 'l mio dottore udito / nomar le donne antiche e' cavalieri, / pietá mi giunse, e fui quasi smarrito" (No sooner had I heard my teacher name / the ancient ladies and knights, than pity / seized me, and I was like a man astray).[32]

Dante the pilgrim (and Dante the reader/interpreter) realizes the moral transgression that such literature may inspire. In the fifth canto, Paolo and Francesca suffer eternal damnation for having succumbed to cupiditous desire, and blame is placed squarely on the "Gallehault" of Arthurian romance. Again the pilgrim is seized by *pietade* (pity) and this time faints. If this second wave of pity is to be taken as a catharsis upon witnessing the "moral tragedy" that is the *cupiditas*-driven romance tradition, the *pathos* expressed might indeed be both pity and fear: Dante faints as he recognizes his own affinity for such literature. Evidence of his appreciation for troubadour poetry was cited earlier in the *De vulgare eloquentia,* and the same discourse of courtly love established by the troubadours is represented as the cause for what he witnesses in Hell's second circle: "piú di mille / ombre mostrommi e nominommi a ditto, / ch'amor di nostra vita dipartille"[33] (more than a thousand / shades were shown to me and their names told, / departed from our life because of love). That the pilgrim personally identifies with the sinful readers and courtly lovers of the circle establishes a literal level of subjective experience to the *Commedia;* the letter to Can Grande's admission that this literal narrative is intended to be read allegorically suggests a metaliterary commentary placing the *cupiditas* of courtly love at the above-mentioned moral crossroads, intersecting with the Platonic option of *caritas.* The charitable *cammin* is for the poet the road less traveled in vernacular literature; it is the virtuous path shown to him by Beatrice (at first through the intercession of Virgil), who assumes the dual function of object of desire and source of inspiration.

Such a role suggests that Beatrice's death as described in the *Vita Nuova* becomes for Dante an act of divine intervention. Because the physical body as object of desire is permanently removed from earthly existence, hence rendering physical fulfillment and union unattainable, Dante is left with no alternative other than to sublimate that desire whose object is permanently absent, to transform the *cupiditas* of his youth to *caritas.* The ethical orientation informing the poet's use of the discourse of courtly love changes dramatically. What this change demonstrates is the moral and ideological malleability of the troubadours' discursive framework: despite the about-face, it still serves Dante's purpose equally well.

> The motif of desire for an absent object as a spur to poetic creation came to Dante through the Provençal and the early Italian lyricists. But rather than a lady in a distant castle, or one trapped in a turret by a terrible monster, or one surrounded in court by dangerously mischievous *lauzengiers,* the object of Dante's desire was a woman of the city, his beloved Beatrice [. . .] he made the stuff of his own life into a narrative [. . .] [and] he "read" this text (with the aid of divine revelation) in a specifically Christian sense.[34]

In other words, Dante finds the discourse of courtly love to be an adequate vehicle for the expression of his own chaste desire for a disembodied object. That this desire as it appears in his *stilnovisti* poetry be interpreted as Christian and orthodox is precisely the argument that the *Vita Nuova* aims to establish.

Lucente explains that in the *Vita Nuova,* the love lyric becomes the locus of an epistemological shift that accompanies the moral shift from *cupiditas* to *caritas.* At first unable to understand the meaning of what he has written, "for Dante knowledge comes through both revelation and reflection."[35] The act of writing love poetry becomes another intermediary in Dante's quest for divine knowledge, and the composition of the *Divina Commedia*—the rescuing of allegory from romance *cupiditas*—is allegorically represented in his ascent to heaven. The epic poem therefore achieves, with the help of Virgil and Statius and with the inspiration of Beatrice, a re-union of the aesthetic pleasure of the classical epic and the moral didacticism of early Christian allegory. In the process, he puts forth a correction to Jean de Meun's presentation of the "abuse" of the discourse of courtly love.

DISCOURSES OF LOVE: BOCCACCIO AND CERVANTES

The ethical and ideological shift traced above, in which the "abuse" of the discourse of courtly love as a means of expressing physical desire was shifted to its allegorical "use" in the *Divina Commedia* to represent *caritas,* paved the way for fourteenth- and fifteenth-century Italian and Spanish sentimental fiction, in which Dante's moral and ideological compass remained the dominant explicit guide for narrative representations of desire. Giovanni Boccaccio's so-called sentimental works (the *Filocolo* and the *Filostrato*) and the morally exemplary narratives from late medieval Spain that constitute the tradition of the *novela sentimental* maintain this explicitly Platonic and spiritual orientation. If, as Lucente argues, we can attribute the shift toward Platonic love to the "internal force of the poet's desire and will," Dante's internal force was felt for generations throughout Western Europe. As a dominant mode of representing desire in a way that can both please and instruct, the discourse of courtly love through Dante became what Augustine would call a "high style," a refined literary register whose message brought moral edification.[36]

Boccaccio's *Decameron,* unlike his earlier sentimental fiction, offers a new perspective on courtly love by placing it in contact with other literary discourses. Courtly love is continually referenced in the collection of tales, and Boccaccio's interest in its conventions and discursive practices, and especially his interest in placing those conventions and practices in contact with those of other source traditions, makes the interpretation of his love stories problematic. The *Decameron* is a pioneer text in the development of prose fiction because of its amalgamation of a variety of medieval literary traditions and sources into a new prose narrative form, resulting in a new kind of novelistic space and, indeed, a new mode of literary discourse that resists the traditional and stable boundaries that normally delimit interpretive possibilities. In other words, Boccaccio does not merely perpetuate a standard medieval courtly presentation of human desire, nor is he committed to an explicit and orthodox judgment of the events that transpire; instead he presents a treatment of literary love that is altogether new and innovative.

Boccaccio's innovation is as much ideological as it is formal. The *Decameron* abandons the *terza rima* of Dante's epic for the prose of medieval *fabliaux* and folktales, and with this formal shift he abandons the theocentric worldview around which the *Divina Commedia* is oriented. The plague that gives occasion for the storytelling in the collection, we are told in the prologue, is *perhaps* of divine origin, perhaps not. The Church plays a role only as an earthly institution, implicitly representative of divine authority but explicitly represented by human beings whose virtue varies dramatically; the clergy are capable of all imaginable behavior, from devout piety to shameless exploitations of ecclesiastical authority to fulfill base carnal desire. Unlike Dante's narration of the divine punishment meted out for such abuses of ecclesiastical authority, Boccaccio's *novelle* narrate the acts of abuse themselves and reserve such condemnation for the reader to make in her or his own right. Dante's divine cosmography is supplanted by a thorough taxonomy of human society: priests and clerics, kings and peasants, queens and prostitutes alike populate the tales. Accompanying this broad cast of characters is the wide array of discursive traditions through which they are conventionally represented, as opposed to the controlling and monologic discourse of the *Divina Commedia,* which assigns all souls to their appropriate place, all according to a fixed and theologically justifiable ideological perspective. If religious figures such as Pope Boniface VII suffer eternal perdition in Dante's epic, it is to reinforce the power of divine justice over all of humanity, regardless of one's rank in any earthly institution. By contrast the celestial sphere is not of concern in the world represented by the *Decameron,* for Boccaccio is interested in treating human behavior in all its variety, by means of the diverse literary discourses traditionally used to describe it, each with its own implicit ideological and interpretive parameters.

The fourth day's prologue and the author's conclusion after the tenth day reinforce the idea that no explicit moral or ethical lesson, no didactic end, motivates the *Decameron*'s composition: it is for the idle reader, especially the *donne* to whom Boccaccio dedicates the work. What he offers them is a catalogue of fictional narrative discourses, including chivalric romance, *exemplum,* and fable. Taken out of their original ideological contexts and placed in contact with one another, these source materials lose their traditional interpretive clues; they undermine the "horizon of expectations" with which the intended reader would approach them. The cautionary tale, for example, offers a predictable and explicit intended meaning, and its rhetorical organization is oriented toward the goal of communicating to the reader that didactic message of caution. When such ideological control is relinquished, the source material may be both reexamined and reformulated with a new priority: entertainment. In lieu of an identifiable authorial ideology, what holds the collection of tales together is the privilege granted to aesthetic pleasure.

The first tale of day four is suggestive of the way in which Boccaccio innovates by way of referencing and manipulating the conventions and discursive practices of the now ethically stabilized (thanks to Dante) courtly love romance narrative. In addition to invoking the discourse of post-Dantean courtly love, this and other tales in the *Decameron* also treat physical love, but without the veil of rhetoric used by the troubadours and Jean de Meun. The presence of a shamelessly cupiditous view of love is especially evident in several of Dioneo's bawdy tales and even in the story offered by Pampinea in the second tale of day four (in which Brother Alberto is able to seduce a lady of questionable intelligence by posing as the angel Gabriel). Any investigation into a Boccaccian assessment of courtly love must take into account this other, noncourtly, physical love whose clearest influence is the oral folktale, a source shared by Apuleius's *The Golden Ass.* Merging and combining these love traditions is ethically problematic, but it is equally problematic in that it necessitates a convergence of distinct discursive traditions. For if the *Decameron,* and in particular the first tale of day four, contains a plurality of approaches to love, it must implicitly involve a plurality of approaches to telling love stories as well.

One can easily imagine the ethical and moral issues at stake when the spiritual love codified by Dante is confronted with tales involving (and tacitly condoning) sexual gratification. Equally important is the confrontation between the discursive traditions that yield such divergent versions of amatory fiction. In other words, we may see in the *Decameron* a problematization of the relationship between what kind of love is described and what kind of tale is used to describe it (between philosophies of love and discourses of love). Ultimately this relationship between form and content, or between a literary discourse and the ethical stance it promotes, helps explain the complexity and frequent ambiguity both of the Boccaccian novella and of the *Decameron* as a unified or organic text. The first tale of day four, particularly in terms of the ambiguous ethical stance of its narration, is an example of this amatory polydiscursivity at work in the *Decameron*.

In compliance with Filostrato's mandate, in this novella Fiammetta narrates a tale of two lovers who meet a tragic end. Tancredi's daughter (Ghismunda) and his valet (Guiscardo) enjoy a brief affair with tragic consequences when it is discovered. The young widow Ghismunda lives with her father, the Prince of Salerno, and her filial love and devotion keep her from seeking a second husband. In order to satisfy her physical needs, she arranges a liaison with Guiscardo.

> e per questo tenero amore, avendo ella di molti anni avanzata l'età del dovere avuto marito, non sappiendola da sé partire, non la maritava: poi alla fine a un figliuolo del duca di Capova datala, poco tempo dimorata con lui, rimase vedova e al padre tornossi. (337)[37]

> [since she was aware that her father, because of the love he bore her, was not concerned about giving her away in marriage again, and since she felt it would be immodest of her to request this of him, she decided to see if she could secretly find herself a worthy lover.] (251)[38]

The illicit meeting is repeated until her father discovers them. An impassioned plea to her father made on her lover's behalf ("non come dolente femina o ripresa del suo fallo, ma come non curante e valorossa, con asciutto viso e aperto e da niuna parte turbato così al padre" [342] [without a trace of feminine sorrow or contrition for her misdeed, she faced her father as a brave and unafraid young lady (254)]) fails to calm the prince's rage, and he has the young man killed. Ghismunda is presented with her lover's heart, and in a desperate act of amorous devotion, she commits suicide, commending herself to her departed lover: "O molto amato cuore, ogni mio uficio verso te è fornito, né più altro mi resta a fare se non di venire con la mia anima a fare alla tua compagnia" (347) [Oh, most beloved heart, now that I have fulfilled all my duties to you, nothing more remains for me but to come to you and join my soul to yours (258)]. The devastated Tancredi regrets his rash decision and has the two lovers buried together honorably.

We may say with certainty, then, that we are dealing with a love story —but certainly not of the fashion envisioned by Dante. Fiammetta's tale and the context in which it is told within the *Decameron* represent a moment of collision between different traditions of amatory discourse, a moment suggestive of Boccaccio's awareness of different traditional "philosophies of love" in literature. It also suggests his awareness of the close relationship between a given genre and the corresponding approach to structuring and telling its love story, or between *what* is told and *how* it is told. Fiammetta's tale demonstrates that the collision of disparate traditions of literary love problematizes form and content, or structure and meaning—ultimately depriving the reader of the generic parameters that would guide his or her interpretation. For the purpose of understanding this problem, we must first outline an admittedly basic dichotomy of literary love traditions to guide such a reading.

This dichotomy pits Dante's idealized and Platonic courtly love against the earthy, physical love hereafter referred to as Apuleian love. The latter is a sexually charged and decidedly unidealized version of love inherited from a variety of traditions, including the Byzantine novel and oral folktales. Courtly love has implied since the troubadours a cast of noble and elite characters (and, moreover, a noble and socially elite audience), especially in the cultural milieu of Boccaccio, in the wake of the *stilnovisti* notion of the *cor gentil.* On the other hand, Apuleian love can be characterized by its socially "low" and common characters (and in turn by a more socially diverse audience of listeners and readers). We may also say that the courtly love of medieval romance is expressed through a predictable narrative formula, in turn based on a love ethic or code of behavior. Of the opposite tradition we may say that in lieu of codified and socially guided behavior, an emphasis is placed on overstepping social boundaries that would restrict the realization of love and sexual pleasure. In other words, courtly love is embraced by the social and literary establishment and may often serve as a reaffirmation of a static social order, while the physical *non*courtly tradition subverts and undermines the social establishment (most clearly in its subversion of the social and religious institution of marriage). The process of achieving this subversive love becomes the object of narrative attention, thereby placing a high value on invention and strategy. It is not, after all, the fact that in the second tale of day four Brother Alberto seduces a naive young lady that entertains us, but rather the ingenious and resourceful strategy employed in the process. Supplanting duty with desire in such instances is not a conflict that informs the plot; it is a given that is presupposed.

This same dualistic treatment of literary love may be perceived in Chaucer's *Canterbury Tales,* but of course the two traditions of this amatory dichotomy existed well before its fourteenth-century combination in frame narratives. Courtly discourse had already been refined and developed for at least three centuries, and although assigning a date to the origins of the primarily oral tradition of Apuleian love is more difficult, we have a long tradition of texts of antiquity and especially late antiquity, including that of Apuleius, that employ such "practical" love stories of folkloric origins. The mischievous tradition of physical love, undoubtedly because of its "low" characters and subject matter, seems utterly irreconcilable to the highbrow courtly tradition before Boccaccio. Telling naughty stories that explicitly objectify sex and the body without the kind of allegorical and rhetorical cloaking employed in *Le Roman de la Rose* involves a completely distinct discourse, rhetorical strategy, and audience than composing a *canson,* romance, or *lai* about a noble and courtly lady.

Indeed the ideological conservatism of Dante widens the gap further: the *Dolce stil nuovo* of Dante and Guinizzelli chooses to highlight those aspects of troubadour love least akin to the love of the physical tradition, while it consciously attempts to purge courtly love of the morally and socially destructive elements found in troubadour poetry. As we have seen, any veiled reference made to cupiditous desire in the troubadour lyric is replaced by a reaffirmation of Augustinian *caritas* in Dante's work. The shift is reflected in the position afforded to the female object of desire: Dantean love is directed toward an idealized and utterly nonphysical object in the figure of Beatrice, who eventually assumes the explicit role of celestial intermediary in the *Divina Commedia.* Her literary descendant, Petrarch's Laura, would later be discussed in similarly nonphysical terms.

The fifth canto of the *Inferno* underscores how far removed the discourse of courtly love is from Apuleian love. Paolo and Francesca suffer an eternal punishment in the *Inferno* that we may take as representative of the general condemnation of desire being physically realized: it is morally destructive (they suffer eternal damnation) and socially destructive (they have destroyed the bonds and social institutions of marriage and family). The *cupiditas* of romance that Francesca blames for her perdition is precisely that element of the courtly tradition that Dante and the *stilnovisti* would eliminate. Paolo and Francesca have subverted social codes in the same way that the unsatisfied wives of the Apuleian tradition must subvert them to attain pleasure. Dante's ethos, of course, condemns such subversion, but its folkloric opposite embraces it.

Before Dante, the courtly lyric and romance did offer a tenuous balance between its high idealism and physical desire. One might even suggest that in the early manifestations of courtly love, Platonic idealism serves as a rhetorical veil through which physical desire is negotiated.[39] The presence of the female body is deferred in both Provençal lyric and romance narrative, and the main concern is the process of striving for physical pleasure—one could say that stories of courtly love-as-suffering must necessarily end when physical and spiritual union is achieved by courtly protagonists, as there remains no conflict to narrate. If boy gets girl, it is typically at the end of the story: the "happily ever after" may be referenced but is not the concern of the narrative itself—unless, as was previously observed in Chrétien de Troyes's *Erec et Enide,* fulfillment of desire breeds new conflict: Erec does get the girl midway through the narrative, but their extensive amorous celebration distracts him from his chivalric duties until his life and position are threatened. Chrétien's text establishes explicitly that the rapture of fulfilled desire cannot maintain a dynamic narrative; it can only give rise to further conflict.

These problems inherent in the medieval courtly love narrative are made explicit in the *Decameron,* and a primary means of achieving this effect may be found in Boccaccio's use of the bawdy physical tradition of Apuleian discourse in tandem with the discourse of courtly love. The morally suspect examples from the traditional canon of courtly literature that Dante would replace with the sweet new style (one need only recall the sexual conquest thinly veiled by Jean de Meun's allegory) are reawakened, as it were, by Boccaccio's mixture of the physical with the spiritual or courtly. If we accept the premise that Boccaccio is aware of the ethical issues in conflict in the physical love of Apuleius and among the various versions of courtly love, then we may see in Fiammetta's tale a collision of these traditions that plays with the ethics of literary love. The tragic fires of passion that doom Dido in the *Aeneid;* the Christian moral stance of Dantean *caritas;* the mixture of a guarded *caritas* with an often thinly veiled *cupiditas* in the troubadour lyric; the blatantly implied *cupiditas* of *Le Roman de la Rose;* and finally the socially subversive *cupiditas* of *The Golden Ass*—the tension between these versions of love may take us far in explaining the ambiguity of Ghismunda's story, in which imagery and structural elements of all of these traditions are fused into one ethically noncommital tale.

Such ethical ambiguity points the reader to question what (if any) implied message Fiammetta's tale bears. And yet such questions yield no answers, but only further questions about the self-contradictory story. Are we to read it as a condemnation of the violation of filial love and piety, as Ghismunda has stained her honor and therefore her father's honor as well? Such are the terms of Tancredi's verbal tirade against his daughter. She has acted dishonorably beyond merely having engaged in an extramarital affair: "E or volesse Idio che, poi che a tanta disonestà conducer ti dovevi, avessi preso uomo che alla tua nobiltà decevole fosse stato" (341) [Since you had to bring yourself to dishonor, would to God you had chosen a man who was worthy of your nobility (254)]. But how, then, do we explain his later repentance and the honor paid to Guiscardo by being buried next to her? Does the tale therefore celebrate the heroic love that leads Ghismunda to sacrifice her life to join Guiscardo in death? The extensive plea she makes to her father, by far the longest speech act quoted by the narrator, and the narrative description of their treatment post mortem that concludes the novella both seem to suggest as much. But if this is the case, how might we account for the illicit sexual union not sanctioned by the institution of marriage? Do the two lovers get what they deserve for giving in to their cupiditous desires, as did Paolo and Francesca? If they do, then what of the sympathetic and even heroic narrative treatment of the female protagonist? What the collision of the physical and spiritual traditions of literary love brings with it is a series of contradictions. With multiple kinds of love at work within the same narrative space, the reader cannot favor one without being confronted with the other.

Even more revealing is the fact that Boccaccio exploits the relationship between these different treatments of love and the narrative frameworks through which they are traditionally represented. In short, the narrative structure of a love story traditionally reflects the ethical stance of that love: the Platonic ascent of Dante's love is reflected in the upward trajectory of the *Vita Nuova* and the *Divina Commedia,* while the moral perdition of sexual gratification determines the tragic conclusion of the cautionary tale. When any such narrative structure is presented in isolation, as in the pre-Boccaccian medieval traditions and the Spanish *novela sentimental,* the reader is tacitly aware of the ethical stance being promoted. But when combined in the narrative space of a *Decameron* novella, one cannot be so certain: does one dominate or subordinate another? Is some sort of ethical compromise reached? And if the novella itself fails to answer these questions conclusively, may we find evidence in the frame around it to point us toward a particular ethical interpretation?

We should first consider the narrative structure imposed upon Fiammetta by Filostrato, the king of day four. To reflect his own personal experience as a perpetually spurned lover, he requires of his subjects that they tell love stories with tragic conclusions. Of course such a narrative structure is not the exclusive domain of any particular strain of literary love, as is demonstrated by the wide variety of tales offered during the fourth day. Marie de France's *Yonec* and the fifth canto of Dante's *Commedia*—not to mention its *Lancelot* subtext—equally satisfy Filostrato's structural requirements. Fiammetta may choose to narrate a cautionary tale or a romantic tragedy—or perhaps both, or perhaps neither.

Although not a narrative tradition per se, we should also consider how the troubadour lyric, the foundation of the discourse of courtly love, might influence narrative structure. The standard lyric treatment codified by the troubadours and perpetuated by Petrarch is that the poet is in a constant state of torment and suffering caused by unfulfilled desire. This is, again, the posture that Filostrato assumes when dictating the narrative structure of the day four novelle. And as if to remind us that the courtly lyric is germane to the tragic structure of the day's stories, at day's end the newly crowned queen Fiammetta orders Filostrato to sing a song of his choosing, "e per ciò che io son certa che tali sono le tue canzoni chenti sono le tue novelle" (415) [since I am certain that your songs will resemble your stories (310)]. His conventional song, a first-person lament of the suffering caused by unrequited love and a call for death to put an end to his suffering, exudes courtly discourse's self-absorption as clearly as any troubadour lyric. Fiammetta notes explicitly that song and story bear a close resemblance; in other words, she states that the structure of a narrative will be a reflection of the philosophy of love implicit in that narrative. Fiammetta recognizes that Filostrato's troubadour-like *ethos* has dictated his structural mandate.

Must we therefore take the fourth day's conclusion as a point of reference to retroactively interpret Fiammetta's story as a heroic but tragic romance with an exclusively courtly ethical posture? I would argue that such an interpretation is overly simplistic, in that it does not account for those conventions of physical love present in the tale. The premise of the story, that a widow must seek a socially subversive means of conspiring to satisfy sexual desire, is clearly of the Apuleian rather than the courtly tradition. The emphasis placed on wit, invention, and strategy as Ghismunda arranges her rendezvous also bespeaks the Apuleian nature of the affair. The narrator takes great pains to emphasize that Guiscardo "non era poco avveduto" (338) [was not slow of wit (251)], which allows him to perceive Ghismunda's secret attraction to him. But it is Ghismunda's invention that brings their mutual desire to fruition: she discovers a secret stairway leading to her chamber and conceals a note to Guiscardo in a hollow reed, passed to him with a cryptic remark, that explains where he might find its entrance. Their subversive love affair owes its success (and its eventual failure) to female agency—very much along the lines of Spanish popular comedy in the seventeenth century. In fact, of the three main characters, it is Guiscardo who is directly quoted the least: he speaks only one line, that "Amor può troppo più che né io possiamo" (341) [Love is more powerful than either you or I (253)], when he is captured by Tancredi. The fact that Ghismunda is the active instigator of the affair, while Guiscardo proves to be little more than a passive participant, is a deviation from the physical tradition which should be kept in mind.

But even if we put aside the noncourtly Apuleian tradition, the tensions implicit in courtly love itself are far from resolved. I have thus far considered Ghismunda as the primary locus of this ethical conflict, as her extensive *apologia* and heroically described suicide would suggest. But who is the story really about? Tancredi is the first personage named and described by Fiammetta in the tale's opening lines, which would suggest that his actions would be of primary interest.

> Tancredi, prencipe di Salerno, fu signore assai umanoe di benigno ingegno, se egli nell'amoroso sangue nella sua vecchiezza non s'avesse le mani brutate; il quale in tutto lo spazio della sua vita non ebbe che una figliuola, e più felice sarebbe stato se quella avuta non avesse. (337)

> [Tancredi, Prince of Salerno, was a most humane lord with a kindly spirit, except that in his old age he stained his hands with lovers' blood. In all his life he had but one daughter, and he would have been more fortunate if he had not had her.] (250)

This would in turn suggest that we are to read the novella as a cautionary tale about a father whose sense of personal and familial honor momentarily eclipses filial love. Indeed Ghismunda's name is not even mentioned until *after* the father has entered the scene in which he will discover the affair—halfway through the story—and then it is only mentioned parenthetically: "Il quale un giorno dietro mangiare là giù venutone, essendo la donna, la quale Ghismunda aveva nome, in un suo giardino . . . in quella senza essere stato da alcuno veduto o sentito entratosene" (340) [One day after eating, while the lady (whose name was Ghismunda) was in her garden . . . he went there without being heard or observed by anyone and entered her bedroom (252)].

But the fact that Ghismunda is only named halfway through the narrative seems to be at odds with the shift in narrative focus from that point forward. After her heroic *apologia,* in which she evokes the "nobility of heart" *topos* to defend her actions and her lover, and then her dramatic Celestinesque suicide, the original narrative focus on Tancredi seems disjointed and out of place. The novella appears to have experienced a metamorphosis from male-centered *exemplum* to female-centered heroic-romantic tragedy.

Just as Ghismunda's agency and resourcefulness (and Guiscardo's silence and passivity) mark an inversion of the standard gender roles of the Apuleian tradition, her absorption of narrative attention midway through the story bespeaks a Boccaccian alteration of romance and of courtly love itself. Notwithstanding twentieth-century recovery of those few and far-between medieval romances authored by women, the romance tradition is by and large a male tradition based on a love ethic from a male poetic tradition. By employing female narrators, the *Decameron* reexamines romance from a position that is perhaps the least traditional in its sympathy toward a feminine point of view: not only do feminine voices such as that of Fiammetta narrate most of the *novelle,* but the introduction to day four (directly preceding Fiammetta's tale) further problematizes the question of a female presence in the male romance tradition from the outset by dedicating the entire collection (ostensibly) to *donne.* Fiammetta's story may begin with a conventional treatment of a male protagonist, but given these circumstances of the frame within which the tale appears, Ghismunda's eventual assumption of narrative focus bespeaks a larger issue of gender being negotiated by Boccaccio throughout the entire collection.

It is worth noting that such a negotiation in prose narrative comes in the aftermath of the *stilnovisti*'s sharpened focus on the *donna,* an often noted departure from the Provençal lyric tradition. Beatrice's explicit identification with divine inspiration and providence is a corrective to the nameless troubadour *domna;* both are objects of desire, but Dante makes clear the sublimated and virtuous nature of his love. It is not likely a coincidence that Dante describes Paolo and Francesca's ordeal through *Francesca*'s words, while Paolo is a silent and passive presence in the *Inferno.* The ethical and ideological impact of Dante's and Boccaccio's use of female voices, however, could not be more different: for the former, the locus of cupiditous male desire gives voice to the lamentable moral quandary she inspires in her male companion. For Boccaccio, however, the female voices of Ghismunda and of his female narrators are used to undermine the ideological parameters of his literary sources.

Other examples of *novelle* in the *Decameron* suggest the consequences of contact between physical and spiritual love, and in fact the same Fiammetta who tells the story of Ghismunda and Guiscardo offers on the following day another such moment of discursive collision. Her tale, the ninth of the fifth day, offers further evidence of this dialogic process: Federigo's story is a mixture of courtly and folk characteristics. As day five's queen, Fiammetta has selected the day's theme (love stories with happy resolutions after a period of misfortune) to be one naturally inclined toward the basic paradigmatic structure of romance. Apart from Boccaccio's choice to employ a female voice as narrator of this transformed male tradition, Fiammetta makes it clear as she begins her narrative that her tale is especially directed toward the female portion of her audience (mirroring Boccaccio's own prologue at the beginning of the *Decameron*), in a push for female agency in matters of love.

> A me omai appartiene di ragionare; e io, carissime donne, da una novella simile in parte alla precedente il faro volentieri, non acciò solamente che conosciate quanto la vostra vaghezza possa ne' cuor gentili, ma perché apprendiate d'essere voi medesime, dove si conviene, donatrici de' vostri guideroni senza lasciarne sempre esser la fortuna guidatrice, la qual non discretamente ma, come s'aviene, smoderatamente il più delle volte dona. (488)

> [It is now my turn to tell a story and, dearest ladies, I shall do so most willingly with a tale similar in some respects to the preceding one, its purpose being not only to show you how much power your beauty has over the gentle heart, but also so that you yourselves may learn, whenever it is fitting, to be the donors of your favors instead of always leaving this act to the whim of Fortune, who, as it happens, on most occasions bestows such favors with more abundance than discretion.] (364)

Here Boccaccio offers even more shifts in his presentation to further destabilize romance, pulling its content out of its social context. In basic terms, the protagonist is of a low social status, as are the protagonists of virtually all preceding tales of the sexualized Apuleian mold. But rather than focus on the strategic use of wit to achieve a fulfillment of sexual desire, Federigo's behavior is of a decidedly *noble* nature: his is a selfless and idealized love. We are therefore faced with the central question of the "nobility of the heart" *topos:* to what extent do lineage and social station determine virtuous conduct? To what extent are traditional assumptions of decorum valid? This is normally considered as a social question, but we may consider it in discursive terms as well: Federigo belongs to a social class traditionally identified with a specific literary tradition (one that privileges physical love), yet his action, and the narration of that action, seem more appropriate to the noble stock of courtly characters that act within the tradition of courtly romance. The decorum expected of his station, in other words, does not match his behavior.

This discrepancy is highlighted in the tale of Federigo: the plot is in fact based on the difference in social status between the two lovers. Courtly love is in this sense brought into contact with economic reality: to be a traditional courtly lover, Federigo must squander his fortune on the elaborate gestures necessary to compete with his rivals for Madonna Giovanna's favor. As a result he is driven to poverty, one could say, by courtly love; his behavior and motives are informed by courtly discourse, which in effect pushes him to live (and to court) beyond his means. The decisive act that finally wins her favor is the relinquishing of his falcon, his last and most prized worldly possession. The narrative structure and the virtue extolled in the lover's behavior follow the well-known patterns of medieval courtly romance —constant and chaste devotion from afar, virtuous conduct ultimately rewarded—and yet it is the story of a man from a social and economic position that would traditionally be the realm of non-courtly literature and its distinct view of love.

Two modes of representing love, and therefore two types of love stories, are thus fused in a way that foreshadows later novelistic developments of the early modern period, including the work of Cervantes and the picaresque novel. The moral, ethical, and discursive ambivalence of Ghismunda's story are to be revisited by later traditions. In the case of the sixteenth century *Lazarillo de Tormes*, the founding work of the picaresque tradition, the combination of preexisting forms of literary discourse does not include courtly love; desire for the feminine, whether Platonic or physical, is not explicitly treated in Lázaro's narrative, although his dubious conjugal arrangement at the end of the narrative does offer veiled references to the folkloric and popular associations with cuckoldry. This original instance of picaresque subjectivity, in part because of its narrative focus on preadolescence, focuses on hunger for food rather than for sexual gratification. But with its ironic and satirical manipulation of folkloric, ecclesiastical, hagiographic, and juridical modes of discourse, not to mention the discourse of honor, the *pícaro*'s first-person life story bears a strong resemblance to the polydiscursivity of the *Decameron*. Boccaccio may have offered us a preview of these issues, but clearly his is not the last word.[40]

A still stronger debt of influence to Boccaccio can be argued for Miguel de Cervantes. Like the *Decameron, Don Quijote* makes use of and responds to the literary discourses that preceded it, in all their variety. Included in Cervantes's assessment and fusion of source materials is the critical assessment of those sources made by Renaissance Humanist scholars contemporary to him.[41] One could therefore say that, if the *Decameron* anthologizes preexisting literary discourses, the *Quijote* is a critical anthology complete with annotations and footnotes. A wide variety of literary forms are brought into contact with one another, each through its own distinctive mode of discourse; the manipulation and combination of these discursive models undermines the ethical and ideological orientation implicit in each one, contaminating them, as it were, through mutual exposure. Among these forms is the discourse of courtly love, and like the *Decameron*, Cervantes's text ultimately manipulates it in collision with other source material in a way that problematizes its interpretation. In general terms, it can be said that the *Quijote* amplifies the *Decameron*'s lack of authorial claims to guide interpretation along predetermined ideological lines; both texts share a refusal on the author's part to explicitly prescribe how his work is to be read.

If we are to believe the narrator's friend and interlocutor in the prologue to the 1605 first part of the *Quijote,* the author's goal is to "deshacer la autoridad y cabida que en el mundo y en el vulgo tienen los libros de caballerías" (9)[42] [shatter the authority of all those tales of chivalry, and their influence on people (6)].[43] Don Quijote would therefore be a character originally employed as a negative example, as a cautionary figure meant to set the reader straight. If we were to believe this, his future association as an idealistic and heroic figure in Spanish popular culture, and indeed in Western popular culture in general,[44] would seem to fly in the face of logic. But the reader learns not to trust the words of this narrator's friend, nor the words of the principal narrator himself, nor those of any other voice involved in the perspectival slew of narrative levels for which the novel is considered so revolutionary. The most prominent of these narrators, translators, and historians, Cide Hamete Benengeli, is of course the least reliable of all, especially since (as Cervantes's narrator warns us) he is a Moor and therefore by nature a liar.[45]

But even if we were to accept him as a reliable transmitter of truth, the fixed signification of language is further destabilized by Don Quijote himself, who sees things as filtered through his particular, romance-tinted perspective. Such perspectivism has fascinated literary critics especially since the rise of poststructuralism: what is for Sancho a windmill is for Don Quijote a giant; a barber's shaving basin is the knight's golden helmet of Mambrino; and of course Don Quijote's noble lady Dulcinea is known to Sancho as a wheat-thrashing peasant girl. Critics have pointed out that this relativism extends into issues of the novel's ethical stance, employing such descriptors as "moral perspectivism" and "fideistic skepticism." Cervantes's combination of literary genres and their implicit worldviews leaves the reader without the guiding voice and ideological orientation that traditional genres supply; in the absence of a controlling authorial *ethos* with which the reader may identify, no single interpretation is privileged.[46] In short, *Don Quijote* is the worst nightmare of New Criticism, the mid-twentieth-century critical approach that privileged a "correct reading" of canonical texts. It is no wonder that today, in an age in which the traditional master narratives of history and culture are regularly challenged and subverted, critical interest has only intensified regarding *Don Quijote,* a novel that denies the reader a stable and fixed perspective, indeed a novel bent on defeating the reader's desire for such a master narrative.

The *Quijote*'s treatment of amatory fiction reflects the process of problematizing interpretation through discursive collision. The most obvious manipulation of courtly love in the novel is the parody of its elevated and idealized construct of the feminine object of desire through the figure of Dulcinea.[47] Her existence is perfunctory, the creation of a madman to fulfill a requirement of the office to which he aspires, what Margaret Doody would call an "eros of eros."[48] Given that she is included in the shopping list of accoutrements for which knights-errant are known (noble steed, armor, illustrious name, lady to whom victories should be dedicated), Don Quijote dedicates himself to a lady so disembodied and absent as to not really exist—a point that is openly conceded by Don Quijote while doing penance in the Sierra Morena in imitation of Amadís of Gaul.[49] As the ethical center of his chivalric quest, this version of the courtly lady is, *in absentia,* the key to his earliest ambitions and to his ultimate disillusion and demise. She is also as absent and voiceless as the troubadour *domna,* Beatrice, or Laura.

An important development of Cervantes's manipulation of the male discourse of courtly love places it in dialogue with the voices of women who do physically exist, and who therefore can speak, in the novel. An example is his taking to task of the courtly love conventions of pastoral romance in the first part of the novel. In chapter 11 Don Quijote and Sancho encounter a community of shepherds, among them would-be shepherds donning the garb of pastoral characters but who are in fact learned aristocrats inspired by the likes of Jorge de Montemayor's *Diana* (and Cervantes's own *Galatea*)—a metaliterary detail that underscores the fictive and artificial nature of the genre. The knight and his squire witness the ceremonial burial of Grisóstomo, a gentleman posing as shepherd who dies of unrequited love, making literal the "death" caused by the courtly *belle dame sans merci*. Ambrosio and his fellow pseudo-shepherds assign the blame for Grisóstomo's suicide to Marcela, the rich and beautiful orphan who has become a shepherdess in order to escape the pressure put on her to choose a spouse. At the memorial, which includes the oral recitation of a poem written by the deceased in expression of his passion, the reader witnesses an extended parody of pastoral motifs and conventions.

The discourse of courtly love is in this case employed to indict the feminine object of desire for her "cruelty." Both the eulogy offered by Ambrosio and Grisóstomo's final poem, pulled from a pile of papers destined to be burned with his corpse, function from within the epistemological parameters of male courtly love: the object's existence is understood as a function of her effect on the male subject. True to the troubadour paradigm, the poem itself focuses especially on the plight of the male subject and the suffering caused by Marcela's disdain, addressing the female object only to announce to her that she has driven him to end his life. Grisóstomo's lyric depiction of her "rigor tan sin segundo" (peerless harshness) is echoed by Ambrosio's comments during the ceremony: her failure to return Grisóstomo's love earns her the successive epithets "enemiga mortal del linaje humano" (mortal enemy of the human race), "fiera" (wild fiend), and "mármol" (block of marble) (91–92). When Marcela appears above the burial site, he addresses her in similar terms: "¿Vienes a ver, por ventura, ¡oh fiero basilisco destas montañas!, si con tu presencia vierten sangre las heridas deste miserable a quien tu crueldad quitó la vida?" (97–98) [Perhaps you've come, o savage stone monument of these mountains, to see if with your presence blood flows from the wounds of this miserable victim, who by your cruelty lost his life?" (70)].

The discourse of courtly love is deliberately voiced from a male perspective, that is to say from a patriarchal ideological stance, in anticipation of Marcela's appearance, which will signal a dramatic discursive shift in the episode. The construction of Marcela's identity from this point of view had already begun the night before the funeral, when Don Quijote first learns of Grisóstomo and her from the goatherd Pedro. His concise and Boccaccian narrative of her life story, despite Don Quijote's frequent interruptions to either correct a misspoken word or compliment Pedro on his pleasureable delivery of the tale,[50] participates in the male representation of her (she is first named as "aquella endiablada moza de Marcela" [that demonic young girl named Marcela]). Pedro's narrative underscores three points worth noting: (1) the decision by her uncle to defer all decisions regarding her marriage to Marcela herself, privileging a willful union between lovers over parentally arranged marriage; (2) Marcela's abuse of that freedom by becoming a shepherdess and shunning her many suitors; and (3) the emphatic assertion that she always preserved her modesty and chastity (i.e., she observed all due decorum), a point reemphasized by Ambrosio in explanation of the jealousy expressed in his dead friend's lyric.

Rhetorically speaking, Cervantes has loaded the dice in favor of Marcela, both in the excessive reproaches of the *pastores* (her "disdain" has brought them to disdain her) and in the logical inconsistency of their construction of her, for it makes her both virgin and whore, both a literal *femme fatale* and a paragon of virtue and chastity. In other words the discourse of courtly love has been manipulated in such a way as to set up the arrival of a feminine counterdiscourse to be employed by Marcela. The voiceless object of courtly desire, whose absence had allowed for the male construction of her, arrives at the funeral scene to respond to such accusations of cruelty in terms that directly call into question the discourse of courtly love, especially in terms of the objectified and ideologically predetermined role it assigns her. In contrast to the archetypal literary treatment that male courtly discourse has afforded her, Marcela claims to speak "con el natural entendimiento que Dios me ha dado" [with the natural understanding God granted me] (98), a posture resembling the art-of-artlessness of Castiglione's *sprezzatura* (and not unlike what Bruckner has called the *trobairitz*'s preference for "the more straight-forward speech of conversation").[51] This plain speaking, in fact logically ordered and persuasively argued, is a juridical assessment and refutation made point by point of the claims against her that reflects a thorough knowledge of the art of rhetoric. She claims for her speech the power to deconstruct and shatter the image of her created by the discourse of courtly love, an image which is inspired by her physical beauty: "A los que he enamorado con la vista he desengañado con las palabras" [Anyone who has been enchanted by the sight of me has been stripped of all illusions by my words] (99).

The discursive exchange between the shepherds and Marcela resembles that offered in the *Decameron* when Ghismunda pleads with Tancredi to spare her life. In both instances, the feminine voice creates a discursive rupture in the narrative, thereby undermining the objectified and ideologically guided treatment of her character that had previously been established by other discursive means. A similar exchange occurs later in the first part of the *Quijote:* Cardenio's autobiographical story paints Luscinda as a fickle girl who gave in to paternal pressure to marry a wealthier suitor, his disloyal and scheming friend Fernando. We meet Cardenio and hear his version of the story as he wanders aimlessly in the wilderness with only temporary flashes of sanity. As Marcela induces death, Luscinda induces insanity (Cardenio admits that only the Christian prohibition against suicide prevents him from imitating Grisóstomo)—at least as the story is told from the male perspective. Later, when the veiled Luscinda arrives at the same inn where Cardenio, Don Quijote, and their companions have been boarded (coincidentally), she tells her own version of the events in question, in which the reader learns of the same events from a dramatically different perspective (and through a discourse diametrically opposed to Cardenio's portrayal of her—a fictional female voice that lays bare the misrepresentation she has suffered under his discourse). Instead of focusing on her alleged betrayal and the destructive effects of the desire she inspires, Luscinda emphasizes her own suffering and forced submission, not to mention that which Cardenio did not witness: her steadfast refusal to accept or consummate the forced nuptials. Cardenio's despair and disdain melt away with Luscinda's words, as does Fernando's resolve to possess her against her will, and the lovers are reunited. In the case of Boccaccio's Ghismunda, the plea of the discursively misrepresented woman fails to avert her tragic fate, but in the cases of Cervantes's Marcela and Luscinda, both women achieve their objectives: liberation from the constraints imposed upon them by male discourse. This fictional liberation of male-authored female voices effectively takes the tradition of courtly discourse to task.

Connecting this use of feminine voices within the *Decameron* and the *Quijote* to the larger *tenso* between male and female writers of the courtly love tradition, however, is a tenuous critical enterprise. We are still talking about the replacement of one male-authored representation of women for another, albeit for a less overtly misogynistic one. If Cervantes's Marcela and Luscinda and Boccaccio's Ghismunda share a rhetorical posture with the *trobairitz* and Marie de France, this fact only underscores the patriarchal origins of such a counter-discourse. The male authors use one mode of discourse (that of classical juridical rhetoric) to subvert another (that of courtly love), voicing the former from the fictional constructions of their female characters because such a maneuver proves most effective for their critique of courtly discourse. Meanwhile the women writers demonstrate that, despite their resistance to the objectification, silence, and enclosure of their gender in the male master narrative of courtly love, they are still discursively contained by the phallogocentric patriarchy—even if only at its margins. Each does serve to substantiate the critique of the other, but the male-authored and female-authored feminine voices are created for distinctive purposes and with distinctive results. For Boccaccio and Cervantes, gendered voices are the means through which courtly love's "discourse of power" and literary authority is subjected to dialogic reappraisal.

The ultimate effects of such dialogism reflect the deeper affinity between the *Quijote* and the *Decameron* noted above: by destabilizing the previously fixed ideological meaning of these discursive systems through their mutual contact, the reader is denied the guidelines for a prescribed interpretation that literary discourse traditionally supplies. Replacing the implied authorial message is the privilege granted to the aesthetic pleasure of the reading experience.[52] The prologue to the first part of the *Quijote* tells the *desocupado lector* [idle reader] as much:

> Acontece tener un padre un hijo feo y sin gracia alguna, y el amor que le tiene le pone una venda en los ojos para que no vea sus faltas, antes las juzga por discreciones y lindezas y las cuenta a sus amigos por agudezas y donaires. Pero yo, que, aunque parezco padre, soy padrastro de don Quijote, no quiero irme con la corriente del uso, ni suplicarte casi con lágrimas en los ojos, como otros hacen, lector carísimo, que perdones o disimules las faltas que en este mi hijo vieres, y ni eres su pariente ni su amigo, y tienes tu alma en tu cuerpo y tu libre albedrío como el más pintado, y estás en tu casa, donde eres señor della . . . Todo lo cual te esenta y hace libre de todo respecto y obligación, y así, puedes decir de la historia todo aquello que te pareciere, sin temor de que te calunien por el mal ni te premien por el bien que dijeres della. (4–5)

> [It sometimes happens that a father has a child that is ugly and without grace, but the love he feels for him veils his eyes so that he can't see his

faults, but instead judges them to be wit and charm, describing them to his friends as clever and graceful. But I, although I seem to be his father, am only Don Quijote's step-father, and I don't want to follow the tendency of current usage, nor will I beg you practically with tears in my eyes, as others do, dearest reader, that you forgive or look beyond the faults you see in my creation; you are not his relative nor are you his friend, and your soul rests in your own body and you have as much free will as anyone, and you're in your own house, where you are in charge . . . All of which exempts you and leaves you free from all duty and obligation, so you can say anything you like about this history, without fear of being held accountable for your criticism nor of being rewarded for the good things you may say about it.] (3)

The passage is indicative of how Boccaccio's repression of authorial claims to control interpretation, and his concurrent promotion of the aesthetic pleasure or entertainment afforded to the reader establish a polydiscursive process that would later thrive in the culture of early modern Spain. As we shall see, further evidence of the phenomenon is to be found in the *Comedia,* the dominant form of popular entertainment that thrived at the time the *Quijote* was written.

DECORUM IN THE *COMEDIA:*
EL CABALLERO DE OLMEDO AND THE *ARTE NUEVO*

As has been cited earlier, Lope's *Arte nuevo* states unequivocally that the primary goal of his theater is to entertain the paying public: "escribo por el arte que inventaron / los que el vulgar aplauso pretendieron; / porque, como las paga el vulgo, es justo / hablarle en necio para darle gusto" (I write according to the art that was invented by those who sought the applause of the people; because, since they pay for it, it is fair and just to speak to them simply, to give them pleasure). Such an agenda privileges the act of interpretation, or the construction of meaning by the audience, whereby it receives pleasure. Just as the prologue to the *Quijote* also professes, positive reception by the audience is more important than the successful transmission of an explicit ideological message. The *Arte nuevo* offers a prescription for how to write comedy in which classical precepts are selectively included or disregarded according to their utility for the author's goal of entertainment.

Hence decorum, which implies for Lope a diverse range of voices that allow for discursive manipulation, is a classical precept embraced by Golden Age dramatists, while the Aristotelian generic separation of tragedy and comedy is discarded: "Lo trágico y lo cómico mezclado / . . . harán grave una parte, otra ridícula; / que aquesta variedad deleita mucho" (174–78) [Tragedy and comedy are mixed . . . they will make one part serious, the other ridiculous; for such variety is very pleasing]. While the observance of decorum would guarantee polydiscursive characterization, the mixture of tragic and comic elements would allow for a broader range of possible character types from which Lope and his new art could draw.

If a discourse implies an ideology, then the *Comedia*'s collision of discourses carries an ideologically destabilizing effect that is only amplified when the spectrum of possible discourses, each bearing its own implicit ideological orientation, ranges from highbrow tragedy to lowbrow comedy. This instability stems in part from the influential Aristotelian association of tragedy with "high" matters and appropriately elevated characters, and of comedy with "low" matters and characters.[53] By combining character types from both modes in the *Comedia,* especially in the dominant forms of comedy and tragicomedy, Lope and his fellow dramatists deny the socially diverse audience of the *corrales* the ideological guidelines for interpretation normally implied in traditional (classical, medieval, and Renaissance) presentations of tragedy and comedy. The interpretation of a play's implied message becomes less a question of what the dramatist intended and more dependent on the social position and ideological orientation of the individual spectator.[54] Questions of to whom the audience should assign the roles of exemplary hero or cautionary scapegoat, and therefore notions such as a play's execution of poetic justice, are often open-ended. Under such circumstances, tensions between the popular theater and institutionalized Counter Reformation Catholicism are quite understandable, as is the disagreement between critics (both in Golden Age Spain and among *Comedia* scholars today) regarding the ideological content of the *Comedia.*[55]

El caballero de Olmedo exemplifies this process of discursive and hence ideological destabilization in that it draws upon the discourses of high tragedy and low comedy so as to elude an overt ideological message.[56] The play continually shifts from moments of "high" and elevated discourse, including the discourses of courtly love and honor, to comic scenes dominated by "low" servants and go-betweens, to moments when the two discursive levels interact with one another. Lope offers a spectacle that plays with his contemporary audience's generic frames of reference: the popular folkloric legend and *coplas* that inspired its composition[57] imply impending doom and tragedy, but the comic discourse of Tello and Fabia undercuts the tension in moments of festive subversion. The drama thus appeals to the distinctive aesthetic sensibilities of tragedy and comedy at different moments in the course of action, as it oscillates between the anticipation of tragic catharsis and a release of tension through laughter or comic relief.

The presence of low and high registers, considered thus far in terms of generic difference, is most immediately recognizable in terms of the play's characters and the social classes they represent. The *galán* and *dama* of the play's love story, Alonso and Inés, pertain to the nobility; as decorum dictates, the language of each is appropriately elevated. The discourse of courtly love, to Lope's audience a highbrow register of literary (written) origin associated with the Petrarchan lyric tradition, emanates through these characters. By contrast, low or comic discourse primarily emanates from characters of a lower social station—the servants Tello and Ana, and the *alcahueta* (go-between) Fabia. If Lope owes the immediate inspiration behind Fabia to the title character of Rojas's *Celestina*,[58] the resemblance of both characters to the pander character type of Roman comedy is no less apparent, just as the *gracioso* (here represented by Tello) is the literary descendent of the slave of Roman comedy. The traditional association of such characters with classical farce is reinforced by the discursive disparity between them and *El caballero de Olmedo*'s upper-class personages.

At the beginning of the second act in *El caballero de Olmedo*, Alonso has come with his lackey Tello for a discreet meeting with his beloved Inés. As they approach, Alonso explains to Tello the nature of his feelings for her.

> ALONSO.   Inés me quiere; yo adoro
>   a Inés, yo vivo en Inés.
>   Todo lo que Inés no es
>   desprecio, aborrezco, ignoro.
>   Inés es mi bien; yo soy
>   esclavo de Inés; no puedo
>   vivir sin Inés. De Olmedo
>   a Medina vengo y voy,
>   porque Inés mi dueño es
>   para vivir o morir.
>
> (lines 987–96)[59]

> [ALONSO.   Inés loves me; I adore
>   Inés, I live in Inés.
>   All that is not Inés
>   I disparage, I hate, I ignore.

> Inés is my well-being; I am
> Inés's slave; I cannot
> live without Inés. From Olmedo
> to Medina I come and go,
> because Inés is my master
> in life or death.]

This invocation of courtly love (complete with the motifs of slavery, suffering, and death) differs from the self-absorbed model we have analyzed thus far in that the beloved is anything but marginalized: Inés's name is given eight times in ten lines. Alonso invokes the discourse of courtly love not as a means for material gain (as does Laurencio in *La dama boba*), nor as a tepid response to a woman's advances (as is the case with Manuel in *La dama duende*). Courtly love is therefore not parodied in this case, but infused with the earnest idealism of early modern Neoplatonism.

Alonso's reverie is interrupted by their arrival at Inés's door; Tello knocks and is answered by Inés's servant Ana.

> ANA.   ¿Quién es?
> TELLO.   ¿Tan presto? Yo soy.
>   ¿Está en casa Melibea?
>   Que viene Calisto aquí.
> ANA.   Aguarda un poco, Sempronio.
>
> (1001–04)

> [ANA.   Who is it?
> TELLO.   So soon? It's me.
>   Is Melibea home?
>   Calisto is here.
> ANA.   Wait a moment, Sempronio.]

With Alonso's lofty and refined (and passionately serious) speech fresh in mind, the audience witnesses an immediate and drastic shift in tone as the servants begin their comic exchange: Tello associates his master with the lovesick Calisto of the *Celestina,* a reference immediately acknowledged by Ana. The reference is both intertextual and metatheatrical in that it invites the spectator/reader to compare the play to Rojas's fifteenth-century tragicomedy—a comparison that calls attention to the conventional nature of the situation in which the characters find themselves, and to the characters' awareness of the roles in which the situation places them. The intertextual relationship between the *Celestina* and *El caballero de Olmedo* can be extended well beyond the Alonso-Tello/Calisto-Sempronio relationship, especially to the role of Fabia, the gypsy go-between whose speech and worldview are clearly drawn from Rojas's title character. Lope's audience would therefore have in mind the tragic conclusion of the *Celestina* as they witness his play: Calisto's interminable pining for Melibea, itself a parody of courtly love, ends when his desire is granted illicit physical fulfillment. He falls to his death shortly thereafter and Melibea, now deprived of honor, commits suicide. Rojas's tragicomic mixture of high and low registers ultimately concludes as a cautionary tale of the tragic consequences that follow the realization of sexual desire outside of wedlock.

Attention is explicitly drawn to *El caballero de Olmedo*'s discursive tensions in the play's opening scene: Alonso appears alone onstage and introduces his plight through the discourse of courtly love. In a direct address to *Amor*, he explains that the desire he feels after seeing Inés for the first time "me encendió / con fuegos tan excesivos" (33–34) [consumed me with such excessive fires]. Immediately following the monologue, Tello appears with Fabia, whom he has brought at his master's request. After diagnosing Alonso's ailment and agreeing to help bring about its cure, Fabia enlists the wary Tello to help her (he fears her reputation for witchcraft and sorcery) by tempting him with "cierta morena / de extremado talle y cara" (lines 211–12) [a certain brunette with extraordinary measurements and face]. Tello is persuaded and the scene ends. The representations of desire offered by Alonso and Fabia/Tello could not be more at odds. Alonso's emotional appeal to Fabia emphasizes that he intends to observe all due decorum in his pursuit of the noble lady: "Es deseo / de su honor" (72–73) [It is desire of her honor]. His depiction of the courtly Inés focuses on her effect on him, in keeping with troubadours' discursive paradigm, and the only reference to her physical body is to her eyes, through which the arrow of love has smitten him. Tello is instead interested in the physical description of the nameless girl with whom Fabia tempts him. The successive representations of the two female objects of desire juxtapose *caritas* and *cupiditas,* traditionally considered (in respective order) morally exemplary and condemnable. The choice by Alonso to enlist the services of Fabia to further his standing with Inés is in this context ethically significant—even more so in light of her association with theological heresy.

The discrepancy between the courtly and comic discourses of desire in this scene reflects the ethical and ideological implications of desire's treatment in the play as a whole. The first representation of love offered by Alonso observes decorum in remaining within the discursive parameters of courtly love; but in terms of action and plot development his desire is static, with Inés occupying the fixed position of the absent object that first appeared in the troubadour lyric. Decorum's affirmation of the established social order, or its ideological orthodoxy, includes restrictions on proper behavior (especially for women) that prevent Alonso from actively pursuing her. The employment of Fabia, a character whose questionable reputation stems from her subversion of decorum (her indecent pandering), may open up strategic possibilities for Alonso, but it ethically undermines his desire as well, removing it from the "high" context of Petrarchan love and placing it at odds with the ideology implicit in Neoplatonic, post-Dantean courtly discourse. Duty and desire are once again in conflict, and Fabia's role suggests a less than heroic resolution. In short, Alonso flirts with the possibility of making the discourse of courtly love socially subversive by demoting the lofty discourse of love as suffering to the role of rhetorical veil for illicit carnal desire, just as Rojas's Calisto and Jean de Meun's narrator had done, and just as Dante had fought against.

In contrast to Alonso's ethical conflict is Rodrigo's desire for Inés. The situation is paradoxical in that his pursuit of desire is far more socially orthodox than is Alonso's, but he is still no doubt the villain of the story. Rodrigo is the title character's rival for the affections of the principle female character, and his desire is expressed in terms that suggest an unhealthy obsession along the lines of Luis in *La dama duende*. He ultimately brings about the play's tragic conclusion by killing the hero, not in a duel but in cold blood. Rodrigo's pursuit of Inés, in spite of its obsessive nature, does observe all due decorum: his approach is to court her father's favor and to win his approval. He engages in a proper (that is, orthodox and decorous) courtship by working within the patriarchal system of exchange that institutional marriage represents in early modern Spain. One could say that he sublimates his desire socially and institutionally, and as the play begins he has convinced Inés's father to encourage her to marry him.

What Rodrigo's desire lacks, of course, is *conformidad* (mutual reciprocity), which Alonso's more problematically pursued desire achieves with the help of Fabia. Inés's disdain for Rodrigo has prevented the contract arranged between suitor and father. As the play opens, and before Inés has ever met Alonso, she complains to her sister Leonor about Rodrigo's unwanted approaches and her father's insistence that he is the proper match for her. Rodrigo's intentions are socially legitimate but emotionally bankrupt because his desire is not felt mutually. Reciprocation, O'Connor emphasizes, is necessary for the felicitous wedding-vow closure of early modern Spanish comedy[60]—a convention that does not necessarily reflect the contemporary social reality of marriage practices. In discursive terms, the implications of *conformidad* are that courtly love holds socially redeeming value in the *Comedia* when it is employed mutually by *galán* and *dama* in reference to and in communication with one another. A dialogic exchange between male and female occurs in such instances, making both man and woman express the subjective experience of desire while at the same time making each the object of the other's desire. Alonso and Inés, whether through letters passed between them or during their brief moments together onstage, share similar feelings and the discursive means to represent them. For both Alonso and his rival, Inés is an object of desire; Rodrigo's societal savvy cannot win Inés favor, while Alonso's employment of the persuasive Fabia succeeds.

Conformidad does not erase the social obstacles that impede the lovers, however, and Alonso and Inés must therefore meet in secret, unbeknownst to her father. Subverting the prescriptions and standards of decorum is the only means by which their relationship may be fostered, a formula already seen as typical of Spanish comedy through the examples of *La dama boba, La dama duende,* and *La traición en la amistad.* Given the limits set for her behavior by decorum, Inés's resistance to the cultural practice of paternally arranged marriage must be passive. When avoiding the issue is no longer an option, she tells her father Pedro that she intends to pursue a religious vocation rather than marry. Similarly, Alonso must subvert the social obligations of honor and decorum that would preclude his seeing an unwed woman without her male guardian's knowledge, all the while protecting the honor and reputation of Inés.

In order to achieve this subversion, the services of the comic intermediaries Fabia, Tello, and Ana are enlisted and the play's *enredo* is developed. They invent a scenario in which the lovers may communicate through written correspondence: because Inés has told her father she intends to take religious vows, Tello may come and go freely posing as a clergyman teaching Latin to the young initiate. Given his social standing, Tello of course has not studied Latin and therefore comically apes the "high" language of literary and institutional authority when in the presence of Inés's father Pedro. When Fabia joins Tello dressed as a nun the irony is amplified, as the social reverence due to the clergy is manipulated for the purpose of the lovers' illicit liaisons. Alonso and Inés are thus able to communicate by exchanging written expressions of desire through the discourse of courtly love, all the while duping the unsuspecting father. The impasse that social circumstances have created for the mutual and dialogic exchange of courtly discourse can only be overcome with the help of "low" characters bound neither in word nor in deed to the same discursive and ideological standards.

The moral trajectory of this love story therefore runs the risk of repeating the *Celestina*'s cautionary invective against "low" *cupiditas*. However, because Alonso and Inés don't seek physical consummation —because they observe decorum—the option of channeling their mutual desire in a more socially acceptable way remains possible. More specifically, Alonso must position himself in such a way as to gain paternal favor and demonstrate his worthiness of her. The bull-fights of the local festival in Medina offer him the opportunity to do this, to put on public display his valor and honor. By contrast, Rodrigo falls from his horse and must be delivered from danger by his rival, an occurrence that undermines his own honor and intensifies his jealousy toward Alonso. These events attest to Alonso's valor, nobility, and worthiness, gaining for him the favor of Inés's father and even the visiting king. By placing chivalric strength at the service of desire, he aligns that desire with decorum and appears to have successfully overcome the obstacles around which the play's *agon* has been built—not unlike Manuel's success in *La dama duende*.

Leading up to the final tragic conclusion, then, the plot appears to have shifted toward the conventional comic denouement of betrothal. In anticipation of such a conclusion, Alonso sets out for his hometown of Olmedo to announce his victory and his intentions to ask for Inés's hand. With the audience's horizon of expectations oriented toward such an optimistic sense of closure, however, Lope reasserts the tragic intertext of the *caballero*'s folkloric legend, made explicit in the repetition of the famous *copla* announcing Alonso's death (the same *coplas* that had originally inspired the play's composition). The murder of Alonso is all the more striking because it is not ideologically necessary: the once questionable ethics of his pursuit of Inés have been legitimized by his heroic actions. It is therefore neither poetic justice nor ideological affirmation that motivates his demise. The discourse of courtly love's tenuous relationship with the comic world of Fabia and Tello has been "corrected" and Alonso's desire rechanneled through the heroic discourse of honor, complete with paternal and even royal approval, making it no longer appropriate to have him killed as a tragic scapegoat in a cautionary tale.[61] The addition of another discursive element, the orally transmitted *copla* that understandably alarms Alonso, undermines the previously anticipated comic resolution of the play's interdiscursive conflicts.

After being courted and pursued by two men throughout the play, Inés is left in the end with no suitors: Rodrigo has been sentenced to death by the king for the murder of Alonso. Before the tragic denouement Inés had successfully resisted paternal pressure to marry against her will, at the same time fostering a clandestine relationship of mutual desire that appeared to move toward social legitimacy and paternal approval. Immediately prior to learning of Alonso's death, Pedro sings the knight's praises and learns of Inés's love for him and of her disdain for Rodrigo. Pedro emphatically denies ever wishing to force his daughter to marry against her will, and he welcomes the news of Alonso's honorable intentions. In short, the audience learns that the *enredo* orchestrated by Fabia and Tello was unnecessary, indeed that Inés's resistance to paternal control was gratuitous, as Edward Friedman explains, "Doña Inés resorts to deception when the course of true love is relatively smooth."[62] In other words Lope's comic formula, with its attendant collision of discourses, has been superimposed on a tragic pretext that renders it ironic—a metatextual acknowledgment of the need for a generic plot replete with separated lovers and overbearing fathers in conformity with the blueprint outlined in his *Arte nuevo* for popular success. This formula's discursive collision with the folkloric pretext of the play both pleases the paying public (as the play's perpetual canonical status would suggest) while ironically commenting on the process. "The language of *El caballero de Olmedo* underscores the role of irony as the medium and the message of the play."[63] I would furthermore privilege irony as the aesthetic experience around which Lope orients the play in order to entertain his paying public. Given such an important role for irony in the play (an irony that is in effect achieved through the play's unsettling discursive juxtapositions), its openness to any number of possible interpretations is understandable.

After they learn of Alonso's murder from Tello, Pedro admonishes his daughter to limit her expression of grief within the bounds of decorum: "Guarda lágrimas y estremos, / Inés, para nuestra casa" (lines 2712–13) [Save your tears and wailing, Inés, for inside our house]. This reassertion of paternal authority reminds the audience of how the social norms informing decorum restrict and enclose women, especially in terms of self-expression. Regardless of the paternal stamp of approval granted to her desire earlier in the scene, Inés's emotions and their expression must still be filtered by decorum. Her response, made in reference to the earlier scheme in which she had feigned a calling to religious vocation (which was itself a strategy for circumventing decorum), punctuates the play's climactic irony: "Lo que de burlas te dije, / señor, de veras te ruego" (lines 2714–15) [What I told you in jest, sir, I now earnestly ask]. Tello's comic and sacrilegious scheme had succeeded in subverting patriarchal authority; now, in the absence of her desire's object, it has become literal truth, furthering the conclusion's tragic irony. From her initial appearance in the play's first act, Inés's character has been defined in terms of Alonso and their mutually reciprocated desire. With the object made permanently absent, there is no desire for the discourse of courtly love to mediate. In response, Inés opts to carry her father's admonition for decorum to the extreme of permanent and institutional enclosure within the cloister.

Friedman argues against the presence of a protofeminist subtext in the play—if Inés's pursuit of desire is a subversion of decorum, it is a temporary one quelled by "fate" or the folkloric intertext that predetermines the play's conclusion. Her empowerment, rhetorically expressed in Alonso's adoration, is discursively manifested in her reciprocations and acted out in her role-playing within the schemes hatched by Fabia and Tello. After Alonso's death, however, this empowerment is rescinded, and for decorum to be observed she must be silenced. The realization of what was originally a comic deception (her calling to a religious vocation) implies a surrendering of the voice through which her desire had been expressed.

Decorum and the *Comedia:* ### *Los empeños de una casa*

The argument for a reading of *El caballero de Olmedo*'s conclusion as an ideological containment of female subversion is suggestive of the ideological orientation of decorum, of its implicit affirmation of the established patriarchal social order. As an object of desire, Inés inspires the passions of two men, one willing to circumnavigate decorum with her and the other willing to kill when her reciprocation cannot be forced through his socially prescribed appeal to paternal authority. Her decision to enter the convent, to vow chastity for life, is a permanent deferral of desire. As such it affirms the power of religious institutions that had previously been threatened by Tello and

Fabia's parody through the discourse of comedy. The readings of female-authored plays from Golden Age Spain in the preceding chapters have noted a different authorial stance vis-à-vis the ideologically informed limits placed upon women by decorum. The act of writing for an early modern woman is itself a subversive gesture that flouts contemporary calls for feminine silence in treatises like Fray Luis de León's *La perfecta casada* (The Perfect Wife). This "unauthorized" authorial position bears distinct implications for the terms in which the discourse of courtly love is refracted by the presence of multiple discursive modes in the *Comedia*.

As her famous epistle to Sor Filotea explains, Sor Juana Inés de la Cruz turned to the cloister for different reasons than does Lope's Inés. Because she claims to never have wanted to participate in the patriarchal rituals of courtship, for Sor Juana the convent is a means of resistance to the patriarchal mandates of decorum that would have her do so at the expense of her true desire, the pursuit of knowledge.

> Entréme religiosa, porque aunque conocía que tenía el estado de cosas (de las accesorias hablo, no de las formales), muchas repugnantes a mi genio, con todo, para la total negación que tenía al matrimonio, era lo menos desproporcionado y lo más decente que podía elegir [. . .] de no querer tener ocupación obligatoria que embarazase la libertad de mi estudio, ni rumor de comunidad que impediese el sosegado silencio de mis libros. (831)[64]

> [I entered religious life because, although I knew that it involved a way of life (speaking in terms of its accessorial and not its formal way of life) in many ways repugnant to my tastes, for my absolute rejection of marriage, it was the least unseemly and most decent choice I could make . . . for not wanting obligatory occupations that would infringe upon my freedom to study, or to hear rumors running through the community that would impede the calming silence of my books.]

Marriage to Christ or to the Church, as religious vocations are often called, allowed Sor Juana's pursuit of knowledge to exceed the limits usually prescribed for secular women, which would include the creation of lyric and allegorical poetry and dramatic literature. Because it works from within the male-authored conventions of the *capa y espada* model of comedy, her *Los empeños de una casa* may be read as a response to Lope's polydiscursive refraction of courtly love from the position of the objectified female. Such an authorial position is reflected in the bifocalization of courtly discourse's ethical implications in terms of both genders. That is to say, Sor Juana reexamines the ethics and ideological function of courtly discourse as it emanates from both male and female voices.

Critics have pointed out close parallels between *Los empeños* and peninsular dramatists, especially Calderón, whose *Los empeños en un acaso* has been identified as an immediate influence on Sor Juana's work.[65] Angel Julián Valbuena-Briones explains that "La escritora mexicana estaba satisfecha de haber dominado y asimilado *sui generis* la estilística de Calderón."[66] More recently, Stephanie Merrim attests to the reliance of *Los empeños* on the stylized conventions of Calderón's comedies. Concrete references to the peninsular model also involve the prominent role of the *gracioso* (Sor Juana's Castaño), a figure like Lope's Tello in that he offers metatheatrical commentary on the events of the play. As if to draw our attention to Sor Juana's close ties with the peninsular convention, Castaño considers how to devise an appropriate scheme to manipulate the play's *enredo:* "alguna traza / que de Calderón parezca / con que salir de este empeño" (297) [some scheme that Calderón would invent to get out of this mess].

One noteworthy feminist reading of Sor Juana's *comedia,* offered by Merrim, reads Sor Juana's subversion of *Comedia* conventions in terms of the gender dynamics of the play's plot structure, more specifically the two love triangles around which the action revolves.[67] In short, Merrim considers Sor Juana's play an attempt to subvert the "deep structure" of the male tradition: her plot reflects a counter structure (which she terms "womanscript") imposed upon the generic structure implicit in male-authored *capa y espada* plays. The female author writing within a patriarchal system must necessarily confront certain artistic and social issues implicit in patriarchal ideology and its cultural manifestations, much as has been observed in the present study regarding the representation of female subjectivity by the *trobairitz,* Marie de France, and other Golden Age *dramaturgas* like María de Zayas and Leonor de la Cueva. Merrim reads this confrontation as the cause of an internal psychological conflict for Sor Juana, as the intellectual and artistic activity to which she is drawn is a transgression of prescribed social norms for feminine behavior. Such an approach implies that the literary text may be read as a product of this tension, or as a means of confronting the repressive demands made of her gender by decorum.

The result of the conflict for Merrim is a "divided self" (the intellectual and artistic female subject vs. the passive object projected by treatises such as *La perfecta casada*), which is in turn projected onto the text as the womanscript. In *Los empeños,* Ana's schemes and plots that catalyze the action represent the creative, subversive, and "dark" side of this split, while Leonor's virtue and submission to male control would represent the "light" side that conforms to the patriarchal system. Merrim therefore reads the play's traditional *capa y espada* closure of reconciliation and a pair of honor-affirming marriages as an unsuccessful transgression of the established patriarchal order.

A closer look at the play, however, suggests that Merrim's generally insightful analysis leaves some questions unanswered. Leonor (the "light" and submissive side of the split) is placed in the house of her admirer Pedro, and the situation does pose a threat to her honor and reputation, but what makes Pedro's capture of her possible in the first place is her decision to flee from her father's house at night to elope with Carlos just before the play's action begins. Like Inés in *El caballero de Olmedo,* then, Leonor is in a relationship based on *conformidad;* she is both subject and object of desire. Her pursuit of desire through elopement is a subversive act that threatens the honor of both her family and herself. This "dark" and subversive female agency is indeed ultimately successful, as she does eventually marry Carlos with her father's begrudging consent. Ana's subversion may therefore be punished by her marriage to Don Juan, but Leonor's subversion appears to be supported and rewarded.

This ethical ambiguity challenges the notion of "deep structure" implicit in Merrim's notion of the womanscript. Poststructuralist theory (and deconstruction in particular) has demonstrated that every argument proposing a text's deep structural unity may be subverted by a counterargument, and Merrim's counterstructure is no exception. The fact that Leonor's motives and actions do not exactly correspond with the structural function that Merrim assigns to her indicates that this reading must be taken with caution. There is little doubt that the issues she raises regarding the ideological implications of a cloistered woman writer in colonial Mexico are valid, and indeed they are essential to the bigger picture of Sor Juana's literary production. However, the conventions of courtly discourse and their reinterpretation by Sor Juana fall outside the scope of the womanscript. The parameters of Merrim's structural approach can be broadened to consider the play's reworking of peninsular conventions on a discursive level.

Merrim does identify a significant departure from the peninsular tradition: whereas the love triangle in the *capa y espada* genre generally involves two men and one woman, in Sor Juana's play the gender distribution is the opposite. The shift has discursive implications in that, if women are to occupy "center stage" and through dialogue negotiate their conflict, they will necessarily dominate what is traditionally a male-dominated discursive space along with the physical, on-stage space. The words of Leonor and Ana assume traditionally male discursive functions: to narrate events that have occurred off-stage, to "plot" the *enredo,* and to resolve it—all through an exercise of the free will so ardently espoused in Sor Juana's poetic and, especially, her epistolary texts. Her inversion of the love triangle in this play allows for much greater emphasis to be placed on feminine presence and dialogue, in particular on the use of courtly discourse to express desire through female voices. In discursive terms, the feminine supplants the masculine, but *Los empeños* maintains its generic identity with the patriarchal tradition in that its *enredo* is in essence a love intrigue. Like her male-authored Golden Age models, Sor Juana represents desire in her comedy through the discourse of courtly love often cited in her non-dramatic poetic corpus,[68] imbedding it in a comic plot structured around the pursuit of that desire; unlike them, she privileges the subjective experience of desire by female personages in a way that resists the male-authored, decorum-guided representation of women that is exemplified by *El caballero de Olmedo*'s Inés.

Leonor, who is unwittingly ensnared in Pedro's trap, makes the connection between her situation and that of the typical *Comedia* heroine explicit. Her extensive monologue in the first act, through which we first learn of her history and of her situation, demonstrates her awareness of this danger while at the same time it suggests the generic conventionality or universality of the situation.

> En fin, yo le amé; no quiero
> cansar tu atención contando
> de mi temerario empeño
> la historia caso por caso;
> pues tu discreción no ignora
> de empeños enamorados,
> que es su ordinario principio
> desasosiego y cuidado,
> su medio, lances y riesgos,
> su fin, tragedias o agravios.

(pp. 642–43)

> [In short, I loved him; I don't want
> to tire your attention by telling you
> of my timorous plight
> and life-story case by case;

> your discretion is not ignorant of love stories,
> which ordinarily begin with care and concern,
> then deal with risky travails,
> and, finally, end with tragedy or injury.]

Leonor spares Ana the details and particulars of her personal experiences, pointing out instead that as a lady of her social milieu she must already be familiar with the courtly narrative and dramatic conventions to which Leonor's life (as told in her narrative) has thus far conformed. All unnecessary particulars aside, she informs Ana that hers is "one of those stories" around which conventional love stories are constructed.

The plot of *Los empeños* draws upon many of the same conventions that are employed in Lope's *El caballero de Olmedo,* albeit with very different results. Pedro, like Rodrigo, suffers from unrequited love for a woman whose own desire is mutually reciprocated by another man, Carlos. Their imminent betrothal drives the jealous Pedro to intercept the lovers as they leave to elope. He poses as a representative of legal authority summoned by Leonor's father to save the family's reputation, depositing Leonor in a nearby house (which just so happens to be his own) so as to avoid public scandal and damage to her reputation, and his sister Ana is charged with her protection and service. Like Lope's Rodrigo, Sor Juana's Pedro is presented as an impediment to the fruition of mutual love, a jealous male antagonist who turns to desperate measures when he cannot win the affections of his desire's object. When he is finally alone with Leonor, his appeal is rhetorically postured after the troubadour model, especially in terms of its objectification of the lady as the *belle dame sans merci.*

> Yo, Señora, he sido vuestro,
> y aunque siempre desdeñosa
> me habéis tratado, el desdén
> más mi fineza acrisola,
> que es muy garboso desaire
> el ser fino a toda costa.

> (p. 661)

> [I, lady, have been yours,
> and although with disdain
> you have always treated me,
> that disdain only sharpens my service,
> for it is very burdensome to appear
> refined at any cost.]

Pedro's lament is consistent with the troubadour *canzon:* although the lady is addressed in the second person, it is only to express his experience of her cruelty and to affirm his virtue in remaining constant and faithful in his love from afar. The discourse of courtly love, then, assigns noble motives behind Pedro's abduction, coercion, and captivity of Leonor—actions which, except for Alonso's murder, are far less decorous than the unwanted advances and dubious dealings of Rodrigo, the villain of *El caballero de Olmedo.* Pedro's rhetorical posture is to explain his perfidy as an expression of the inner workings of his *cor gentil.*

Another of Sor Juana's additions to the popular formula (one with which Lope occasionally experimented as well) is that Ana is also an unrequited lover from afar, a double of Pedro's role of jealous lover. Her willingness to comply with her brother's deceptive and manipulative scheme is due to the fact that the object of her own desire just so happens to be Carlos, Leonor's would-be husband. Carlos's situation resembles that of *El caballero de Olmedo*'s Inés: he is the object of desire for two women, the second of whom conspires with her brother to prevent his union with the first. Thus Carlos is to Pedro what Leonor is to Ana: the recipient of the affections that jealous brother and sister covet in vain. The doubling of the plot is seamlessly framed in the conventions of domestic comedy when Carlos's search for the abducted Leonor leads him to the house of Ana and Pedro, where he is promptly hidden by Ana in her room. The *empeños* of this house, the schemes and plot complications that will entertain Sor Juana's implied audience, will make the domestic setting a house of mirrors in which each male expression of desire through courtly discourse will be juxtaposed against its feminine double. Sor Juana's double plot allows her to represent all sides of conventional literary desire, all subject and object positions created by the discourse of courtly love, through characters of both sexes. The brother and sister represent the jealous and isolated lover as man and woman, each of whom objectifies the person s/he desires through the discourse of courtly love. Carlos and Leonor, by contrast, enjoy the mutually felt desire of *conformidad,* which is also verbally expressed and dialogically exchanged through courtly discourse. And yet their perilous situation, it should be remembered, is at least in part of their own doing, an unforeseen consequence of their indecorous elopement. All four characters experience and express desire in a manner that is in one way or another morally and ideologically compromised. The resolution of the conflict, predetermined by generic convention to involve betrothal, will not resolve the problematization of courtly discourse offered over the course of the play.

A focal point of this questioning of the motives behind the discourse of courtly love is female desire. Placing a female character within the conflicts and tribulations of a love story discursively grounded in what José Pascual Buxó calls the "culto de amor"[69] generally involves presenting her with a possible threat to her honor if she is to pursue the object of her desire. Mediating these demands—one social, the other literary—is something akin to walking a tightrope. As Zayas's conclusion to the *Desengaños amorosos* illustrates, the surest way for a woman to avoid both the abuses of patriarchal misogyny and any compromise of one's honor (chastity) is to leave the battlefield of courtly love altogether and seek a cloistered refuge, much as Sor Juana herself chose to do. Otherwise the standard female *Comedia* protagonist is faced with choosing either to suppress her desire and remain passive, leaving the fate of her love in the hands of her lover (if indeed her love is reciprocated), or to act on that desire and risk perceived impropriety. In short, her dilemma is that she must either conform to decorum and its implicit ideology or attempt to subvert it.

Sor Juana is therefore faced with an ideological quandary in conforming to generic conventions while attempting to represent her own gender from a protofeminist perspective. Generic conventional provisions do exist and are at her disposal to avoid this conflict: two alternative modes of female representation used extensively by peninsular dramatists that allow for active female agency are the *mujer esquiva* and the *mujer varonil*.[70] Both conventions maintain the established social order in that they are treated as anomalies to the norm, outside standard and accepted social behavior. But rather than opt for either means of escape, Sor Juana faces the conflict head-on by writing within the *capa y espada* tradition in *Los empeños*, in part to call attention to the problem itself and recognize it as such. The *capa y espada* plays, known especially for confusion, chaos, and plot complication, seem to present courtly discourse in the most problematic light, precisely because of the attention paid to the desire of their heroines and their attempts to act upon it. Such is the case of the genre's more famous examples, such as Lope's *La dama boba* and *La discreta enamorada*, and Calderón's *La dama duende* and *Casa con dos puertas, mala es de guardar*. It should come as no surprise, then, that Sor Juana's version should also privilege female desire.

What sets Sor Juana's play apart from these male-authored staples of the genre, then, is not that a female protagonist should express desire or even that she should act upon it, but that we are presented with *two* such characters whose negotiations of desire come into direct conflict. How, then, are we to interpret the fact that one character's successful fulfillment of her desire must come at the other's failure? Teresa Soufas's book-length study of several peninsular female-authored comedias suggests that a principal concern of Zayas, Cueva, and Caro is to undermine the implicit essentialism in the patriarchal representation of women. Their texts constitute "an encoded pattern of disruption for the ideological category 'Woman,' challenging the patriarchal insistence on the inherently natural quality of the two-gendered hierarchy that assigns women to enclosure and silence."[71] A key method of this disruptive practice is the portrayal of female characters that flout the essentialist stereotype imposed upon them —a method also applied throughout *Los empeños*. Such essentialism, I would argue, is intrinsic to the objectified representation of women engendered by the discourse of courtly love. In response, Sor Juana presents two heroines, each facing a moral and social dilemma.

The dilemma for Leonor is partially of her own doing, and partially due to factors beyond her control, such as Pedro's abduction of her; in other words she is at the same time both an active subject pursuing desire and a passive object of Pedro's desire. Although her decision to seek a clandestine union with the man she loves clearly flouts decorum, her ultimate goal of codifying the union through the sacrament of marriage is considered noble. Her first speech, the longest monologue by far of the entire play, includes a verbal portrait of Carlos (an inversion of the troubadour male's portrait of the passive and distant female object) that reflects the orthodox and ennobling version of Dante's Neoplatonic *caritas*. If Leonor has subverted decorum by eloping with Carlos, it is intended to be a temporary subversion that would ultimately seek institutional approbation. Because her amorous relationship with Carlos is based on *conformidad* and not on possessive and obsessive jealousy, her successful betrothal at the end of the comedy can be interpreted as a fitting reward—just as the *conformidad* of desire between Inés and Alonso makes the denouement of *El caballero de Olmedo* so ironically tragic.

The same cannot be said for Ana, who provides evidence for a negative interpretation of courtly love as a codified mode of self-expression that, when abused, can say more about the speaking subject than about the beloved object of desire. Her narcissistic, socially destructive, and self-reflexive desire operates within the parameters of courtly discourse in that it depends upon the absence of the beloved, but its base is self-interest, not *conformidad*. Rather than direct her sentiments toward the orthodox goal of sacramental union with one devoted lover, Ana seeks novelty and excitement in love for its own sake. She has chosen to love Carlos from afar rather than to direct her affections toward her previous lover Juan, whose arrival at Ana's house helps to further intensify the play's *enredo*. Her justification for choosing to pursue Carlos, who does not know her, over fostering her relationship with Juan, who is so devoted to her that he followed her from Toledo to Madrid, is particularly telling: "porque si él es ya tan mío / ¿qué tengo que desear?" (639) [For if he is already in my possession, what is left for me to desire?]. She later reinforces her preference for love from afar when she asserts that Carlos "tiene de más galán el ser ajeno" (644) [he is more attractive in being unknown]. The ethical implications of Ana's desire are clearly placed in opposition to those of her rival—one could even say that her desire more closely resembles the destructive force of love that was the norm in classical antiquity, exemplified by figures such as Dido and Medea. Ana admits that her newly discovered *galán* has rendered her will *ciega* (blind); her passion is likened to fire ("ya otro fuego en mi pecho se acrisola" [now another fire is kindled in my breast]); and its cause, whether good or bad, is deemed unimportant ("no sé si es gusto o capricho" [639] [I don't know if it is preference or caprice]). In a stunning reversal of Leonor's ethically orthodox stance, Ana exclaims to her *criada:* "¿Pues no he de llorar / ¡ay infeliz de mí!, cuando / conozco que estoy errando / y no me puedo enmendar?" (639) [Am I not to cry, oh unhappy me!, when I know that I err and cannot correct myself?].

Such a discrepancy between the two female characters and their expression of desire establishes *Los empeños* as a comedy whose dilemma largely hinges on two women and their conflicting approaches to love, which serve as distinctive motives for which the same discourse of courtly love is employed. This conventional love-language offers the terms through which contradictory representations of the female subject may be offered. It also suggests that Sor Juana's response to the male-authored *Comedia*'s representation of women shares common ground with that of the peninsular female playwrights: Soufas's identification of their anti-essentialism may apparently be extended across the Atlantic to Sor Juana. Neither Ana nor Leonor is "Woman" per se, but both represent a possible way in which a woman might negotiate her desire (one is exemplary, the other cautionary). Neither one is neither wholly pure nor wholly impure, neither Mary nor

Eve; instead both fall somewhere in between these two dichotomous and ideologically paradigmatic extremes. By exploiting the often obscure and ethically ambiguous discourse of the courtly love tradition, Sor Juana is able to offer both praiseworthy and condemnable behavior from within the same literary context—and in the process she renders such conventional notions as heroism and villainy ambiguous and discursively indistinguishable.

The self-reflexive conventionality of *Los empeños,* which comes to a climax in its denouement, makes Sor Juana's response to the male-authored *Comedia*'s representation of women through the discourse of courtly love both subtle and complex. One could certainly argue for an interpretation of the play along the lines of A. A. Parker's seminal notion of poetic justice, through which the *Comedia* is said to maintain its "thematic unity."[72] Such a reading depends on treating the play's denouement as the meting out of justice by the author, a gesture that would ostensibly reflect the dramatist's ideological stance. Although we have seen that *El caballero de Olmedo* resists such a reading, *Los empeños* seems more amenable to it. The final scene includes the arrival of Rodrigo, Leonor's father and the clearest representative of patriarchal authority in a comedy whose primary players are all implicated in ideologically unorthodox and even subversive behavior. His presence does make possible a resolution of paternally approved betrothal, but after finding his daughter in the presence of the man with whom she had eloped, his tersely expressed consent ironically reveals the conventional transparency of the "all's well that ends well" conclusion. Despite the threat that Carlos's actions pose to his daughter's (and his own) honor and reputation, the father is satisfied that they will marry, that Carlos will enter the family, and that therefore family honor will be preserved.

This reading would imply that Ana's behavior merits punishment while Leonor's merits reward; of the two female protagonists, one's agency is condemned while the other's is rewarded. The discrepancy can be explained in terms of how each female character negotiates desire through the discourse of courtly love, and in terms of the morality of their motives for using it. However, it would also imply a tacit condemnation of the generic conventions with which Sor Juana has worked so closely throughout her comedy: what is traditionally rewarded in the male-authored *capa y espada* model is in fact punished in this case. The scheming Ana follows the mold of other female protagonists that have been treated in earlier chapters of this study, namely *La dama boba*'s Finea and *La dama duende*'s Angela—

both of whom succeed in circumventing decorum's gender restrictions in order to realize their pursuit of desire. An audience aware of this generic convention would therefore expect similar success for Ana. By reversing the fate of the female lover/agent, Sor Juana implicitly rejects the patriarchal tradition's standard justification for the morally and ethically questionable use of courtly discourse. In this case, all is *not* fair in love and war. What at first glance appears to be a casual discrepancy is in fact an explanation point appended to a statement (if we consider the play a statement) whose underlying message is critical of how the literary status quo (both the *Comedia* and the broader courtly love tradition) objectifies and essentializes women.

If the interpretation of courtly discourse is problematized in *El caballero de Olmedo* by its collision with alternate modes of discourse, especially that of low comic farce as voiced by Tello and Fabia, *Los empeños* takes courtly love itself to task by representing it as duplicitous and relative to the gendered and ideological position from which it is voiced (among the various voices used to establish such relativity is that of the comic *gracioso* Castaño). This instability of the "message" of courtly discourse has been at issue ever since the troubadours first fashioned it, and it explains the divergent ways in which it has been employed over the centuries leading up to the Spanish Golden Age, from *caritas* to *cupiditas*, from jealous self-interest to *conformidad*. Dante's attempts to purge courtly discourse of its potential for abuse (in the Augustinian sense of the word) toward "dark" and subversive ends, and to instead infuse it with the spiritual idealism of Neoplatonic love, met only temporary success that did not extend beyond Petrarch. Especially since the fourteenth-century appearance of the *Decameron*, the ambiguity and malleability intrinsic to the discourse of courtly love have allowed writers to elude the ideological service expected of them by decorum. They could instead privilege the act of interpretation by the individual reader or spectator and appeal to his or her aesthetic demands. A good love story, after all, is highly entertaining and the stuff of best-sellers; it is all the better if, free from ideologically predetermined interpretive guidelines, it teaches us to question the social conditions it describes.

Conclusion: Furthering the *Tenso*

> De todos instrumentos yo, libro, só pariente:
> bien o mal, qual puntares, tal diré ciertamente;
> qual tú dezir quisieres, ý faz punto, ý tente;
> si me puntar sopieres, sienpre me avrás en miente.
> —Juan Ruiz, *Libro de buen amor,* 27

[I, the book, am a relative of all the musical instruments: well or badly, however you play me, so I will surely sound; whatever kind of poem you want, play it thus, and you will have it; if you know how to play me, you will always have me in mind.][1]

IN HIS CHARACTERIZATION OF THE *LIBRO DE BUEN AMOR* AS LIKE A MUSIcal instrument that can be "played" (that is to say, read) any number of ways, Juan Ruiz offers a compelling metaphor for the interpretational open-endedness of courtly discourse that this book has explored. We have seen that despite the myriad ways in which this instrument has since been played, the troubadours forged an amatory discourse whose self-reflective subject position and corresponding displacement of the female object persisted over centuries of male performances of desire. The court cultures of Trastámaran Spain fostered a mode of lyrical expression, recorded for posterity in poetic anthologies known as *cancioneros,* that celebrated desire in all its various manifestations—including the sexual desire that Jean de Meun had allegorized before them. Conversely, Dante begins a long line of poets (following the model of some troubadour poets and poems, at least as those models have been commonly interpreted) who chose to play the courtly instrument as a means of sublimating desire to a more spiritual and Neoplatonic plane; in Spain the legacy of this reading or "playing" would reverberate for centuries, from fifteenth-century sentimental fiction to Petrarchism, San Juan de la Cruz's mystical poetry, and even Lope de Vega's own *Rimas sacras.* While beyond the parameters of this book, these examples of religious-amorous poetry *a lo divino* (in the divine style) present the extreme but logical consequence of the spiritualized and Neoplatonic trajectory of the European love lyric: the idealized female object of desire displaced by the male subject's self-reflection is literally removed from the equation, replaced by God. The opposite extreme of this ethical or ideological spectrum is well represented by such masterpieces as the *Libro de buen amor* and *Celestina*, and it is frequently exploited for comic effect in the *Comedia*—as for example when the adulation of the chaste Marcia voiced by the *galán* Liseo is ironically inverted by the *gracioso* León's praise of promiscuous servant-girls in the first act of Zayas's *La traición en la amistad.*

We may extend Ruiz's musical analogy to suggest that the discursive interplay that was the subject of the last chapter is tantamount to casting that musical instrument into a kind of literary orchestra, in which a matrix of other discursive "instruments" condition the presentation of courtly discourse and suggest new interpretive possibilities for it. Any given play will generate its *agon* from the creative selection and arrangement of the many discursive practices (both literary and nonliterary, both new and inherited) which inspire its author and, more importantly, with which the paying public of the *corrales* may identify. The dynamic play between these discursive practices, in effect a linguistic manifestation of early modern Spanish society's underlying cultural and ideological conflicts and tensions, constitutes the orchestral arrangement that is the polymetric and polydiscursive *Comedia*. This book has perhaps focused disproportionately on only one instrument, the discourse of courtly love, in part because of its thematic and dramatic importance to the bestselling comedies of early modern Spain, but also because its intrinsic linguistic indeterminacy lends itself to many ways in which it may be played—just as changes in manual technique, tuning, and sociocultural performance context can make what is a violin for some be a fiddle for others. The dependence on interpretation that Ruiz claims of his book is true of the period's dramatists, as their invocation of courtly discourse constitutes an act of interpretation of inherited literary forms, but it is also true of early modern theatergoing publics, be they the paying *vulgo* of the *corrales,* the institutional authorities monitoring public performances for their social and ideological implications, or the patron-publics who commissioned private performances for royal, courtly, and private consumption.

Such ideologically antithetical contemporaries as the *Celestina* and Petrarchism, or the *cancioneros* and sentimental fiction, are indicative of the complicated and multifaceted cultural legacy of courtly discourse from the Middle Ages into early modern Spain. To be sure, cultural and socioeconomic factors too complicated to receive substantial treatment here underlie the dramatic shift from the ethically prescribed and guided readership of Dante to the ideologically guideless readership of Cervantes—factors such as the arrival of the printing press in the fifteenth century, the rise of free market economies in the early modern period, and the subsequent emergence of a literate bourgeois class whose purchase of books was often guided by the thirst for pleasurable entertainment rather than moral instruction. Boccaccio's prologue to the *Decameron* and his day 4 prologue underscore the emergence of a female readership to whom he offers his *novelle,* both as a source of solace or comfort from the painful experiences of love, and as a means of entertainment that works within the confines of the lifestyle of enclosure imposed upon them by men. His reconfigured presentation of courtly desire, like Lope de Vega's reformulation for the largely illiterate *corral* audience three centuries later, demonstrates the extent to which the survival of courtly discourse as an economically viable object of popular consumption is largely due to its adaptability to new orchestral arrangements tailor-made to meet the demands of emerging demographic targets.

That readers, especially female readers, would continue to represent an economically viable target audience for early modern Spanish writers is substantiated by the *Vida* of St. Teresa of Avila. Among the many sins of which she would later repent, she confesses to having relished the reading of the wild and imaginative books of chivalry that had inspired *Don Quijote*'s parody. Such a mode of reading resembles Francesca in the *Inferno* far more closely than it does Dante's "ideal reader," Can Grande della Scala. Certainly Cervantes and Lope de Vega both appeal to the aesthetic pleasure of their respective readers and spectators in a way that would concern Augustine and the medieval literary culture he so heavily influenced, especially in light of how such an appeal involves the exchange of an ideologically controlling authorial voice for the reader/spectator's free interpretation. The *Comedia* was especially adaptive to the tastes of its popular culture, as the production of dramatic spectacle was fast becoming a market-driven industry.

At the same time that the Spanish people's economic capital set its own aesthetic demands on the professional theater, the Church was in the process of reasserting its control over Spanish popular culture, an effort that included the Inquisition's vigilant monitoring and censorship of public theatrical performances. The cultural debate being waged over the licitness of the public theater in early modern Spain should serve as a reminder that, despite the increasing privilege granted to entertainment in the acts of reading literature and witnessing dramatic performance, the cultural climate of the Spanish Golden Age was by no means a moral or ethical free-for-all. The reader/spectator's individual construction of meaning, no longer so explicitly guided (in ethical or ideological terms) by religious authority, was problematic for the Counter Reformation Church. The Protestant Reformation among other things was a rejection of papal authority and a call for the individual to pursue his relationship with God independent of such authority. This emphasis on individual autonomy included biblical exegesis—in other words, reading scripture became an act of empowerment for the individual, a rejection of how the Vatican and its representative local institutions would have one read it. For the Church, responding to the international religious struggle pioneered by Martin Luther was, in a sense, responding to a challenge against a prescribed and controlled mode of reading. One such response was the Inquisition's index of prohibited books, which temporarily included such ideologically elusive works as the *Decameron* and the *Lazarillo*. Writers in early modern Spain thus faced two conflicting demands: to succeed in the literary marketplace while avoiding institutional censure.

The discourse of courtly love offered an immediate and attractive framework for meeting the conflicting demands of Church and society while offering the paying public a time-honored literary tradition, a conventional mode of discourse with which all were familiar. The fact that courtly love was an equally important source for Dante, whose manipulation of it prescribed a fixed reading at the service of Augustinian *caritas,* and for Cervantes, who used it to problematize such notions of authorial control over interpretation, suggests how protean its discourse has always been. Such caprice is intrinsic to courtly love, I have argued, because that is precisely how the troubadours wanted their discourse to function: as an open-ended system of tropes and conventions riddled with ambiguity. Their game of love depended on the ability of the poet to manipulate courtly discourse so as to demonstrate his wit, skill, and capacity for innovation. Little did the troubadours know that this game would profoundly influence the representation of desire in the Western world for centuries to come, or that their discursive indeterminacy would generate the longstanding tensions and problems that have been the subject of this book.

From this perspective, Jean de Meun's playful manipulation of courtly discourse stands as an accurate narrative adaptation of the troubadour lyric: it is among other things a celebration of the male libido and of his verbal dexterity in representing it. The controversy and debate that the *Roman de la Rose* inspired, through which Christine de Pizan offered a distinctively feminine perspective on the discourse of courtly love, is demonstrative of how uneasy the more conservative voices of the late Middle Ages were with the free interpretability and manipulability of the discourse of courtly love. That debate can be seen as a foreshadowing of the later controversy surrounding the moral licitness of the *Comedia*, in which the representation of desire through the discourse of courtly love would again be perceived as a threat to the established moral and social order of institutional authority. In this sense Dante's authoritative voice, in its attempt to rescue courtly discourse from the moral peril of both the libido and linguistic indeterminacy (the dangers of both physical desire and its verbal representation), was only temporarily successful. Although he could create an epic and divine cosmography in which courtly discourse was assigned a fixed and ideologically orthodox function, he could not fundamentally transform the nature of the discourse itself, for he (like Boccaccio, Cervantes, and Lope de Vega) inherited it as a literary tradition. Dante could not rewrite a literary history that was destined to repeat itself in the centuries to follow.

The voices of the *trobairitz*, Marie de France, and the female dramatists of Golden Age Spain bear witness to this diachronic continuity. While each of these women writers thinks and writes from her own particular cultural and ideological circumstances, they all share the marginal position to which their gender is assigned by the patriarchal courtly tradition. The perpetuation of the same implicit problems in courtly discourse concerning how women are represented, from the troubadours to the *Comedia*, has elicited gendered responses from these historically and culturally isolated women that bear striking similarities to one another. The pattern of questioning the underlying assumptions of male courtly love, of engaging in its discursive conventions for the purpose of subverting them, shows that the Provençal *domna*, medieval Italian *donna*, and Golden Age Spanish *dama* are all treated by male authors as passive and objectified fictions of the male imagination. My reading of courtly discourse has seen this critique from the feminine margins of the tradition as a valid and valuable source of insight on its ideological implications. The feminine periphery, of whose existence Gaston Paris, Denis de Rougemont, and C.S. Lewis were unaware, is now a useful tool for better defining the phallogocentric center.

The "poetics of exclusion" whereby the lady is marginalized and objectified in troubadour poetry, and ultimately in all of courtly discourse, was well perpetuated by the ideological climate of Counter-Reformation Spain. Humanist treatises like Fray Luis de León's *La perfecta casada* are indicative of a cultural and especially institutional misogyny whose manifestations in Spanish didactic literature date at least as far back as the medieval *Corbacho* by the Archpriest of Talavera. This tradition's institutionalized and essentialist classification of women as either virgin or whore, as either Mary or Eve, is reflective of the same patriarchal attitudes toward women shown in Provençal poetry. The troubadours' idealized and dehumanized *domna,* described either through lofty superlatives or as the cruel *belle dame sans merci* (a contrast amplified in both Humanist didactic prose and Petrarchism by what is often called the Renaissance's "rhetoric of praise and blame"), would constitute an attractive prescriptive model for representing women onstage to more conservative dramatists of early modern Spain, in a time of intense institutional scrutiny from the Inquisition.

Given these circumstances, it is no surprise that women writers would take issue with the way in which courtly discourse was used to represent their gender. While this book has by no means offered an exhaustive study of the variety of responses given by women writers to the patriarchal standards and conventions of the courtly tradition or of the *Comedia,* it has at least attempted to indicate the importance of such study in the future, as well as the utility of focusing it on the discourse of courtly love's representation of desire. Such a focus has demonstrated that strong parallels exist between Golden Age *dramaturgas* and their predecessors, such as the *trobairitz* and Marie de France—all of whom challenge the authority of male courtly discourse, particularly in terms of its objectification and silence of women. Whether or not we treat female responses to the male position as a distinctive literary tradition (or counter-tradition), they point to a problem that persisted over the centuries and across national boundaries. That problem is the discourse of courtly love itself, as it is engendered by male writers; *La traición en la amistad, La firmeza en la ausencia,* and *Los empeños de una casa* point to the fact that it was no less problematic in early modern Spain than it had been in twelfth-century Provence.

I have not attempted to catalogue all responses by women writers concerned with their gender's representation from the Middle Ages through the Spanish Golden Age, simply because they resist a reduced and procrustean collective reading or a master narrative that would be fully representative of "Woman's voice." If there is a common message to be gleaned, it is that "Woman" is not representable, for women poets, novelists, and dramatists of the Western world from the twelfth through the seventeenth century resist the essentialist classification offered by courtly discourse (whether in medieval romance narrative, the early modern *novella,* lyric poetry, or the *Comedia*) and the patriarchal institutions that exercised ideological influence over it. The common ground shared by these women writers is their writing against the grain of the essentialized notion of Woman, rejecting the assignment of a fixed and conclusive meaning to their sex.

This study has operated from the premise that the *Comedia* tradition is a kind of gendered *tenso*—a dialogic exchange between the sexes, at least in part linguistically grounded in the discourse of courtly love. Such a premise suggests that for twenty-first century scholars and critics, the value of historically distant works authored by women extends beyond their own intrinsic academic or aesthetic merit. The traditional Golden Age canon authored by Lope de Vega and his male contemporaries, for example, resonates differently when considered in tandem with contemporary plays of female authorship, which in their own right echo and respond to the formal conventions established by the male authors. While this dialectic has been identified by feminist critics in their reading of female-authored texts, the preceding pages suggest that the implications of the *tenso* analogy extend beyond their scope into our understanding of the male-authored comedies to which they respond. If one accepts that the collective effort of these women authors resists a common master narrative, or that they elude essentialist reduction, then in this sense they are no different than their male interlocutors. To bring their work into contact with the patriarchal tradition is to recognize the dialogic nature of the *Comedia* and the scholarship it inspires. As Amy Williamsen explains in her study of another early modern Spanish *dramaturga,* Ana Caro, "Instead of representing dialectical opposites, margin and center will be increasingly perceived as fluctuating, interdependent constructs."[2] This holds true for the medieval discursive tradition of courtly love, the popular theater of early modern Spain, and for those of us in the twenty-first century who study them, examining the courtly dialogue through a *tenso* of our own.

Notes

INTRODUCTION

1. Lope de Vega, *El arte nuevo de hacer comedias en este tiempo,* ed. Juana José de Prades (Madrid: Consejo Superior de Investigaciones Científicas, 1971). Subsequent quotations from this work are cited parenthetically in the text according to the line numbers indicated in this edition. All translations are mine.

2. Donald Gilbert-Santamaría, *Writers on the Market: Consuming Literature in Early Seventeenth-Century Spain* (Lewisburg: Bucknell University Press, 2005), 24.

3. See, for example, Nancy L. D'Antuono, *Boccaccio's Novelle in the Theater of Lope de Vega* (Madrid: Porrúa Turanzas, 1983); Frederick A de Armas, ed., *A Star-Crossed Golden Age: Myth and the Spanish Comedia* (Lewisburg, PA: Bucknell University Press, 1998); Michael McGaha, "Guarini's *El pastor fido* and Lope de Vega's *El verdadero amante,*" *Journal of Hispanic Philology* 10, no. 1 (1985): 51–60; and Manuel Criado de Val, ed., *Lope de Vega y los orígenes del teatro español* (Madrid: EDI-6, 1981).

4. Denis de Rougemont, *L'amour et l'Occident* (Paris: Union générale d'éditions, 1939); Gaston Paris, "Lancelot du Lac, II. *Le Conte de la Charrette,*" *Romania* 12 (1883): 459–534; C. S.Lewis, *The Allegory of Love: A Study in Medieval Tradition.* (Oxford: Clarendon Press, 1936). For a comprehensive overview of the development of courtly love scholarship from its origins through the 1970s, see Roger M. Boase, *The Origin and Meaning of Courtly Love: A Critical Study of European Scholarship* (Manchester, England: Manchester University Press, 1977).

5. Foucault treats this notion most extensively in *Les mots et les choses: une archéologie des sciences humaines* (Paris: Gallimard, 1966).

6. Some of the pivotal studies in this disciplinary transformation are Paul Julian Smith's *Writing in the Margin: Spanish Literature of the Golden Age* (Oxford: Oxford University Press, 1988); Walter Cohen, *Drama of a Nation: Public Theater in Renaissance England and Spain* (Ithaca: Cornell University Press, 1985); George Mariscal's *Contradictory Subjects: Quevedo, Cervantes, and Seventeenth-Century Spanish Culture* (Ithaca: Cornell University Press, 1991); and Anthony Cascardi's *Ideologies of History in the Spanish Golden Age* (University Park: Pennsylvania State University Press, 1997). Barbara Mujica, in "Golden Age/Early Modern Theater: *Comedia* Studies at the End of the Century," *Hispania* 82, no.3 (1999), 397–407, offers an excellent narrative of this process. For a more recent survey of current trends in *Comedia* scholarship, see Laura R. Bass and Margaret R. Greer, ed., *Approaches to Teaching Early Modern Spanish Drama* (New York: MLA, 2006).

7. Thomas A. O'Connor, *Love in the 'Corral': Conjugal Spirituality and Antitheatrical Polemic in Early Modern Spain* (New York: Peter Lang, 2000).

8. Ibid., p. 30.

9. Ibid., p. 22.

10. Ibid., p. 30.

11. See, for example, Teresa Soufas, *Dramas of Distinction: A Study of Plays by Golden Age Women* (Lexington: University of Kentucky Press, 1997).

12. Three excellent studies of Petrarch's impact on Spanish poetry are Anne J. Cruz, *Imitación y transformación: El petrarquismo en la poesía de Juan de Boscán y Garcilaso de la Vega* (Philadelphia: John Benjamins, 1988); Daniel Heiple, *Garcilaso and the Italian Renaissance* (Lewisburgh, PA: Bucknell University Press, 1994); and Ignacio Navarrete, *Orphans of Petrarch: Poetry and Theory in the Spanish Renaissance* (Berkeley: University of California Press, 1994).

13. Laura Kendrick, *The Game of Love: Troubadour Wordplay* (Berkeley: University of California Press, 1988).

14. José Antonio Maravall, *Teatro y literatura en la sociedad barroca* (Madrid: Seminarios y Ediciones, 1972); Bruce Wardropper, "La comedia española del Siglo de Oro," in Elder Olsen, *Teoría de la Comedia,* trans. Salvador Oliva and Manuel Espín (Barcelona: Ariel, 1978), 183–242.

CHAPTER 1. TROUBADOUR SELF-ABSORPTION

1. All citations from *La dama boba* are taken from the edition by Alonso Zamora Vicente (Madrid: Espasa-Calpe, 1946), and are listed by line number. English translations are my own.

2. Catherine Larson offers an insightful reading of this statement and the role of language in *La dama boba.* " 'Yo quiero hablar claro': Language as the Motivating Force of Lope's *La dama boba*" in *Things Done with Words: Speech Acts in Hispanic Drama,* ed. Elias L. Rivers, 29–39 (Newark, DE: Juan de la Cuesta, 1986).

3. For an analysis of Lope's parodic treatment of Petrarchan conventions and motifs, see Iris M. Zavala, "Burlas al amor," *Nueva Revista de Filología Hispánica* 29, no. 2 (1980): 367–402.

4. The case of Nise is undoubtedly more complex than it is presented here, as Nise herself is an intellectual who would be well acquainted with the rhetorical flourishes of Petrarchism. The point nonetheless is that Nise's alienation from male amatory discourse reflects her concern throughout the play for holding men accountable for their use of such language.

5. As James Holloway argues, Lope appears to espouse a Neoplatonic model of desire that reflects the currents of Renaissance writers like Marsilio Ficino and Giovanni Pico della Mirandola, despite his willingness to poke fun at its formal poetic expression in the Petrarchan tradition. "Lope's Neoplatonism: *La dama boba,*" *Bulletin of Hispanic Studies* 49 (1972): 236–55. While this Renaissance reconfiguration differs significantly from the medieval Neoplatonic tradition that influenced such figures as Augustine and Dante, the implicit argument of this chapter is that such differences do not extend to the underlying discursive paradigm of courtly love. In other words, Lope endorses a more "updated" model of Neoplatonic desire that nonetheless retains the implicit gender dynamics of the medieval (troubadour) tradition. While by no means do I dismiss as insignificant the differences between the

varieties of Neoplatonism at play during the Middle Ages and the Renaissance, I do find such differences to be peripheral to the discursive analysis of courtly discourse that is the focus of this chapter.

6. *Bernart de Ventadour, Troubadour du XIIe Siècle: Chansons d'Amour,* ed. Moshé Lazar (Paris: Librairie C. Klinksieck, 1966). All subsequent citations of Bernart de Ventadorn are taken from this edition and are listed parenthetically by line number. Unless otherwise noted, all translations are mine.

7. See introduction, n. 4.

8. Sarah Kay, "Rhetoric and Subjectivity in the Troubadour Lyric," in *The Troubadours and the Epic: Essays in Memory of W. Mary Hackett,* ed. Simon Gaunt and Linda Paterson (Coventry: University of Warwick, 1987).

9. Matilda Bruckner, "Fictions of Female Voice: The Women Troubadours," *Speculum* 67, no. 4 (1992): 866.

10. See introduction, n. 13.

11. E. Jane Burns, "The Man Behind the Lady in Troubadour Lyric," *Romance Notes* 25, no. 3 (1985): 254–70.

12. For some prominent examples of this general trend of mid- to late-twentieth century troubadour criticism, see E. Jane Burns as well as Simon Gaunt, "Poetry of Exclusion: A Feminist Reading of Some Troubadour Lyrics," *Modern Language Review* 85, no. 2 (1990): 310–29; and Linda Paterson, *Troubadours and Eloquence* (Oxford: Clarendon Press, 1975).

13. Kendrick, *The Game of Love: Troubadour Wordplay,* (Berkeley: University of California Press, 1988), 184.

14. An important contribution to our understanding of *cancionero* culture is the collection of essays edited by E. Michael Gerli and Julian Weiss, *Poetry at Court in Trastamaran Spain: From the* Cancionero de Baena *to the* Cancionero General (Tempe, AZ: Medieval & Renaissance Texts & Studies, 1998).

15. Roy Rosenstein and Jay Wolf, eds. and trans., *The Poetry of Cercamon and Jaufre Rudel.* (New York: Garland, 1983).

16. Ibid., 101.

17. All citations of Jaufre Rudel, including English translations, are taken from Rosenstein and Wolf, *The Poetry of Cercamon and Jaufre Rudel,* and are listed parenthetically by line number.

18. Translation from Bernard O'Donoghue, *The Courtly Love Tradition* (Manchester: Manchester University Press, 1982), 117.

19. Linda M. Paterson's *Troubadours and Eloquence* thoroughly treats this tendency in troubadour poetry (see above, n. 12).

20. Simon Gaunt, "Sexual Difference and the Metaphor of Language in a Troubadour Poem," *Modern Language Review* 83, no. 2 (1988): 304.

21. Meg Bogin, *The Women Troubadours* (New York: Norton, 1980), 56.

22. Burns, "Man Behind the Lady," 268.

23. Roger Boase, *The Troubadour Revival: A Study of Social Change and Traditionalism in Late Medieval Spain* (London: Routledge and Kegan Paul, 1978).

24. See especially Gerli and Weiss, as well as Ingrid Bahler and Katherine Gyékényesi Gatto, eds., *Of Kings and Poets: Cancionero Poetry of the Trastámara Courts* (New York: Peter Lang, 1992).

25. See esp. Bogin, Bruckner, "Fictions" (see above, n. 9) and "Na Castelloza, Trobairitz, and Troubadour Lyric" (*Romance Notes* 25, no. 3 [1985]: 239–53), as well

as Carol Nappholz, "(Re)locating Lost Trobairitz: The Anonymous Female Voice in Provençal Debate Poems," *Tenso* 7, no. 2 (1992): 125–41.

26. Bogin, *The Women Troubadours*, 72.

27. Eva Rosenn, "The Discourse of Power: The Lyrics of the Trobairitz," *Comitatus* 21 (1990): 1.

28. Mikhail Bakhtin, "Discourse in the Novel," in *The Dialogic Imagination: Four Essays by M.M. Bakhtin* (Austin: University of Texas Press, 1981).

29. Bruckner, "Fictions," 875.

30. Bogin, *The Women Troubadours*, 13.

31. Nappholz, "(Re)locatig," 130.

32. Ibid., 72.

33. Bruckner, "Fictions," 878.

34. The poem is cited from Bogin, *The Women Troubadours*, 114–17. My reading of this *tenso* is based upon Tilde Sankovitch's insightful analysis in *The Voice of the Trobairitz: Perspectives on the Women Troubadours*, ed. William D. Paden (Philadelphia: University of Pennsylvania Press, 1989), 183–96.

35. Bogin, *The Women Troubadours*, 116–17. All subsequent citations of *trobairitz* poetry and their English translations are taken from Bogin's anthology.

36. Rosenn, "The Discourse of Power," 10.

37. Dante Alighieri, *Il Purgatorio*, ed. and trans. John D. Sinclair (New York: Oxford University Press, 1961), 342. All subsequent citations and translations from the *Purgatorio* are from this dual-language edition.

38. Douglas Radcliff-Umstead, "Love in the Italian Sweet New Style," in *Innovation in Medieval Literature: Essays to the Memory of Alan Markman*, ed. Douglas Radcliff-Umstead (Pittsburgh: University of Pittsburgh Medieval Studies, 1971, 63–64.

39. Dante Alghieri, *Purgatorio*, 310–11.

40. Ibid.

41. Ibid.

42. Burns, "Man Behind the Lady," 268.

43. Guido Guinizelli, *Rime*, ed. Pietro Pelosi (Naples: Liguori, 1998). English translation taken from Radcliff-Umstead (see above, n. 32), 65.

44. Mark Musa, *Selections from the Canzoniere and Other Works* (Oxford: Oxford University Press, 1986), introduction, xvii.

45. Francesco Petrarca, *Il Canzoniere*, ed. G. A. Scartazzini (Leipzig: F. A. Brockhaus, 1883), 112.

46. Musa, *Selections*, xvii.

47. Ignacio Navarrete, *Orphans of Petrarch: Poetry and Theory in the Spanish Renaissance* (Berkeley: University of California Press, 1994). See above, introduction n. 12.

48. Iris M. Zavala, "Burlas al amor," *Nueva Revista de Filología Hispánica* 29, no. 2 (1980): 367–402, 374.

49. Elias J. Rivers, *Renaissance and Baroque Poetry of Spain* (New York: Dell, 1966), 38. All subsequent citations from Garcilaso are taken from this source, including English translations.

50. Ibid., 55.

51. Heiple's *Garcilaso and the Italian Renaissance* (see above, introduction n. 12) marks an important turning point in Garcilaso scholarship, away from the traditional biographical approach.

52. Zavala, "Burlas al amor," 375.

53. Alexander A. Parker, *The Philosophy of Love in Spanish Literature: 1480–1680* (Edinburgh: Edinburgh University Press, 1985), 12.

54. While Edward Friedman's observation is well taken that in drama "Each of the characters speaks in a voice which appears to be unmediated but which bears the marker of authorial intervention" ("Girl Gets Boy: A Note on the Value of Exchange in the *Comedia*," *Bulletin of the Comediantes* 39, no. 1 [1987]: 77), we may look beyond Lope's ostensible intention of subverting Petrarchan discourse to the nature of the Neoplatonic discourse with which he would replace it. In this play, the features of courtly discourse outlined thus far are held in common by the supplanted and its proposed alternative.

55. Friedman refers to the play's denouement as "a type of *enamoramiento ex machina* and a barrage of Neoplatonic imagery" (Ibid., 81).

56. Among the many critical assessments of Neoplatonic love in *La dama boba*, those offered by Emilie Bergmann, "*La dama boba*: temática folklórica y neoplatónica" in *Lope de Vega y los orígenes del teatro español*, ed. Manuel Criado de Val, 409–14 (Madrid: EDI-6, 1981); David Gómez-Torres, "*La dama boba* de Lope de Vega: Un caso de subversión aparente o el proceso de formación de un discurso monológico," *Bulletin of the Comediantes* 48, no. 2 (1996): 315–27; and James E. Holloway ("Lope's Neoplatonism") are especially insightful. Friedman, however, cautions that "a view of the play as dramatized neoplatonism . . . fails to consider the conventionalized and ultimately hypocritical use of these lofty ideals" ("Boy Gets Girl," 80).

57. Friedman, "Boy Gets Girl," 80.

58. Robert ter Horst, in "The True Mind of Marriage: Ironies of the Intellect in Lope's *La dama boba*," *Romanistisches Jahrbuch* 27 (1976): 347–63, treats the way in which men in *La dama boba* manipulate Neoplatonic love conventions for the sake of material gain.

59. See Bergmann for a thorough reading of the mirror motif in *La dama boba*.

60. Bergmann, *La dama boba*, 411.

61. Gómez-Torres also treats Finea's transformation as a primarily discursive one, from the "low" discourse of Carnival to a language he terms "serio," that is, more appropriate to her social station. His interpretation does not, however, consider the sources of Finea's "serious" or more decorous register, let alone its debt to the discourse of courtly love.

62. Catherine Connor, "Prolegomena to the 'Popular' in Early Modern Public Theater: Contesting Power in Lope and Shakespeare," in *The Golden Age Comedia: Text, Theory, and Performance*, ed. Charles Ganelin and Howard Mancing, 262–75 (West Lafayette, IN: Purdue University Press, 1994) discusses the applicability of a neo-historical approach to the *Comedia* that makes use of Foucault's work regarding power and Bakhtin's notions of dialogism and the carnivalesque. Particularly pertinent to my argument of the function of ideolect in *La dama boba* is her emphasis on ideology as a process (p. 269).

63. This dialogical relationship with Lope's patriarchal model, noted here in reference to the action and discursive negotiation within the play itself, is echoed in more general terms by Teresa Soufas ("María de Zayas's [Un]Conventional Play, *La traición en la amistad*," in Ganelin and Mancing, 148–64), who considers Zayas's purpose to be the offering of "dialectical responses to the established theatrical conventions" of the *Comedia* (p. 148).

64. This treatment of courtly discourse in the case of Zayas's play parallels Soufas's

more general assessment of the satirical nature of *La traición en la amistad:* "She communicates a cynical regard for the literary stereotypes that make the process of falling in love and devoting oneself to a beloved simply part of a predictable, cyclical game of insincerity and trickery whose end is the standard pairings of often mismatched couples in the last act" ("María de Zayas's [Un]Conventional Play," 149).

65. All citations of *La traición en la amistad,* including English translations, are taken from María de Zayas y Sotomayor, *La traición en la amistad/Friendship Betrayed,* ed. Valerie Hegstrom and trans. Catherine Larson (Lewisburg: Bucknell University Press, 1999), and are listed by line number.

66. Two cogent arguments to this effect may be found in Teresa Soufas, "María de Zayas's [Un]Conventional Play," and Constance Wilkins, "Subversion through Comedy? Two Plays by Sor Juana Inés de la Cruz and María de Zayas," in *The Perception of Women in Spanish Theater of the Golden Age,* ed. Anita K. Stoll and Dawn L. Smith, 107–20 (Lewisburg: Bucknell University Press, 1991).

67. Mary Gaylord-Randel offers an insightful analysis of the patriarchal construct of decorum and its implications for women in the *Comedia* in " 'Las damas no desdigan su nombre': decoro femenino y lenguaje en el *Arte nuevo y La dama boba,*" in *Justina: Homenaje a Justina Ruiz de Conde en su ochenta cumpleaños,* ed. Elena Gascon-Vera, 71–81 (Erie: ALDEEU, 1992).

68. Alexander A. Parker, "The Approach to the Spanish Drama of the Golden Age," *The Tulane Drama Review* 4, no. 1 (1959): 42–59, offers a seminal discussion of the notion of poetic justice in the *Comedia.* "Spanish dramatic plots are constructed on the principle of poetic justice" (45). Such an approach may seem outdated and simplistic in light of the myriad theoretical approaches applied to the *Comedia* since Parker's article was published, but the thematic presence of poetic justice is duly noted.

69. Matthew Stroud, in a study that relates *La traición en la amistad* to Zayas's prose fiction, finds the sense of closure offered in the denouement dissatisfying: "Love, Friendship, and Deceit in *La traición en la amistad,* by María de Zayas," *Neophilologus* 69 (1985): 539–47.

70. Lisa Vollendorf, "The Future of Early Modern Women's Studies: The Case of Same-Sex Friendship and Desire in Zayas and Carvajal," *Arizona Journal of Hispanic Cultural Studies* 4 (2000): 265–84, considers Zayas's representation of this friendship as an exploration of homosocial desire, an alternative to the heterosexual desire that proves to be so problematic in the play.

71. Wilkins explains the solidarity between women in Zayas's play as follows: "The women's actions in support of each other and in condemnation of Fenisa constitute a forceful affirmation of female community" (115).

72. Wilkins, "Subversion through Comedy," 115.

CHAPTER 2. DUTY AND DESIRE

1. Wardropper's seminal article "La comedia española del siglo de oro" (see introduction, n. 14) examines this issue and its implications for female characters. In Golden Age comedy, he argues, the agency of the female individual works subversively against the patriarchal society that would contain her. Although I am wary of the supposition of a "deep structure" in the *Comedia,* Wardropper's analysis is crit-

ical for suggesting a way to read Spain's popular comedy that deals with its relationship to the prevailing ideology of the period.

2. One might also add to this list of texts the so-called honor plays of Calderón, which include *A secreto agravio, secreta venganza, El médico de su honra*, and *El pintor de su deshonra*. William C. McCrary, "The Theatricality of Male Orientation in the *Comedia*," in *Studies in Honor of William C. McCrary*, ed. Robert Fiore and Everett W. Hesse, 27–33 (Lincoln, NE: Society of Spanish and Spanish-American Studies, 1978), takes the first of these as exemplary of Calderón's use of tragedy to "theatricalize males becoming men" (32), an assessment which underscores the phallocentrism intrinsic to how honor is treated in traditional *Comedia* scholarship. Another such "standard" assessment is offered by Frank P. Casa in "Honor and the Wife-Killers of Calderón," *Bulletin of the Comediantes* 29 (1977): 6–23, in which once again the emphasis is placed on the husbands of these conflicts, not the wives. A notable reversal of this trend is Yvonne Yarbo Bejarano, *Feminism and the Honor Plays of Lope de Vega* (West Lafayette, IN: Purdue University Press, 1994), which shifts the focus from the husbands of such conflicts to the broader issues of gender and sexuality that are engaged in Lope's honor plays.

3. Both Teresa Soufas ("María de Zayas's [Un]Conventional Play") and Matthew D. Stroud, "Social-Comic Anagnorisis in *La dama duende*," *Bulletin of the Comediantes* 29 (1977): 96–102, point to the dubious future that such a marriage arrangement suggests.

4. Joan Ferrante offers a thorough analysis of this issue in medieval romance in "The Conflicts of Lyric Conventions and Romance Form," in *In Pursuit of Perfection: Courtly Love in Medieval Literature*, ed. Joan Ferrante and George Economou, 135–73 (Port Washington, NY: Kennikat, 1975). Her particular emphasis is on the French *roman* dealing with classical subject matter.

5. Wardropper ("La comedia española del Siglo de Oro," 183–242) explains this emphasis on community succinctly: "Un individuo no puede amar, odiar o despreciar a otro sin despertar el interés de una sociedad que tiene ideas preconcebidas sobre cómo deben obrar los dos. La religión, la ley, la costumbre y el prejuicio actúan todos ellos como normas sociales; desviarse de estas normas es incurrir en la desaprobación—y algunas veces en el castigo—de la sociedad" (225). Earlier in the essay he connects such a procommunity stance with the standard marriage couplings that typically end the action of early modern Spanish comedy: "quién vence al final no es la joven enamorada, sino la sociedad" (224).

6. It is worth noting here that many scholars make a distinction that I have chosen to omit in this study, between the "courtly love" of the troubadours and Andreas Cappellanus and the "chivalric love" of contemporary romance narrative. In particular, the former's explicit exclusion of marriage is seen at odds with the fact that many romance protagonists, from Erec to Amadís, do not pursue a clandestine relationship with their lady and often are married to their objects of desire. In my view, the distinction has little to do with the discursive model of courtly love, at least in terms of its positioning of self-absorbed male as subject and passive female as object. As this chapter argues, the larger issue of the troubadours' discursive legacy should not be delimited to those channels in which the explicit laundry-list of "requirements" outlined by Cappellanus are followed.

7. O'Connor, *Love in the 'Corral,'* 4.

8. Irving P. Rothberg discusses the relationship between Lope de Vega and the two classical dramatists who most influenced his work, Plautus and Terence. "Algo

más sobre Plauto, Terencio y Lope, " in *Lope de Vega y los orígenes del teatro español,* ed. Manuel Criado de Val, 61–65 (Madrid: EDI-6, 1981).

9. All original citations of *Erec et Enide* are from Jean-Marie Fritz's edition (Paris: Le Livre de Poche, 1992).

10. All translations of *Erec et Enide* are from D. D. R. Owen, ed. and trans., *Arthurian Romances* (London: J. M. Dent, 1993).

11. Ferrante, "The Conflicts of Lyric Conventions," 147.

12. Ibid., 165.

13. Anita Benaim Lasry, "The Ideal Heroine in Medieval Romances: A Quest for a Paradigm," *Romance Quarterly* 32, no.3 (1985): 227.

14. Eva Rosenn, "The Discourse of Power: The Lyrics of the Trobairitz." *Comitatus* 21 (1990): 227.

15. Ibid., 228.

16. All original citations from *Eliduc* are from Glyn Burgess's edition of Marie de France's *Lais* (London: Bristol Classical Press, 1995).

17. All translations of "Eliduc" are from Glyn Burgess and Keith Busby's edition and translation of *The Lais of Marie de France* (London: Penguin, 1986).

18. For a current assessment of the *novela sentimental* tradition, see Gerli and Gwara's edited collection of essays entitled *Studies on the Spanish Sentimental Romance (1440–1550): Redefining a Genre* (London: Tamesis, 1997).

19. The inexhaustible list of critical voices that have treated the code of honor in the *Comedia* cannot be enumerated here. The traditional "debate" among critics dealing with Calderón's treatment of honor has focused on whether or not he valued and approved of it, as well as on whether the representation of honor in Calderonian drama and in the *Comedia* more generally reflects the actual social norms, customs, and values of seventeenth-century Spain, or whether honor instead functions as a sensationalistic theatrical convention. The latter suggestion is substantiated by Lope de Vega's explanation in the *Arte nuevo* that cases of honor are crowd-pleasers. Important contributions to this debate include Frank P. Casa, "Honor and the Wife-Killers of Calderon," *Bulletin of the Comediantes* 29 (1977): 6–23; Peter Dunn, "Honour and the Christian Background in Calderon," *Bulletin of Hispanic Studies* 37 (1960): 75–105; Edwin Honig, *Calderon and the Seizures of Honor* (Cambridge: Harvard University Press, 1972); C. A. Jones, "Honor in Spanish Golden Age Drama: Its Relation to Real Life and Morals," *Bulletin of Hispanic Studies* 35 (1958): 199–210; Melveena McKendrick, "Honour/Vengeance in the Spanish 'Comedia': A Case of Mimetic Transference?" *Modern Language Review* 79, no. 2 (1984): 313–35; and A. A. Parker, "On Edwin Honig's *Calderon and the Seizures of Honor,*" *Bulletin of the Comediantes* 26 (1974): 68–71. Melveena McKendrick's more recent reflections on the issue may be found in "Communicating the Past" (Bass and Greer, 29–38).

20. While I do not pretend to do justice to the complexity of *Celestina*'s treatment of courtly desire in the present study, two important representatives of this field of study are A. D. Deyermond's *The Petrarchan Sources of La Celestina* (Oxford: Oxford University Press, 1961) and Dorothy Sherman Severin's *Tragicomedy and Novelistic Discourse in Celestina* (Cambridge: Cambridge University Press, 1989).

21. Alexander A. Parker discusses the abstract nature of neoplatonism and its difficult integration into Golden Age narrative and drama in *The Philosophy of Love in Spanish Literature: 1480–1680* (Edinburgh: Edinburgh University Press, 1985).

22. O'Connor, *Love in the 'Corral',* 7.

23. Ibid., 16.

24. Arthur Holmberg gives a convincing reading of the role that honor plays in *La dama duende,* although not in terms of its conflict with courtly discourse, in "Variaciones sobre el tema del honor en *La dama duende* de Calderón" in *Actas del Congreso Internacional sobre Calderón y el teatro español del siglo de oro,* ed. Luciano García Lorenzo, 913–23 (Madrid: Consejo Superior de Investigaciones Científicas, 1983). He does consider it along Freudian lines, as a social code that may serve as a buffer for the individual whose primitive desires would otherwise disrupt the community. This is especially true in the case of Luis, whom he sees as "ejemplo de necesidad cultural del código del honor como freno a la agresividad instintiva" (917). See also Edwin Honig, *Calderón and the Seizures of Honor* (Cambridge: Harvard University Press, 1972), who considers the play a triumph of love over honor (34).

25. See Wardropper, "La comedia española del Siglo de Oro," 221–32.

26. Thomas O'Connor sees honor as a positive social force asking of men that they aspire to a heroic masculine ideal in *Love in the Corral: Conjugal Spirituality and Antitheatrical Polemic in Early Modern Spain* (New York: Peter Lang, 2000). What he does not mention is the feminine corollary, that honor prescribes an essentially defensive posture for women to protect and preserve chastity and fidelity. Male honor is a tangible objective, while female honor is an absence of transgression, an intrinsically defensive posture. Or, as Mary Gaylord-Randel puts it: "La mujer es cuna y sepultura del honor" [Woman is the cradle and grave of honor] ("Amor y honor a través del espejo" in *Actas del Congreso Internacional sobre Calderón y el teatro español del siglo de oro,* ed. Luciano García Lorenzo, 869–79 [Madrid: Consejo Superior de Investigaciones Científicas, 1983], (871).

27. All citations from *La dama duende* are taken from the edition prepared by Pilar Diez y Jiménez de Castellanos (Madrid: Ebro, 1968) and are listed by line number. All English translations are mine.

28. Margaret Rich Greer, "The (Self) Representation of Control in *La dama duende*" in *Golden Age Comedia: Text, Theory, and Performance,* ed. Charles Ganelin and Howard Mancing (West Lafayette, IN: Purdue University Press, 1994), 103.

29. A thorough treatment of the issue is offered by Frederick de Armas in *The Invisible Mistress: Aspects of Feminism and Fantasy in the Golden Age* (Charlottesville, VA: Biblioteca Siglo de Oro, 1976).

30. Stroud's comments on Manuel's personal sense of honor are worth citing: "It is not Angela he cares about; it is the image of his honor. When he gives her his hand in marriage, it is true that he is doing the noble, socially dignifying (if individually troublesome) thing to do, but it is nonetheless true that his duty in this case, as with most of Manuel's actions, is marked by an acute bloodlessness and lack of conviction. He does the correct thing but only by seeing that any other course of action would cause him to lose that ultimate bloodless, brittle commodity, honor" ("Social-Comic Anagnorisis in *La dama duende,*" 101).

31. Critical interest in *La firmeza en la ausencia* is only a recent phenomenon in comparison to that paid to the male-authored *Comedia* canon. In formulating my own analysis of the play I have found particularly useful three pieces by Teresa Soufas: "Regarding the Woman's Response: Leonor de la Cueva y Silva's *La firmeza en la ausencia*" *Romance Language Annual* 1 (1989): 625–30; "The Absence of Desire in Leonor de la Cueva's *La firmeza en la ausencia*" in *Gender, Identity, and Representation in Spain's Golden Age,* ed. Anita K. Stoll and Dawn L. Smith, 142–55 (Lewisburg: Bucknell University Press, 2000); and "Bodies of Authority" (*Dramas of Distinction,* 37–69), as well as two articles by Sharon Voros: "Armesinda's Dream: Leonor de la Cueva's

Challenge to the Patriarchy in *La firmeza en la ausencia*," *Monographic Review* 13 (1997): 74–86; and "Fashioning Feminine Wit in María de Zayas, Ana Caro, and Leonor de la Cueva" in *Gender, Identity, and Representation in Spain's Golden Age,* ed. Anita K. Stoll and Dawn L. Smith, 156–77. A broader discussion of issues intrinsic to the study of plays by Golden Age women is offered by Catherine Larson in "Valor Judgments, or Women Writers and the *Comedia*" in *Brave New Words: Studies in Spanish Golden Age Literature,* ed. Edward Friedman and Catherine Larson, 259–70 (New Orleans: University Press of the South, 1996).

32. In "You Can't Always Get What You Want: Gender, Voice, and Identity in Women-Authored *Comedias*" in *Gender, Identity, and Representation in Spain's Golden Age,* ed. Anita K. Stoll and Dawn L. Smith, 127–41, Catherine Larson suggests the same subtlety with which women dramatists of the Golden Age challenge patriarchal conventions: "identity, gender and voice unite in a product that closely resembles those authored by men but that also advances something slightly different, slightly provocative, slightly radical" (135).

33. Despite this difference, the two men do share, according to Soufas, the fact that they are "lovers whose own amorous feelings become more compelling than the well-being of the woman they desire" ("Regarding the Woman's Response," 626).

34. All citations of *La firmeza en la ausencia* are taken from Teresa Soufas, ed., *Women's Acts: Plays by Women Dramatists of Spain's Golden Age* (Lexington: University Press of Kentucky, 1997), 198–224, and are indicated by line number. English translations are mine.

35. "In this play, Cueva reveals male discourse to be the medium of lies and mistrust" (Soufas, "Regarding the Woman's Response," 627).

36. In "The Absence of Desire," Soufas relates Filiberto's desire for Armesinda to contemporary Neoplatonic theories of love, especially that of Ficino. According to this philosophical model, desire is inspired by lack—which would explain the obsessive passion of the king and its continual augmentation over the course of the play. With each instance of rejection, Filiberto's passion intensifies.

37. Soufas also sees an economic element to this stereotype, that in seventeenth-century Spain a woman was the "objectified commodity bought by the wealthiest and highest bidder" ("The Absence of Desire," 145).

38. "Perhaps most interesting, the focus of attention is clearly on the woman, Armesinda, and the ways in which she describes and defines herself, analyzes her various courses of action (escape, suicide, the convent, etc.), and insists on maintaining her fidelity, even in her dreams; in this manner, Cueva offers a stark contrast with the majority of plays authored by men, in which the spotlight is clearly on how the male decides to respond to the suspected infidelity of his mate" (Larson, "You Can't Always Get What You Want," 136).

39. Cueva's representation of Armesinda's "subjectivity" is critical to the readings of the play offered by both Soufas and Voros. "What Cueva offers in her drama, however, is a more fully developed female subjectivity through her character's critical and reflective intellectual engagement of internal and external forces that allows her to articulate an effective alternative to the patriarchal discourse" (Soufas, "Regarding the Woman's Response," 626).

40. In making this point I take exception to Soufas's statement that "Even though she believes that he is no longer eligible to marry her, she remains resolute in her devotion to the man she loves" ("Regarding the Woman's Response," 625–26). Armesinda's

words cited after this note support the notion that she in fact disdains her purportedly unfaithful lover.

41. See Soufas, "Bodies of Authority," 37–69 in *Dramas of Distinction.*

CHAPTER 3. DISCURSIVE INTERPLAY

1. In *How to Do Things with Words* (Cambridge: Harvard University Press, 1962), J. L. Austin defines performative speech acts as those which accomplish a transaction in their very utterence; for example, "I do" during a religious or legal wedding ceremony (pp. 5–7, cf. Elias L. Rivers, ed. "The *Comedia* as Discursive Action" in *Studies in Honor of Bruce W. Wardropper,* 250 [Newark, DE: Juan de la Cuesta, 1989]). Manuel offers his hand in marriage to Angela with Luis as witness, a performative speech act that satisfies the brother's concerns for Angela's honor (and by extension, that of her family).

2. George Mariscal, *Contradictory Subjects: Quevedo, Cervantes, and Seventeenth-Century Spanish Culture.* Ithaca: Cornell University Press, 1991, p. 3.

3. *Poetics,* cf. Keir Elam, *Shakespeare's Universe of Discourse: Language-Games in the Comedies* (Cambridge: Cambridge University Press, 1984), 6.

4. Cf. O'Connor, *Love in the "Corral",* 30.

5. While this general principle of Foucault's thinking applies to many of his texts, see especially *Surveiller et punir* (Paris: Gallimard, 1975) and *Language, Countermemory, Practice* (Ithaca: Cornell University Press, 1977).

6. The association of speech and behavior implicit in the notion of decorum was formally codified in Castiglione's *Cortegiano.*

7. The first half of Thomas O'Connor's *Love in the "Corral,"* entitled "Social Discourse on the *Comedia,*" treats this polemic extensively. It is the primary source for my summary of the debate. It should be noted, however, that José Antonio Maravall's *Teatro y literatura en la sociedad barroca* (Madrid: Seminarios y Ediciones, 1972) essentially argues for an interpretation of Spanish Golden Age theater as didactic by considering it a propagandistic medium for the prevailing ideology of Church and State. The most extensive source of the public documents through which this debate was waged is Emilio Cotarelo y Mori's *Bibliografía de las controversias sobre la licitud del teatro en España* (Madrid: Revista de Archivos, Bibliotecas y Museos, 1904).

8. O'Connor, *Love in the "Corral,"* 66.

9. Ibid., 52.

10. Ibid., 47.

11. O'Connor's *Love in the "Corral"* also examines at length the presence and function of professional dramatists and actors within some institutional structures of the Church itself, including charitable hospitals administered by the clergy.

12. Description of literary discourse as "low" or "high" is ultimately attributable to classical Greece and was reformulated by Augustine, who establishes a tripartite (low, middle, and high) division of style in the *De doctrina Christiana.* For a thorough treatment of Augustine's impact on biblical exegesis and on literary interpretation and composition in general, see Sarah Spence's *Rhetorics of Reason and Desire: Virgil, Augustine, and the Troubadours* (Ithaca: Cornell University Press, 1988).

13. The bibliography dealing with Cervantes and Spanish Golden Age theater is immense. I would especially suggest Jean Canavaggio's "Cervantes dramaturgo," in

Rileggere Cervantes: Antologia della Critica Recente, ed. Mariarosa Scaramuzza-Vidoni, 167–82 (Milan: LED, 1994); and two articles by Anthony Close, "Cervantes' Arte Nuevo de Hazer Fábulas Cómicas en Este Tiempo" *Cervantes* 2, no. 1 (1982): 3–22; and "Characterization and Dialogue in Cervantes's 'Comedias en prosa'" *Modern Language Review* 76, no. 2 (1981): 338–56.

14. It should be clarified that Boccaccio's ideological elusiveness is not without precedent. Indeed many medieval romance narratives, and especially the works of Chaucer, exhibit what Rosemarie P. McGerr terms a "resistance to closure" in *Chaucer's Open Books: Resistance to Clousure in Medieval Discourse* (Gainesville: University Press of Florida, 1998). Laura Kendrick attributes a similar tendency to subvert traditional medieval conventions of closure in troubadour poetry in *The Game of Love: Troubadour Wordplay* (Berkeley: University of California Press, 1988); and Matilda Bruckner makes a similar point regarding Chrétien's romances in "*An Interpreter's Dilemma: Why Are There So Many Interpretations of Chrétien's Chevalier de la charrette?*" *Romance Philology* 40, no. 2 (1986): 159–80. What is different with Boccaccio, and what therefore leads me to treat him as the beginning of this process, is the use of varied modes of literary and nonliterary discourse to subvert fixed notions of interpretation. The polyphonic secular lyric poetry beginning in the thirteenth century, and some examples of Latin satire dating back as early as the twelfth century, also pave the way for Boccaccio's discursive cacophony.

15. It should be noted that this open-endedness of Boccaccio's novelle does not exclude him from the observation made in the first chapter, namely that all manifestations of courtly discourse are ultimately gender-inflected. While the *Decameron* does take up the issue of a female readership, it does so from the pen of a male writer, despite the innovative employment of female narrators within the collection. A study of the *Decameron* in comparison with a female-authored collection of *novelle* (such as Margarite de Navarre's *Heptameron*), while not feasible within the parameters of this study, would help to clarify this point.

16. Kendrick, *The Game of Love,* 6.

17. Ibid., 21–22.

18. Ibid., 17–19.

19. Gregory L. Lucente, "Lyric Tradition and the Desires of Absence: Rudel, Dante, and Michelangelo," *Canadian Review of Comparative Literature* 10, no. 3 (1983): 307.

20. For an explanation of the debate over the epistle's authenticity see Robert Hollander, *Dante's Epistle to Cangrande.* Ann Arbor: University of Michigan Press, 1993.

21. Guillaume de Lorris and Jean de Meun, *Le roman de la rose,* ed. Daniel Poiron (Paris: Garnier-Flammarion, 1974), 44. All subsequent citations are from this edition. English translation is taken from Harry W. Robbins (New York: E. P. Dutton, 1962), 4. All subsequent tranlations are from this edition.

22. de Lorris and de Meun, *Le roman,* 572.

23. Robbins (trans.), *The Romance of the Rose,* 462.

24. De Lorris and de Meun, 144–216.

25. Ibid.

26. Ibid., 113–14; translation from Robbins, 64.

27. Ibid., 183; 123.

28. Ibid., 155; 103.

29. Ibid., 571; 461.

30. All citations from the *Inferno* in this chapter are taken from the 1988 edition

of the *Divina Commedia* edited by Emilio Pasquini and Antonio Quaglio (Milan: Garzanti, 1988). English translations are mine.

31. Ibid., 23.

32. Ibid., 52.

33. Ibid., pp.51–52.

34. Lucente, "Lyric Tradition," 315.

35. Ibid., 316.

36. See book 1 of *On Christian Doctrine*, trans. D. W. Robertson (New York: Liberal Arts Press, 1958).

37. All original citations from the *Decameron* are from the 1985 edition edited by Vittore Branca (Milan: A. Mondadori, 1985).

38. All English translations from the *Decameron* are from Mark Musa and Peter Bondanella (New York: Penguin, 1982).

39. See Spence, *Rhetorics of Reason and Desire*, for an effective presentation of this argument.

40. Although Juan Ruiz's *Libro de buen amor* is roughly contemporary to Boccaccio, it was only discovered and put into circulation centuries later. Its distinctive method of discursive cross-fertilization and interpretive open-endedness suggests that further research would help us better understand the role of the *Decameron*'s innovations in Spain.

41. For a thorough treatment of how Cervantes includes the voices and arguments of contemporary critics, see especially Alban K. Forcione's *Cervantes, Aristotle, and the Persiles* (Princeton: Princeton University Press, 1970) and E. C. Riley's *Cervantes's Theory of the Novel* (Oxford: Clarendon Press, 1962).

42. All Spanish citations from the *Quijote* are from the 1998 edition edited by Salvador Fajardo and James A. Parr (Asheville, NC: Pegasus, 1998).

43. English translations of the *Quijote* are from Burton Raffel's 1995 translation (New York: Norton, 1995).

44. For an explanation of Don Quijote's idealization, see Anthony Close, *The Romantic Approach to Don Quixote: A Critical History of Quixote Criticism* (Cambridge University Press, 1977); and James Fernández, "The Bonds of Patrimony: Cervantes and the New World," *PMLA* 109, no. 5 (1994): 969–86.

45. Cide Hamete Benengeli is first introduced in chapter 8 of the 1605 installment of *Don Quijote*, at which point his unreliability as a narrator and his ethnicity are directly associated with one another. The seminal study on the *Quijote*'s narrative and narratological complexity remains James A. Parr's *Don Quixote: An Anatomy of Subversive Discourse* (Newark, DE: Juan de la Cuesta, 1988).

46. The term "moral perspectivism" is taken from Oscar Kenshur, "Skepticism and the Form of the *Quijote*," *Dispositio* 2 (1977): 254–61. Donald R. Wehrs's term "fideistic skepticism" ("Sterne, Cervantes, Montaigne: Fideistic Skepticism and the Rhetoric of Desire" *Comparative Literature Studies* 25, no. 3 [1988]: 127–50), is employed to argue that the novel's "generic equipollence" is in fact grounded in the philosophical tradition of Renaissance Humanism and especially Erasmus, who converted the arguments of the classical Greek skeptics into a defense of religious faith. We may certainly agree that if Cervantes is ideologically "slippery" and noncommittal, it is only in literary terms—not in religious terms.

47. An excellent, if somewhat dated, assessment of the vast critical attention paid to Dulcinea is offered by Javier Herrero in "Dulcinea and her Critics," *Bulletin of the Cervantes Society of America* 2, no. 1, (1982): 23–42.

48. See Margaret Doody's *The True Story of the Novel* (New Brunswick, NJ: Rutgers University Press, 1996).

49. *Don Quijote,* part I, chapter 25.

50. The exchange is a common type of discursive collision and metadiscursive commentary appearing throughout the *Quijote.* The orally transmitted story of Marcela ("in little villages like these everything is chewed over and people whisper about everything" (58), discursively rooted in folklore, comes into contact with Don Quijote's learned and authoritarian discourse. An overview of folklore's function in the novel is given by Mac E. Berrick, "The Form and Function of Folktales in *Don Quijote," Journal of Medieval and Renaissance Studies* 6, no. 1 (1976): 101–38.

51. Bruckner, "Fictions," 13.

52. While the present study does not allow for an extensive treatment of Cervantes's other works, it is well worth noting that critics have argued a similar point about the *Novelas ejemplares.* Nicholas Spadaccini and Jenaro Talens offer the following explanation in "Cervantes and the Dialogic World" in *Cervantes's Exemplary Novels and the Adventure of Writing,* ed. Michael Nerlich and Nicholas Spadaccini, 205–45 (Minneapolis, MN: Prisma House, 1989): "The notion of exemplarity inscribed (and gathered) by the reader in Cervantes's *novelas* would seem to be tied to two interrelated factors: a new way of writing fiction in the Castilian language and the idea that meaning ultimately depends on the role assumed by the reader in its construction . . . The burden of shaping or harvesting the 'provecho' is placed on the discerning eye ('bien mirar') of the receiver whose imagination becomes the very instrument for turning an activity—reading—that was traditionally associated with idleness, leisure and passivity into a productive enterprise connected to an exploration of the self in the world" (220). See also Ruth El Saffar's *Novel to Romance: A Study of Cervantes' Novelas ejemplares.* Baltimore: Johns Hopkins University Press, 1974.

53. Aristotle's *Poetics* establishes this generic division: tragedy treats "high" matters and comedy treats "low" ones. More specifically, in chapter 2 he makes this high/low distinction in terms of character. Tragedy is an imitation of men of a "higher type" and comedy is an imitation of men of a "lower type." It is explicitly noted by Aristotle that such a distinction is made in terms of moral character: "for moral character mainly answers to these divisions, goodness and badness being the distinguishing marks of moral differences" (cf. Bernard F. Dukore, *Dramatic Theory and Criticism: Greeks to Grotowski* [Orlando, FL: Harcourt Brace & Co., 1974], 32). All of the generic differences between tragedy and comedy follow from this fundamental distinction, as "Comedy aims at representing men as worse, Tragedy as better than in actual life" (33). All subsequent citations from Aristotle's *Poetics* are from this source. See James Parr, *'Don Quixote': An Anatomy of Subversive Discourse* (Newark, DE: Juan de la Cuesta, 1988), for an extended discussion of the tragic/comic duality as it pertains to the *Comedia.*

54. Roger Chartier makes a similar point in reference to the French classical theater of the seventeenth century in *Forms and Meanings: Texts, Performances, and Audiences from Codex to Computer* (Philadelphia: University of Pennsylvania Press, 1993). Specifically his "thick description" of multiple performance contexts for Molière's *George Dandin* emphasizes that in a performance before the courtly audience of Versailles, complete with dances and one-act pastoral dialogues, the play mocked the insubordination of the title character for having married above his station. For the popular (and paying) urban audience of Paris, however, *Dandin* was a character with whom the audience might identify, a man outside of the nobility but wealthy. In

"Hacia una teoría sociocultural del espectador aurisecular" (*El texto puesto en escena: estudios sobre la Comedia del Siglo de Oro en honor a Everett W. Hesse,* ed. Bárbara Mujica and Anita K. Stoll, 3–13 [London: Tamesis, 2000]), Catherine Connor explores the implications of reception as a function of the individual's social position in the context of the *Comedia.*

55. My earlier discussion of the polemic surrounding the licitness of the public theater, drawn heavily from O'Connor's *Love in the "Corral,"* indicates this disagreement in early modern Spain. Evidence of a similar dispute among twentieth century *Comedia* scholars can be seen in Maravall's argument for a reading of the *Comedia* as a propagandistic affirmation of Counter Reformation ideology, in contrast to the assertion by Wardropper ("La comedia española") that the *comedia nueva* is ideologically subversive. The more recent readings of the *Comedia* offered by Cascardi and Gilbert-Santamaría suggest that Maravall's "propagandistic" reading of the tradition still resonates with critics today.

56. A predictable disagreement regarding the play's message, especially in terms of what moral and lesson it offers, still occupies critics today. See Bruce W. Wardropper's "The Criticism of the Spanish Comedia: *El caballero de Olmedo* as Object Lesson" in *Hispanic Studies in Honor of Edmund de Chasca,* 177–96 (Iowa City: University of Iowa Press, 1972).

57. The lines appear just before Alonso's murder, sung by an anonymous passerby: "Que de noche le mataron / al caballero, / la gala de Medina, / la flor de Olmedo" (lines 2371–75) [At night they killed the gentleman, the champion of Medina, the flower of Olmedo]. Joseph Pérez's introduction to the Castalia edition of the play (Madrid: Castalia, 1983) explains the historical origins of the legend and its widespread dissemination throughout popular Spanish culture in the latter part of the sixteenth century (7–13).

58. A standard explanation of the Fabia-Celestina relationship is offered by J. Oliver Asín in "Más reminiscencias de *La Celestina* en el teatro de Lope," *Revista de Filología Española* 15 (1928): 67–74.

59. All citations of *El caballero de Olmedo* are taken from the edition edited by Joseph Pérez (Madrid: Castalia, 1983) and are listed by line number. English translations are mine.

60. See the chapter entitled "The Meaning of *Conformidad*" in *Love in the "Corral,"* 225–82.

61. This play does have a long critical history of being read in such terms, but I suspect that such crtitcs' own horizons of expectations regarding tragedy are the cause for such an interpretation. Alonso's death is indeed puzzling and unsettling, given the decidedly nontragic trajectory of the plot being outlined here, and a tempting line of interpretation is to take the murder as cause to retroactively apply the problematic notion of *hamartia* (the so-called "tragic flaw" taken from Aristotle's *Poetics*) to his character and behavior in the first two acts. If the flawed character of Alonso was killed in an act of poetic justice, Rodrigo's condemnation by the king (the ultimate earthly arbiter of justice) in the final scene would make little sense: the monarch's judgment implies wrongdoing on Rodrigo's part, but the application of *hamartia* would imply that the murder is just. Whether one accepts such a reading or not, the presence of comic elements in the play makes it clear that *El caballero de Olmedo* is not a traditional Aristotelian tragedy, nor is it so easily reconciled to the notions of catharsis and *hamartia* as is, for example, Shakespearean tragedy. For an example of what may be called a "Shakespearean" reading of the play, see John G.

Weiger's "Don Alonso's Tragic Flaw in *El caballero de Olmedo,*" *Hispanic Journal* 7, no. 1 (1985): 41–49; Alice E. Schafer's "Fate versus Responsibility in Lope's *El caballero de Olmedo,*" *Revista Canadiense de Estudios Hispánicos* 3 (1978): 26–39; and Peter W. Evans's "Alonso's Cowardice: Ambiguities of Perspective in *El caballero de Olmedo,*" *Modern Language Review* 78, no. 1 (1983): 68–78. For a more theoretically current reading of the play that questions such a traditional line of interpretation, see Friedman's "Theater Semiotics and Lope de Vega's *El caballero de Olmedo.*"

62. Friedman, "Theater Semiotics," 76.

63. Ibid.

64. All citations of Sor Juana are from her collected works, *Obras completas,* ed. Francisco Monterde (México: Porrúa, 1969). English translations are mine.

65. Despite this general recognition by critics, however, emphasis is generally placed on how Sor Juana departs from the male-authored model. Examples of such a tendency can be seen in the scholarship on Sor Juana done by Stephanie Merrim and Wilkins.

66. Angel Julián Valbuena-Briones, "La particularidad de *Los empeños de una casa,* de Sor Juana Inés de la Cruz, ante la tradición calderoniana," *Hispanic Journal* 18, no. 1 (1997): 166.

67. Stephanie Merrim, *Early Modern Women's Writing and Sor Juana Inés de la Cruz* (Nashville: Vanderbilt University Press, 1999).

68. A thorough treatment of the role of courtly love in Sor Juana's lyric poetry can be found in Octavio Paz's *Sor Juana Inés de la Cruz: o las trampas de la fe* (Mexico: Fondo de Cultura, 1977).

69. In "Sor Juana Inés de la Cruz: Amor y Cortesanía," *Colonial Latin American Review* 4, no. 2 (1995): 85–100, José Pascual Buxó cites Castiglione's *Il Cortegiano* as representative of the mileu in which Sor Juana received her literary education, and his reading of both *Los empeños* and her love poetry suggests that her representation of love is inseparably intertwined with seventeenth-century courtly culture and all the ideological implications connoted by its "culto de amor." He explains that her participation in this discursive tradition is the expression of her "competencia cultural, que lo liga a una tradición a la vez ideológica y formal, esto es, de conocimientos modelizados del mundo y de expresión igualmente modelizada de tales conocimientos" (86).

70. The terms *mujer esquiva* (a woman who shuns love altogether) and *mujer varonil* (literally a "manly woman," or a woman who assumes male attributes or behavior, including the conventional cross-dressed woman) were originally coined by Melveena McKendrick in *Woman and Society of the Spanish Golden Age: A Study of the Mujer varonil* (Cambridge: Cambridge University Press, 1974).

71. Soufas, *Dramas of Distinction,* 12.

72. See Parker's "The Approach to the Spanish Drama of the Golden Age."

Conclusion

1. Translation mine.

2. Amy Williamsen, "Re-Writing in the Margins: Caro's *Valor, agravio y mujer* as Challenge to Dominant Discourse." *Bulletin of the Comediantes* 44, no. 1 (1992): 29.

Bibliography

Albrecht, Jane. "The Golden Age Playgoing Public: From the Highest to the Lowest?" *Bulletin of the Comediantes* 49, no. 1 (1997): 89–96.

Alcalá, Antonio Torres. "Fin' Amors: Código poético y contexto en los primeros trobadores." *Anuario Medieval* 6 (1994): 185–92.

Alighieri, Dante. *La divina commedia.* Milan: Garzanti, 1988.

———. *Il Purgatorio.* Edited and translated by John D. Sinclair. New York: Oxford University Press, 1961.

———. *Vita nuova.* Notre Dame, IN: University of Notre Dame Press, 1995.

Anonymous. *El abencerraje.* Madrid: Cátedra, 1982.

———. *Sir Gawain and the Green Knight.* Chicago: Northwestern University Press, 1970.

Augustine of Hippo. *On Christian Doctrine.* Translated by D. W. Robertson. New York: Liberal Arts Press, 1958.

Austin, J. L. *How to Do Things with Words.* Cambridge: Harvard University Press, 1962.

Bahler, Ingrid, and Katherine Gyékényesi Gatto. *Of Kings and Poets: Cancionero Poetry of the Trastámara Courts.* New York: Peter Lang, 1992.

Bakhtin, Mikhail. *The Dialogic Imagination: Four Essays by M.M. Bakhtin.* Austin: University of Texas Press, 1981.

———. *La cultura popular en la Edad Media y en el Renacimiento: El contexto de Francois Rabelais.* Madrid: Alianza Universidad, 1987.

Bass, Laura R., and Margaret R. Greer, eds. *Approaches to Teaching Early Modern Spanish Drama.* New York: MLA, 2006.

Beecher, Don A. "Translating Renaissance Comedy by Its Codes of Decorum." *Yearbook of Italian Studies* 7 (1988): 109–18.

Bergmann, Emilie. "*La dama boba:* temática folklórica y neoplatónica." In *Lope de Vega y los orígenes del teatro español.* 409–14. Madrid: EDI-6, 1981.

Berrick, Mac E. "The Form and Function of Folktales in *Don Quijote.*" *Journal of Medieval and Renaissance Studies* 6, no. 1 (1976): 101–38.

Blue, William R. *Spanish Comedy and Historical Contexts in the 1620s.* University Park: Pennsylvania State University Press, 1996.

Blumenfeld-Kosinski, Renate, ed. *The Selected Writings of Christine de Pizan.* New York: Norton, 1997.

Boase, Roger. *The Origin and Meaning of Courtly Love: A Critical Study of European Scholarship.* Manchester, England: Manchester University Press, 1977.

———. *The Troubadour Revival: A Study of Social Change and Traditionalism in Late Medieval Spain*. London: Routledge and Kegan Paul, 1978.

Boccaccio, Giovanni. *Decameron*. Milan: A. Mondadori, 1985.

———. *The Decameron*. Translated by Mark Musa and Peter Bondanella. New York: Penguin, 1982.

———. *Il Filocolo*. Bari: G. Laterza, 1938.

Bogin, Meg. *The Women Troubadours*. New York: Norton, 1980.

Bossy, Michel-André. "The *Trobar Clus* of Raimbaut D'Aurenga, Girautde Bornelh, and Arnaut Daniel." *Mediaevalia* 19 (1996): 203–19.

Boyce, Elizabeth S., and Julián Olivares, eds. *Tras el espejo la musa escribe: Lírica femenina de los Siglos de Oro*. Mexico City: Siglo Veintiuno, 1993.

Bruckner, Matilda. "Fictions of Female Voice: The Women Troubadours." *Speculum* 67, no. 4 (1992): 865–91.

———. "An Interpreter's Dilemma: Why Are There So Many Interpretations of Chrétien's Chevalier de la charrette?" *Romance Philology* 40, no. 2 (1986): 159–80.

———. "Na Castelloza, Trobairitz, and Troubadour Lyric." *Romance Notes* 25, no. 3 (1985): 239–53.

Burns, E. Jane. "The Man Behind the Lady in Troubadour Lyric." *Romance Notes* 25, no. 3 (1985): 254–70.

Buxó, José Pascual. "Sor Juana Inés de la Cruz: Amor y Cortesanía." *Colonial Latin American Review* 4, no. 2 (1995): 85–100.

Calder, Andrew. "Molière, Plautus, Terence and Renaissance Theories of Comedy." *New Comparison* 3 (1987): 19–32.

Calderón de la Barca, Pedro. *Obras completas*. Madrid: Aguilar, 1960.

———. *La dama duende*. Madrid: Ebro, 1968.

Campbell, Gwyn E. "(En)Gendering Fenisa in María de Zayas's *La traición en la amistad*." *RLA* 10, no. 2 (1998): 482–87.

Campbell, Jodi. *Monarchy, Political Culture, and Drama in Seventeenth-Century Madrid: Theater of Negotiation*. Burlington, VT: Ashgate, 2006.

Canavaggio, Jean. "Cervantes drammaturgo." In *Rileggere Cervantes: Antologia della Critica Recente*, 167–82. Milan: LED, 1994.

Cappellanus, Andreas. *The Art of Courtly Love*. Translated by John Jay Parry. New York: Continuum, 1985.

Caro, Ana. *Las comedias de Ana Caro: Valor, agravio y mujer y El conde Partinuplés*. New York: Peter Lang, 1997.

Casa, Frank P. "Honor and the Wife-Killers of Calderón." *Bulletin of the Comediantes* 29, no. 1 (1977): 6–23.

Cascardi, Anthony. *Ideologies of History in the Spanish Golden Age*. University Park: Pennsylvania State University Press, 1997.

Castells, Ricardo. "Bakhtin's Grotesque Realism and the Thematic Unity of *Celestina*, Act I." *Hispanófila* 35 (1992): 9–20.

Cervantes Saavedra, Miguel de. *Entremeses*. Madrid: Taurus, 1981.

———. *El ingenioso hidalgo Don Quijote de la Mancha*. Asheville, NC: Pegasus, 1998.

———. *The History of that Ingenious Gentleman Don Quijote de la Mancha*. Translated by Burton Raffel. New York: Norton, 1995.

———. *Novelas ejemplares.* Madrid: Cátedra, 1995.

Chartier, Roger. *Forms and Meanings: Texts, Performances, and Audiences from Codex to Computer.* Philadelphia: University of Pennsylvania University Press, 1993.

Close, Anthony. "Cervantes's Arte Nuevo de Hazer Fábulas Cómicas en Este Tiempo." *Cervantes* 2, no. 1 (1982): 3–22.

———. "Characterization and Dialogue in Cervantes's 'Comedias en prosa.' " *Modern Language Review* 76, no. 2 (1981): 338–56.

———. *The Romantic Approach to Don Quixote: A Critical History of Quixote Criticism.* Cambridge: Cambridge University Press, 1977.

Coassin, Flavia. "Female Voice-Male Rhetoric." *Spunti e Ricerche: Rivista d'Italianistica* 9 (1993): 45–55.

Cohen, Walter. *Drama of a Nation: Public Theater in Renaissance England and Spain.* Ithaca: Cornell University Press, 1985.

Connor (Swietlicki), Catherine. "Marriage and Subversion in Comedia Endings: Problems in Art and Society." In *Gender, Identity, and Representation in Spain's Golden Age.* Lewisburg: Bucknell University Press, 2000.

———. "The Preceptistas and Beyond: Spectators Making 'Meanings' in the *Corral de comedias.*" *Hispania* 82, no. 3 (1999): 417–28.

———. "Toward a New Socio-Cultural Theory of Baroque Theater." In *Hispanic Essays in Honor of Frank P. Casa.* New York: Peter Lang, 1987.

Cooper, Kate. "Elle and L: Sexualized Textuality in *Le Roman de Silence.*" *Romance Notes* 25, no. 3 (1985): 341–60.

Cortez, Beatriz. "El travestismo de Rosaura en *La vida es sueño* y de Leonor en *Valor, agravio y mujer:* el surgimiento de la agencialidad femenina y la desnaturalización del binarismo del género." *Bulletin of the Comediantes* 50, no. 2 (1998): 371–85.

Cotarelo y Mori, Emilio. *Bibliografía de las controversias sobre la licitud del teatro en España.* Madrid: Revista de Archivos, Bibliotecas y Museos, 1904.

Criado de Val, Manuel. *Lope de Vega y los orígenes del teatro español,* Madrid: EDI-6, 1981.

Cruz, Anne J. *Discourses of Poverty: Social Reform and the Picareque Novel in Counter-Reformation Spain.* Toronto: University of Toronto Press, 1999.

———. *Imitación y transformación: El petrarquismo en la poesía de Juan de Boscán y Garcilaso de la Vega.* Philadelphia: John Benjamins, 1988.

Cruz, Anne J, and Elizabeth Perry, eds. *Culture and Control in Counter-Reformation Spain.* Minneapolis: University of Minnesota Press, 1992.

Cueva y Silva, Leonor de la. *La firmeza en la ausencia.* In *Women's Acts: Plays by Women Dramatists of Spain's Golden Age.* Lexington: University Press of Kentucky, 1997.

D'Antuono, Nancy L. *Boccaccio's Novelle in the Theater of Lope de Vega.* Madrid: Porrúa Turanzas, 1983.

De Armas, Frederick. *The Invisible Mistress: Aspects of Feminism and Fantasy in the Golden Age.* Charlottesville, VA: Biblioteca Siglo de Oro, 1976.

——— ed. *A Star-Crossed Golden Age: Myth and the Spanish Comedia.* Lewisburg: Bucknell University Press, 1998.

De France, Marie. *Lais.* London: Bristol Classical Press, 1995.

———. *The Lais of Marie de France.* Translated by Glyn Burgess and Keith Busby. London: Penguin, 1986.

De Lorris, Guillaume, and Jean de Meun. *Le roman de la rose.* Paris: Garnier-Flammarion, 1974.

———. *The Romance of the Rose.* Translated by Harry W. Robbins. New York: E. P. Dutton, 1962.

De Rougemont, Denis. *L'amour et l'Occident.* Paris: Plon, 1939.

De Troyes, Chrétien. *Arthurian Romances.* Translated by D. D. R. Owen. London: J. M. Dent, 1993.

———. *Erec et Enide.* Paris: Le Livre de Poche, 1992.

———. *Romans.* Paris: H. Champion, 1952.

Deyermond, A. D. *The Petrarchan Sources of La Celestina.* London: Oxford University Press, 1961.

Donnell, Sidney. *Feminizing the Enemy: Imperial Spain, Transvestite Drama, and the Crisis of Masculinity.* Lewisburg: Bucknell University Press, 2003.

Doody, Margaret. *The True Story of the Novel.* New Brunswick, NJ: Rutgers University Press, 1996.

Dronke, Peter. *The Medieval Lyric.* Rochester, NY: D. S. Brewer, 1996.

Economou, George, ed. *Proensa: An Anthology of Troubadour Poetry.* New York: Paragon House, 1978.

Egido, Aurora. "La universidad de amor y *La dama boba.*" *Boletin de la Biblioteca Menéndez Pelayo* 54 (1978): 351–71.

Elam, Keir. *Shakespeare's Universe of Discourse: Language-Games in the Comedies.* Cambridge: Cambridge University Press, 1984.

Evans, Peter W. "Alonso's Cowardice: Ambiguities of Perspective in *El caballero de Olmedo.*" *Modern Language Review* 78, no. 1 (1983): 68–78.

Fergusson, Francis. *The Idea of a Theater.* Princeton: Princeton University Press, 1949.

Fernández, James. "The Bonds of Patrimony: Cervantes and the New World." *PMLA* 109, no. 5 (1994): 969–86.

Ferrante, Joan: "The Conflicts of Lyric Conventions and Romance Form." In *In Pursuit of Perfection: Courtly Love in Medieval Literature.* Port Washington, NY: Kennikat, 1975.

Foucault, Michel. *Language, Counter-memory, Practice.* Ithaca: Cornell University Press, 1977.

———. *Les mots et les choses: une archéologie des sciences humaines.* Paris: Gallimard, 1966.

Frank, Donald K. *Naturalism and the Troubadour Ethic.* New York: Peter Lang, 1988.

Friedman, Edward. "Girl Gets Boy: A Note on the Value of Exchange in the Comedia." *Bulletin of the Comediantes* 39, no. 1 (1987): 75–83.

———. "Theater Semiotics and Lope de Vega's *El caballero de Olmedo.*" In *El arte nuevo de estudiar comedias: Literary Theory and Spanish Golden Age Drama.* Lewisburg: Bucknell University Press, 1996.

Ganelin, Charles, and Howard Mancing, eds. *The Golden Age Comedia: Text, Theory, and Performance.* West Lafayette, IN: Purdue University Press, 1994.

García Lorenzo, Luciano, ed. *Cuadernos de teatro clásico: La comedia de capa y espada.* Madrid: Compañía Nacional de Teatro Clásico, 1988.

Gaunt, Simon. "Sexual Difference and the Metaphor of Language in a Troubadour Poem." *Modern Language Review* 83, no. 2 (1988): 297–313.

———. "Poetry of Exclusion: A Feminist Reading of Some Troubadour Lyrics." *Modern Language Review* 85, no. 2 (1990): 310–29.

Gaylord-Randel, Mary. "Amor y honor a través del espejo." In *Actas del Congreso Internacional sobre Calderón y el teatro español del siglo de oro.* Madrid: Consejo Superior de Investigaciones Científicas, 1983.

———. "'Las damas no desdigan de su nombre': decoro femenino y lenguaje en el *Arte nuevo* y *La dama boba.*" In *Justina: Homenaje a Justina Ruíz de Conde en su ochenta cumpleaños.* Erie: ALDEEU, 1992.

Gerli, E. Michael, ed. *Poesía cancioneril castellana.* Madrid: Ediciones Akal, 1994.

———. *Triste Deleytación: An Anonymous Fifteenth Century Castilian Romance.* Washington: Georgetown University Press, 1982.

Gerli, E. Michael and Joseph J. Gwara, eds. *Studies on the Spanish Sentimental Romance (1440–1550): Redefining a Genre.* London: Tamesis, 1997.

Gerli, E. Michael and Julian Weiss, eds. *Poetry at Court in Trastamaran Spain: From the* Cancionero de Baena *to the* Cancionero General. Tempe, AZ: Medieval & Renaissance Texts & Studies, 1998.

Gilbert-Santamaría, Donald. *Writers on the Market: Consuming Literature in Early Seventeenth-Century Spain.* Lewisburg: Bucknell University Press, 2005.

Girard, René. "Comedies of Errors: Plautus-Shakespeare-Molière." In *American Criticism in the Poststructuralist Age.* Ann Arbor: University of Michigan Press, 1981.

Gómez-Torres, David. "*La dama boba* de Lope de Vega: Un caso de subversión aparente o el proceso de formación de un discurso monológico." *Bulletin of the Comediantes* 48, no. 2 (1996): 315–27.

Green, Otis. *Spain and the Western Tradition: The Castilian Mind from El Cid to Calderón.* Madison: University of Wisconson Press, 1963.

Guinizelli, Guido. *Rime.* Naples: Liguori, 1998.

Gunn, Alan Murray Finlay. *The Mirror of Love: A Reinterpretation of "The Romance of the Rose."* Lubbock: Texas Tech University Press, 1952.

Harrison, Ann. "Arthurian Women in Jaufre." In *Studia Occitanica in Memoriam Paul Remy.* Vol. 2. Kalamazoo, MI: Medieval Institute, 1986.

Hathaway, Robert. *Love in the Early Spanish Theater.* Madrid: Playor, 1975.

———. "Frustrated Lovers' Farewells in the Early Iberian Theater." In *From Dante to García Márquez.* Williamstown, MA: Williams College, 1987.

Hegstrom, Valerie, and Amy R. Williamsen, eds. *Engendering the Early Modern Stage: Women Playwrights in the Spanish Empire.* New Orleans: University Press of the South, 1999.

Heiple, Daniel. *Garcilaso and the Italian Renaissance.* Lewisburg: Bucknell University Press, 1994.

Hernández-Araico, Susana. "La innovadora fiesta barroca de Sor Juana: *Los empeños de una casa.*" In *El escritor y la escena, V: Estudios sobre teatro español y novohispano en los Siglos de oro.* Ciudad Juarez, Mexico: Universidad Autónoma de Ciudad Juarez, 1997.

———. "Sor Juana's *Los empeños de una casa:* A Baroque Fete and a Theatrical Feat." In *Hispanic Essays in Honor of Frank P. Casa.* New York: Peter Lang, 1997.

Hollander, Robert. *Dante's Epistle to Cangrande.* Ann Arbor: University of Michigan Press, 1993.

190   BIBLIOGRAPHY

Holloway, James E. "Lope's Neoplatonism: *La dama boba.*" *Bulletin of Hispanic Studies* 49, no. 3 (1972): 236–55.

Holmberg, Arthur. "Variaciones sobre el tema del honor en *La dama duende* de Calderón." In *Actas del Congreso Internacional sobre Calderón y el teatro español del siglo de oro.* Madrid: Consejo Superior de Investigaciones Científicas, 1983.

Honig, Edwin. *Calderón and the Seizures of Honor.* Cambridge: Harvard University Press, 1972.

Inés de la Cruz, Sor Juana. *Obras completas.* México: Fondo de Cultura Económica, 1994.

Jones, C. A. "Honor in Spanish Golden Age Drama: Its Relation to Real Life and Morals." *Bulletin of Hispanic Studies* 35, no. 2 (1958): 199–210.

Kaminsky, Amy K., ed. *Water Lilies / Flores del agua. An Anthology of Spanish Women Writers from the Fifteenth through the Nineteenth Centuries.* Minneapolis: University of Minnesota Press, 1996.

Kay, Sarah. *Subjectivity in Troubadour Poetry.* Cambridge: Cambridge University Press, 1990.

———. "Rhetoric and Subjectivity in the Troubadour Lyric." In *The Troubadours and the Epic: Essays in Memory of W. Mary Hackett,* edited by Simon Gaunt and Linda Paterson. Coventry: University of Warwick Press, 1987.

Kendrick, Laura. *The Game of Love: Troubadour Wordplay.* Berkeley: University of California Press, 1988.

Kenshur, Oscar. "Skepticism and the Form of the *Quijote.*" *Dispositio* 2 (1977): 254–61.

Kocher, Suzanne. "Undermining Oppositionality: *The Romance of Silence*'s Nature/Nurture Debate Complicated by the Rhymes of Apieler (to Name) and Celer (to Conceal)." *Romance Language Annual* 7 (1995): 95–99.

Krauel, Ricardo. "Amor de nobles, amor de plebeyos: Análisis de dos episodios de *La Celestina.*" *Anuario Medieval* 6 (1994): 127–38.

Krueger, Roberta. *Women Readers and the Ideology of Gender in Old French Verse Romance.* Cambridge: Cambridge University Press, 1993.

Labrador, José J., ed. *Cancionero de poesías varias: manuscrito 1587 de la Biblioteca Real de Madrid.* Madrid: Visor, 1994.

Larson, Catherine. "'Yo quiero hablar claro': Language as the Motivating Force of Lope's *La dama boba.*" In *Things Done with Words: Speech Acts in Hispanic Drama.* Newark, DE: Juan de la Cuesta, 1986.

———. "Valor Judgments, or Women Writers and the *Comedia.*" In *Brave New Words: Studies in Spanish Golden Age Literature.* New Orleans: University Press of the South, 1996.

———. "You Can't Always Get What You Want: Gender, Voice, and Identity in Women-Authored *Comedias.*" In *Gender, Identity, and Representation in Spain's Golden Age.* Lewisburg: Bucknell University Press, 2000.

Lasry, Anita Benaim. "The Ideal Heroine in Medieval Romances: A Quest for a Paradigm." *Romance Quarterly* 32, no. 3 (1985): 227–43.

Lewis, C. S. *The Allegory of Love: A Study in Medieval Tradition.* Oxford: Clarendon Press, 1936.

Lida de Malkiel, María Rosa. "Juan Rodríguez del Padrón. Vida, Obras." *Nueva Revista de Filología Hispánica* 6 (1952): 313–51.

López-Castro, Armando. "El pensamiento del amor en la obra de Dante." *Insula* 38, no. 443 (1983): 12–13.

López Grigera, Luisa. *La retórica en la España del Siglo de Oro*. Salamanca: Ediciones Universidad de Salamanca, 1994.

Lucente, Gregory L. "Lyric Tradition and the Desires of Absence: Rudel, Dante, and Michelangelo." *Canadian Review of Comparative Literature* 10, no. 3 (1983): 305–32.

Maravall, José Antonio. *Teatro y literatura en la sociedad barroca*. Madrid: Seminarios y Ediciones, 1972.

Mariscal, George. *Contradictory Subjects: Quevedo, Cervantes, and Seventeenth-Century Spanish Culture*. Ithaca: Cornell University Press, 1991.

Mazzaro, Jerome. "From *fin amour* to Friendship: Dante's Transformation." In *The Olde Daunce: Love, Friendship, Sex, and Marriage in the Medieval World*. Albany: SUNY Press, 1991.

McCrary, William C. "The Theatricality of Male Orientation in the *Comedia*." In *Studies in Honor of William C. McCrary*. Lincoln, NE: Society of Spanish and Spanish-American Studies, 1978.

McGaha, Michael. "Guarini's *El pastor fido* and Lope de Vega's *El verdadero amante*." *Journal of Hispanic Philology* 10, no. 1 (1985): 51–60.

McGerr, Rosemarie P. *Chaucer's Open Books: Resistance to Closure in Medieval Discourse*. Gainesville: University Press of Florida, 1998.

McKendrick, Melveena. *Woman and Society of the Spanish Golden Age: A Study of the Mujer varonil*. Cambridge: Cambridge University Press, 1974.

———. "Breaking the Silence: Women and the Word in the *Comedia*." *Revista Canadiense de Estudios Hispánicos* 29, no. 1 (2004): 13–30.

———. "Honour/Vengeance in the Spanish 'Comedia': A Case of Mimetic Transference?" *The Modern Language Review* 79, no.2 (1984): 313–35.

Melczer, William. "Neoplatonismo y el *Quijote*." *Anales Cervantinos* 26 (1988): 313–25.

Merrim, Stephanie. *Early Modern Women's Writing and Sor Juana Inés de la Cruz*. Nashville: Vanderbilt University Press, 1999.

———. "*Mores Geometricae:* The Womanscript." In *Feminist Perspectives on Sor Juana Inés de la Cruz*. Detroit, MI: Wayne State University Press, 1991.

Moi, Toril. "Desire in Language: Andreaus Capellanus and the Controversy of Courtly Love." In *Medieval Literature: Criticism, Ideology, and History*. New York: St. Martin's, 1986.

Moreto, Agustín. *El desdén con el desdén*. Barcelona: Planeta, 1987.

Mourgues, Odette de. "Love in Moliere and in Restoration Comedy: Literature or Sociology?" *The Seventeenth Century* 1, no. 1 (1986): 57–67.

Mujica, Barbara. *Calderón's Characters: An Existential Point of View*. Barcelona: Puvill, 1980.

———. "Golden Age/Early Modern Theater: *Comedia* Studies at the End of the Century." *Hispania* 82, no. 3 (1999): 397–407.

———. "Honor from the Comic Perspective: Calderón's *Comedias de capa y espada*." *Bulletin of the Comediantes* 38, no. 1 (1986): 7–23.

Nappholz, Carol. "(Re)locating Lost Trobairitz: The Anonymous Female Voice in Provençal Debate Poems." *Tenso* 7, no. 2 (1992): 125–41.

Navarrete, Ignacio. *Orphans of Petrarch: Poetry and Theory in the Spanish Renaissance.* Berkeley: University of California Press, 1994.

Nichols, Stephen G. "Amourous Imitation: Bakhtin, Augustine, and *Le Roman d'Enéas.*" In *Romance: Generic Transformation from Chrétien de Troyes to Cervantes.* Hanover, NH: University Press of New England, 1985.

O'Connor, Thomas A. *Love in the 'Corral': Conjugal Spirituality and Antitheatrical Polemic in Early Modern Spain.* New York: Peter Lang, 2000.

————. "'Putting Sex into Discourse' in Golden Age Theater: The Case of Fray Gaspar de Villaroel." *Bulletin of the Comediantes* 48, no. 1 (1996): 5–14.

O'Donoghue, Bernard. *The Courtly Love Tradition.* Manchester: Manchester University Press, 1982.

Oliver Asin, J. "Más reminiscencias de *La Celestina* en el teatro de Lope." *Revista de Filología Española* 15 (1928): 67–74.

O'Meara, John J. "St. Augustine's Attitude to Love in the Context of His Influence on Christian Ethics." *Arethusa* 2 (1969): 46–60.

Packer, Mark. "The Conditions of Aesthetic Feeling in Aristotle's Poetics." *British Journal of Aesthetics* 24, no. 2 (1984): 138–48.

Paden, William D., ed. *The Voice of the Trobairitz: Perspectives on the Women Troubadours.* Philadelphia: University of Pennsylvania Press, 1989.

Padrón, Juan Rodríguez del. *Siervo libre de amor.* Madrid: Castalia, 1986.

Paris, Gaston. "Lancelot du Lac, II. *Le Conte de la Charrette.*" *Romania* 12 (1883): 459–534.

Parker, Alexander A. "The Approach to the Spanish Drama of the Golden Age." *The Tulane Drama Review* 4, no. 1 (1959): 42–59.

————. "On Edwin Honig's *Calderon and the Seizures of Honor.*" *Bulletin of the Comediantes* 26, no. 2 (1974): 68–71.

————. *The Philosophy of Love in Spanish Literature: 1480–1680.* Edinburgh: Edinburgh University Press, 1985.

Parr, James. *'Don Quixote': An Anatomy of Subversive Discourse.* Newark, DE: Juan de la Cuesta, 1988.

Paterson, Linda M. *Troubadours and Eloquence.* Oxford: Clarendon Press, 1975.

Paz, Octavio. *Sor Juana Inés de la Cruz: o las trampas de la fe.* Mexico: Fondo de Cultura, 1977.

Pérez-Romero, Antonio. *The Subversive Tradition in Spanish Renaissance Writing.* Lewisburg: Bucknell University Press, 2005.

Perry, Mary Elizabeth. *Gender and Disorder in Early Modern Seville.* Princeton: Princeton University Press, 1990.

Petrarca, Francesco. *Il Canzoniere.* Leipzig: F. A. Brockhaus, 1883.

————. *Selections from the Canzoniere and Other Works.* Translated by Mark Musa. New York: Oxford University Press, 1986.

Poe, Elizabeth W. "A Dispassionate Look at the Trobairitz." *Tenso* 7, no. 2 (1992): 142–64.

Radcliff-Umstead, Douglas. "Love in the Italian Sweet New Style." *Innovation in Medieval Literature: Essays to the Memory of Alan Markman.* Pittsburgh: University of Pittsburgh Medieval Studies, 1971.

Riley, E. C. "Cervantes: A Question of Genre." In *Medieval and Renaissance Studies on Spain and Portugal in Honor of P. E. Russell*. Oxford: Society for the Study of Medieval Languages and Literature, 1981.

————. *Cervantes's Theory of the Novel*. Oxford: Clarendon Press, 1962.

Riquer, Martín de, (ed.). *La lírica de los trovadores, antología comentada*. Barcelona: Escuela de Filología, 1948.

Rivers, Elias L. "The *Comedia* as Discursive Action." In *Studies in Honor of Bruce W. Wardropper*. Newark, DE: Juan de la Cuesta, 1989.

————, ed. *Renaissance and Baroque Poetry of Spain*. New York: Dell, 1966.

Rojas, Fernando de. *La Celestina*. Madrid: Espasa-Calpe, 1968.

Rosenn, Eva. "The Discourse of Power: The Lyrics of the Trobairitz." *Comitatus* 21 (1990): 1–20.

————. "The Sexual and Textual Politics of Marie's Poetics." In *In Quest of Marie de France, a Twelfth-Century Poet*. Lewiston, NY: Mellen Press, 1992.

Rosenstein, Roy and Jay Wolf, eds. and trans. *The Poetry of Cercamon and Jaufre Rudel*. New York: Garland Press, 1983.

Rothberg, Irving P. "Algo más sobre Plauto, Terencio y Lope." In *Lope de Vega y los orígenes del teatro español*. Madrid: EDI-6, 1981.

Ruiz, Juan. *Libro de buen amor*. Madrid: Cátedra, 1992.

San Pedro, Diego de. *Cárcel de amor*. Madrid: Castalia, 1971.

Sánchez de León, María José Rodríguez, ed. *La crítica ante el teatro barroco español*. Salamanca: Ediciones Almar, 2000.

Schafer, Alice E. "Fate versus Responsibility in Lope's *El caballero de Olmedo*." *Revista Canadiense de Estudios Hispánicos* 3 (1978): 26–39.

Segre, Césare. "What Bakhtin Left Unsaid: The Case of the Medieval Romance." In *Romance: Generic Transformation from Chrétien de Troyes to Cervantes*. Edited by Kevin Brownlee and Marina S. Brownlee. Hanover, NH: University Press of New England, 1985.

Serés, Guillermo. *La transformación de los amantes: imágenes del amor de la antigüedad al siglo de oro*. Barcelona: Crítica, 1996.

Severin, Dorothy Sherman. *Tragicomedy and Novelistic Discourse in Celestina*. London: Cambridge University Press, 1989.

Sharman, Gillian. "The Love Match: Complication and Resolution of Plot in Italian Renaissance Comedy." In *The Cultural Heritage of the Italian Renaissance: Essays in Honour of T. G. Griffith*. Lewiston, NY: Mellen Press, 1993.

Simerka, Barbara, ed. *El arte nuevo de estudiar comedias: Literary Theory and Spanish Golden Age Drama*. Lewisburg: Bucknell University Press, 1996.

Smith, Paul Julian. *Writing in the Margin: Spanish Literature of the Golden Age*. New York: Oxford University Press, 1988.

Soufas, Teresa. "The Absence of Desire in Leonor de la Cueva's *La firmeza en la ausencia*." In *Gender, Identity, and Representation in Spain's Golden Age*. Lewisburg: Bucknell University Press, 2000.

————. *Dramas of Distinction: A Study of Plays by Golden Age Women*. Lexington: University of Kentucky Press, 1997.

————. "Regarding the Woman's Response: Leonor de la Cueva y Silva's *La firmeza en la ausencia*." *Romance Language Annual* 1 (1989): 625–30.

Spadaccini, Nicholas, and Jenaro Talens. "Cervantes and the Dialogic World." In *Cervantes's Exemplary Novels and the Adventure of Writing*. Minneapolis, MN: Prisma House, 1989.

Spence, Sarah. "Rhetoric and Hermeneutics." In *The Troubadours: An Introduction*. Cambridge: Cambridge University Press, 1999.

———. *Rhetorics of Reason and Desire: Vergil, Augustine, and the Troubadours*. Ithaca: Cornell University Press, 1988.

Stoll, Anita K., and Dawn L. Smith, eds. *The Perception of Women in Spanish Theater of the Golden Age*. Lewisburg: Bucknell University Press, 1991.

Stroud, Matthew D. "Love, Friendship, and Deceit in *La traición en la amistad*, by María de Zayas." *Neophilologus* 69 (1985): 539–47.

———. "Social-Comic Anagnorisis in *La dama duende*." *Bulletin of the Comediantes* 29, no. 2 (1977): 96–102.

Ter Horst, Robert. "The True Mind of Marriage: Ironies of the Intellect in Lope's *La dama boba*." *Romanistisches Jahrbuch* 27 (1976): 347–63.

Tirso de Molina. *El burlador de Sevilla*. Binghamton, NY: Medieval & Renaissance Texts and Studies, 1994.

———. *El vergonzoso en palacio*. Barcelona: Planeta, 1982.

Valbuena-Briones, Angel Julián. "La particularidad de *Los empeños de una casa*, de Sor Juana Inés de la Cruz, ante la tradición calderoniana." *Hispanic Journal* 18, no. 1 (1997): 159–68.

Varela, José Luis. "Revisión de la novela sentimental." *Revista de Filología Española* 48 (1965): 351–82.

Vega Carpio, Félix Lope de. *El arte nuevo de hacer comedias en este tiempo*. Madrid: Consejo Superior de Investigaciones Cienti'ficas, 1971.

———. *El caballero de Olmedo*. Madrid: Castalia, 1983.

———. *La dama boba*. Madrid: Espasa Calpe, 1946.

———. *Obras de Lope de Vega*. Madrid: Ediciones Atlas, 1965.

Ventadorn, Bernart de. *Bernart de Ventadour, Troubadour du XIIᵉ Siècle: Chansons d'Amour*. Paris: Librairie C. Klinksieck, 1966.

Vicente, Gil. *Don Duardos*. Madrid: Taurus, 1966.

Vollendorf, Lisa. "Cervantes and His Women Readers." *Romance Quarterly*, 52, no. 4 (2005): 312–27.

———. "Desire Unbound: Women's Theater of Spain's Golden Age." In *Women in the Discourse of Early Modern Spain*. Gainesville: University Press of Florida, 2003.

———. "The Future of Early Modern Women's Studies: The Case of Same-Sex Friendship and Desire in Zayas and Carvajal." *Arizona Journal of Hispanic Cultural Studies* 4 (2000): 265–84.

———. *Reclaiming the Body: María de Zayas's Early Modern Feminism*. Chapel Hill: University of North Carolina Press, 2001.

———. *Recovering Spain's Feminist Tradition*. New York: MLA, 2001.

———. "The Value of Female Friendship in Seventeenth-Century Spain." *Texas Studies in Literature and Language* 47, no. 4 (2005): 425–45.

Voros, Sharon. "Fashioning Feminine Wit in María de Zayas, Ana Caro, and Leonor de la Cueva." In *Gender, Identity, and Representation in Spain's Golden Age.* Lewisburg: Bucknell University Press, 2000.

———. "Armesinda's Dream: Leonor de la Cueva's Challenge to the Patriarchy in *La firmeza en la ausencia.*" *Monographic Review* 13 (1997): 74–86.

Wardropper, Bruce. "La comedia española del Siglo de Oro." Elder Olsen. *Teoría de la Comedia.* Translated by Salvador Oliva and Manuel Espín. Barcelona: Ariel, 1978.

———. "The Criticism of the Spanish Comedia: *El caballero de Olmedo* as Object Lesson." In *Hispanic Studies in Honor of Edmund de Chasca.* Iowa City: University of Iowa Press, 1972.

Wehrs, Donald R. "Sterne, Cervantes, Montaigne: Fideistic Skepticism and the Rhetoric of Desire." *Comparative Literature Studies* 25, no. 3 (1988): 127–50.

Weiger, John G. "Don Alonso's Tragic Flaw in *El caballero de Olmedo.*" *Hispanic Journal* 7, no. 1 (1985): 41–49.

Weimer, Christopher B. "Ana Caro's *El Conde Partinuplés* and Calderón's *La vida es sueño:* Protofeminism and Heuristic Imitation." *Bulletin of the Comediantes* 52, no. 1 (2000): 123–46.

Wilkins, Constance. "Subversion through Comedy?: Two Plays by Sor Juana Inés de la Cruz and María de Zayas." In *The Perception of Women in Spanish Theater of the Golden Age.* Lewisburg: Bucknell University Press, 1991.

Williamsen, Amy. "Re-Writing in the Margins: Caro's *Valor, agravio y mujer* as Challenge to Dominant Discourse." *Bulletin of the Comediantes* 44, no. 1 (1992): 21–30.

Wilson, Katharina M., ed. *Medieval Women Writers.* Athens: University of Georgia Press, 1984.

Yarbro-Bejarano, Yvonne. *Feminism and the Honor Plays of Lope de Vega.* West Lafayette, IN: Purdue University Press, 1994.

Zavala, Iris M. "Burlas al amor." *Nueva Revista de Filología Hispanica* 29, no. 2 (1980): 367–402.

Zayas y Sotomayor, María de. *La traición en la amistad/Friendship Betrayed.* Translated by Catherine Larson. Lewisburg: Bucknell University Press, 1999.

Index